BILL CLINTON:

THE INSIDE STORY

Part of Robert E. Levin's share of profits from the sale of this book will be donated to the Robin Hood Foundation, the Children's Defense Fund, the Environmental Defense Fund, the Anti-Defamation League of B'nai Brith and the Simon Wiesenthal Center of Los Angeles.

Photo credits:

Front cover photograph: copyright © 1991 by
Rick Friedman/Black Star.
Photo section: courtesy of Max Parker, Clinton For
President; also copyright © 1992 T. L. Litt/Impact
Visuals; copyright © 1991, 1992 Black Star.

Permission to use essays by Michael B. Cornfield,
Edwin Diamond and Marion R. Just
is gratefully acknowledged.

Permission to use *Memoir of Bill Clinton,* by
William A. Fletcher copyright © 1992,
is gratefully acknowledged.

Permission to excerpt portions from *Travelling Blind,*
by Dr. Harold W. Snider, copyright © 1992,
is gratefully acknowledged.

Permission to excerpt portions from the statement of
Tom Williamson, copyright © 1992,
is gratefully acknowledged.

BILL CLINTON

☆ THE INSIDE STORY ☆

by
Robert E. Levin

with Introduction by
Senator David Pryor

Edited by
J. Shawn Landres

Associate Editors:
Jason Albert Wertheim

Kathy M. Shandling

A division of Shapolsky Publishers, Inc.

Bill Clinton: The Inside Story

S.P.I. BOOKS

A division of Shapolsky Publishers, Inc.

Copyright © 1992 by Robert Levin

For any additional information, contact:
S.P.I. BOOKS/Shapolsky Publishers, Inc.
136 West 22nd Street
New York, NY 10011
(212) 633-2022
FAX (212) 633-2123

ISBN: 1-56171-177-2

10 9 8 7 6 5 4 3 2 1

Printed and bound in the United States of America

CONTENTS

Preface

By

Robert E. Levin

Never doubt that a small group of thoughtful, committed citizens can change the world. Indeed, it's the only thing that ever has.

Margaret Mead

The Cold War ended in 1991 and the changes just don't stop. A phrase from a recent movie reflects the turbulent *zeitgeist* — the spirit of the times: "The 1990s are going to make the 1960s look like the 1950s."

There are cycles in American and world history, just as there are cycles in nature. The 1980s ended with a major credit and real estate cycle going bust. It has led to a more sober era. Still, there are reasons to be hopeful. A few prominent historians have predicted that the United States may enter an era of progressive reform in the 1990s after a period of domestic neglect in the 1980s. Just as the U.S. entered a progressive era from 1900 to 1917 after two decades of neglect and the excesses of the Robber Baron era, so must the America of the 1990s reinvent itself in order to move forward. Political leaders, if they are to succeed, must not only redefine the political values which have dominated the past twenty-five years but they must also convince the baby-boomer generation and its children that those values are valid and effective.

In a recent article called "Beyond Left and Right: A New Political Paradigm," published in *The Responsive Community*, David Osborne noted that these new political values are already being defined on state and local levels. He wrote:

What we need today is not more or less government: we need different government. Outside Washington, beyond the beltway, mayors and governors have begun to evolve ways to deal with the new realities and to give people what they want. These state and local executives are creating a third way, which blends the activism of traditional Democratic politics with the aversion to big government of traditional conservatism.

. . . A paradigm is really nothing more than a set of assumptions about how the world works; it's a world view. And although there are many different ways to describe the kind of new world view that our more innovative governors and mayors are beginning to articulate, they all seem to share a few common assumptions.

. . . Six assumptions provide a rough sketch of where American politics is heading. We are moving toward government that steers more than it rows, that catalyzes others into action; that's market oriented; that avoids bureaucracy and uses more entrepreneurial governance; that stresses empowerment rather than simply giving people services; that stresses opportunity and responsibility rather than entitlement; and that decentralizes authority.

Bill Clinton could have the opportunity to be the first post Cold-War president to launch an ambitious domestic agenda under such a new paradigm. His generation grew up during the Cold War, and baby boomers from both parties are anxious to move beyond it to tackle the long-neglected problems which have accumulated over the past thirty years: the infrastructure, health care, the economy, and the environmental crisis. The American challenge will be to work smarter and harder, to be patient, diligent, committed, self-sacrificing, and persistent to rebuild, preserve, and protect the American Dream.

Clinton and his running mate, Senator Al Gore, are national leaders who understand that their generation has the shared experience of events and moods which fundamentally shaped today's political arena — the influence of television, the assassinations of great leaders, the fear of nuclear war, the tragedy of Vietnam, urban riots, the civil rights struggle, the women's movement, Watergate, and the disenchantment with politics in general and government in particular. They recognize that the agenda of the baby-boomer generation is based on issues which do not fit the traditional liberal/conservative labels. Watergate fostered mistrust of government and a yearning for the optimism which had prevailed during the Kennedy Administration.

Those of the current generation who are now becoming national leaders all lived through the Vietnam era and faced the same dilemmas. Bill Clinton had the courage of his convictions at a time when Americans were divided over the war and the majority of Americans were turning against it. Al Gore made his own difficult decision — he enlisted and served in Vietnam. Some were expecting Bill Clinton to choose a vice-presidential running mate who would "balance" the ticket geographically, a traditional criterion. Clinton chose Gore despite the fact that both are from the South. Although Gore complements Clinton and brings balance to the ticket in a number of important ways, the Clinton-Gore slate may inadvertently symbolize a different kind of "balance": a reconciliation between the baby boomers who served in Vietnam and those who served in the protests to stop the war, one which symbolizes a growing concern that although Americans have diverse values and beliefs, they must come together if they are to solve vital problems.

And there are problems which must be solved. From the bombing of Baghdad in 1991 to the burning of Los Angeles in 1992 the mood of America has swung from euphoria to deep frustration. Sadly, this is happening at a time when economic dislocations are giving many Americans the impression that the country is on the wrong track.

In the introduction to his ground-breaking book *Why Americans Hate Politics*, journalist E.J. Dionne, Jr., noted:

After two centuries in which the United States stood proudly as an example of what an engaged citizenry could accomplish through public life, Americans view politics with boredom and detachment. . . . Election campaigns [are dominated by] approaches that treat individual voters not as citizens deciding their nation's fate, but as mere collections of impulses waiting to be stroked and soothed.

. . . At its best, democratic politics is about what Arthur Schlesinger, Jr., calls "the search for remedy." The purpose of democratic politics is to solve problems and resolve disputes. But since the 1960s, the key to winning elections has been to reopen the same divisive issues over and over again. The issues themselves are not reargued. No new light is shed. Rather, old resentments and angers are stirred up in an effort to get voters to cast yet one more ballot of angry protest. . . . At the end of it all, the governing process, which is supposed to be about real things, becomes little more than a war over symbols.

The people want to have a government they can trust. They want bold, direct leadership to tell them the truth, present a clear plan of action to solve America's serious economic, environmental and health care problems. They yearn for a president who can get the nation moving again in the right direction.

This book is the result of my attempt to discover whether Bill Clinton has what America needs. We have read his myriad of policy papers. We know which way he wants the country to go. Does he have the strength of character to lead us, to take us there, or are the problems too big for one man to solve, as the nation faces fiscal constraints which may hamper even the best laid plans?

The author of *Hard Times*, Studs Terkel, pioneered an oral history technique in which he would paint a lucid composite picture of a personality, time, or place in history through extensive quotations from primary sources. I borrowed from that technique in this biography in order to give readers an authentic first-hand account of Bill Clinton's life. In this book you will meet Clinton's many associates and friends. These are extraordinary people who knew him well as a child, as a student and as a young leader. So diverse and yet so united in their commitment to Bill Clinton, they have been affectionately dubbed FOBs: Friends of Bill. The sources interviewed for this book represent a wide variety of income levels, many different professions — even opposing political parties.

To know Bill Clinton's personal convictions and beliefs, as well as the values that guide his decisions, one must talk to the people who know him best. Even though I have met and spoken with Bill Clinton several times, I believe that I learned much more about him from the hundred or so primary and secondary sources consulted as part of the research process in this book. Not only did they provide valuable insight into Bill Clinton the person, but they also revealed much about the spirit of the times during which Bill Clinton grew up. Consider the words of a lifelong friend whom Clinton met in high school, Carolyn Yeldell Staley:

> We lived in the days of President John Kennedy and American hope and pride. This was before the escalation of the war in Vietnam, before Watergate, before cynicism and doubt in our country's systems crept into the mainstream of public thought. That same belief in

America and in our system of government has really not returned to the full glory we knew then; however, it is that same sense of respect in our country and belief in public service through elected office which motivates Bill Clinton to seek the Presidency. The decades of cynicism and greed, of lost hope and American pride of the '70s and '80s did not replace the hopes and dreams of a better tomorrow for America which were planted in Bill Clinton's heart as a young man in the 60's. He still believes our best days are yet to be.

Admittedly, political issues are not the only matter at hand. The question of which personal issues are relevant to judgements about presidential character, however, was not adequately addressed in 1992. Chronic alcoholism, drug abuse, or a habit of lying and stretching the truth certainly qualify as character issues relevant to judging presidential qualifications. But the character issue focused on litmus test questions which were too narrowly defined and which perhaps lacked relevance to presidential character. The common denominator in character-related questions during the 1992 campaign boiled down to "Have you ever indulged in the following victimless personal vices?" The questions failed to define the kind of public character which the presidency requires to address the important issues facing the nation.

On the one hand, the office of the president by definition commands respect and should be a repository for the public trust. Therefore, the argument goes, the president should be a paragon of private and public virtue if that person is to be credible moral leader and role model for the nation's youth. On the other hand, public character flaws can sometimes result in millions of potential victims. Private character questions are more relevant if you are electing a saint or if there is a direct relationship between private character and public character. During the presidential campaign of 1884, Republican candidate and former Secretary of State James G. Blaine had a reputation for private morality but questions remained about his business dealings; conversely, Grover Cleveland, the governor of New York, had been accused of fathering a child out of wedlock but was known to be utterly scrupulous in his public duties. As the campaign progressed, one commentator suggested that Cleveland be elevated to the public office for which he was so well-suited, and that Blaine be restored to the private life for which he was extremely qualified. With the slogan *A Public Office is a Public Trust*, Cleveland won.

Certain values a president may or may not hold dear *do* have a direct impact on our national security, but others do not. Would a Clinton administration make the polluter or the taxpayer pay to clean up an environmental disaster? Would a Clinton administration advocate abstinence and/or "safe sex" as the primary method of preventing transmission of the AIDS virus? With over 100,000 cancer deaths each year attributable to cigarette smoking, would a Clinton administration continue USDA subsidies to tobacco farmers? These questions about public ethics and public moral standards certainly are as relevant to presidential character as private ethics and moral standards.

Some readers may already have preconceived notions about Bill Clinton. While many of these perceptions may be valid, others may be mistaken, especially if they are the result of media sensationalism or of a lack of information. Such erroneous first impressions tend to crystallize opinions despite the availability of important additional information and thus can impair voters' abilities to make informed choices. This book is intended both as a basic but comprehensive introduction for readers who know little or nothing about Bill Clinton and as a second look for those who know more and would like to increase their understanding of him.

Many people presume, for example, that Bill Clinton grew up in a well-off family which could afford to send him to Yale Law School and Oxford University. In fact, Clinton had humble beginnings as a small-town boy who didn't always have it easy growing up and had to survive the stormy dynamics of a broken family. He was raised in the small Arkansas towns of Hope and Hot Springs. His widowed mother had to struggle and study to achieve the American Dream. There is no doubt that facing up to violence, alcoholism and drug abuse in his own family strengthened his character, contributed to his moral development and fostered an ambition to help people help themselves. Clinton's concern for the educational, economic and health care needs of America's children and their families is rooted in a genuine caring for people who need help.

The question, then, is whether Bill Clinton has a commitment to change and to effective government. The record speaks for itself: over 26 years ago, while still a junior at Georgetown University he wrote, "If elected representative government is to have any meaning at all," he wrote, "it must make a deep commitment to meet [issues] head-on. . . . We cannot adopt a policy of isolation or inaction, or our politics will be without substance. We . . . must urge our representatives to enter and support them in those fields where they are most needed -- to plant the seeds of improvement, to reap the harvest of beneficial change. The times demand it." Much about him has changed since then, but not his spirit of commitment and innovation. Clinton remains among a breed of political leaders on both sides of the aisle who believe that government can be an effective catalyst for change and can be made to work for the common good of the people.

In his inaugural address, President John F. Kennedy said: "Now the trumpet summons us again — not as a call to bear arms, though arms we need — not as a call to battle, though embattled we are — but as a call to bear the burden of a long twilight struggle, year in and year out, 'rejoicing in hope, patient in tribulation' — a struggle against the common enemies of man: tyranny, poverty, disease, and war itself. Can we forge a grand and global alliance, North and South, East and West, that can assure a more fruitful life for all mankind? Will you join me in that historic effort?" Such was the challenge of the man Bill Clinton met in 1963 at the White House — the one man who more than any other inspired Clinton to devote his life to public service.

This book contains the evidence and the story of a man with a restless spirit of can-do idealism which is rare in American politics today. The sources herein go beyond the media filter to reveal the *real* Bill Clinton, a man of integrity and compassion who believes in the values which have made America great.

Bill Clinton, I have come to believe, has what it takes. This book tells us why.

Robert E. Levin
New York City
September 1992

Introduction

By

Senator David Pryor

The Arkansas Democratic Primary elections used to be held in July, with run-off elections in August. So it was in July 1966, in front of the fire station in Arkadelphia, when I first saw and spoke with a 19-year-old college student named Bill Clinton. I was running for Congress, and he was a volunteer for a candidate for Governor. Incidentally, I won my race and Bill Clinton's man lost to an arch right-winger who was later defeated in November by Winthrop Rockefeller.

I had a strange feeling about that first meeting with Bill on that hot July afternoon. Although our visit lasted only two or three minutes, I knew I'd just met someone very special. In fact, when I got back into the car and headed for our next stop, I told my wife Barbara we were going to hear a lot from Bill Clinton in future years.

For years since then, our lives and paths have been personally and politically interwoven into the Arkansas landscape. After meeting him, anyone would immediately know he was not going to spend his life sitting on the sidelines.

He was a doer. He had the fire. He would wait for his time, yes, but as great leaders do. They don't just wait for opportunities; they create them.

As a student at Georgetown University, Bill visited Senator Fulbright's office in search of a job. Lee Williams, the Senator's Administrative Assistant, recalled telling him: "We don't have a full time job, but we do have open two part time slots."

"I'll take 'em both," Bill Clinton replied.

He was immediately hired in the mailroom and devoured stacks of mail each day on Vietnam and other issues. Between classes, he read six newspapers daily and his voracious appetite for learning was insatiable. One staff member told me, "there's nothing he's not interested in."

In 1974, Bill challenged a very popular Republican Congressman. It was then I heard him make his first speech. It was 3 minutes long. It was the traditional Pope County Democratic Women's dinner and rally in Russellville, a ritual held every two years for several hundred democratic loyalists — and a must appearance for any democratic politician. It always falls on the first Saturday night after the filing deadline (we call it "ticket closing day").

Dale Bumpers and Bill Fulbright had spoken. Senator Robert C. Byrd (West Virginia) was the evening's feature speaker. Candidates for Sheriff and Coroner and Governor had all spoken. The crowd was exhausted, but at near 11 PM, the young Bill Clinton was recognized, but because of the late hour was limited to only 3 minutes at the podium. Bill who? What's he running for? Against whom?

He had no notes. He wore a heavy gray flannel suit that was far too hot for the May evening. He had a new pair of shoes. Within seconds the slumped audience snapped to attention. Total silence fell throughout the steamy, hot school cafeteria. It was crowd hypnosis; he had it and we knew it.

His close defeat in the Fall would have caused many others to drop out of politics, but Bill Clinton went to work to build upon the foundation of support he had laid. To-day, in Arkansas politics, his political "root system" is deep and strong in each county. His unique ability to bring opposing sides and forces together is legend.

Well, you know the rest. Attorney General two years later. Governor two years after that. Seventeen times on the Arkansas ballot. As we like to say, Bill Clinton knows every person in Arkansas by their first name.

In September of last year, I played golf with Bill Clinton late one afternoon. There was much speculation about his plans and no one seemed to think he would actually throw his hat in the ring. He had been on "the list" before, and besides, Arkansas is too small, Clinton was not known, and all the other hundreds of reasons.

We talked about everything as we played, but I was very surprised that we had gone through 17 holes of play without him ever mentioning presidential politics. Then on the 18th hole, Bill sliced his drive into the rough behind a pine tree. We walked over to survey the ball and Bill looked up at me and asked:

"What should I do?"

"Use a 2 iron and hit the ball back in the fairway," I suggested.

"No," he replied. "What I want to know is should I run for President?"

Shortly after that, we sat together at a friend's funeral. I was seated on Hillary's right and Bill sat to her left. On the back of the funeral program, I wrote one word and passed it over to him, in big letters: "RUN." Of course, I'll always believe his mind had been made up long before. He had to do it.

His enormous energy and campaign skills drew wins in early primaries. His magnetism transformed mere supporters into passionate believers. His schedule defied human tolerance. Accusations that would kill off lesser mortals only steeled his resolve.

Days and nights, weeks and months, criss-crossing America staggers one's imagination. On February 17, the day before the New Hampshire primary vote, he made 17 stops over the state. At 11:30 that night, schedule completed, he asked, "Isn't there a bowling alley that's open all night? We need to shake some hands."

Wherever he went, large crowds or small, he constantly scanned his audience for the Arkansas Travelers, that loyal band of followers from home who joined him in each state. During the darker days of the campaign, those from home who knew him best came to his side and stayed. There was a bonding, a relationship which made the statement: "He's ours, no matter what."

When he would lose his voice, I heard one say: "Don't waste your voice on me, Bill — save it for someone else." He pulled him close, choked with gratitude. From Hillary and those who stood at his side, he drew the strength and courage to hold on and persevere.

A recent cover story of a news magazine had the picture and ghastly headline: "Perot — The Quitter." That's a word Bill Clinton doesn't know.

In American politics, we usually get to eventually know just 'bout every public position a candidate has taken on an issue. However, too seldom do we ever get "inside" the candidate, especially a candidate for president. This is one of those rare looks at a young man who may become our next president. It is written in simple language and it goes directly to Bill Clinton, the *human being*. It's the "inside story" on this unique person, because it is written by those who know both the public and the private person.

Bill Clinton's Life and Times:

A Chronology of Important Events

1942
Bill Clinton's parents, Virginia Cassidy and William Blythe are married.

1946
Clinton's father is killed and Clinton is born four months later.

1948
Clinton's mother, Virginia, leaves Hope to study and Clinton stays with his grandparents, Eldridge and Edith Cassidy, where he is raised from age 2 to 4. Truman defeats Dewey and calls for Fair Deal.

1950

Virginia marries Roger Clinton when Bill is 4 and moves back to Hope. The Korean war begins with invasion of South Korea on June 25. President Truman authorizes production of H-bomb.

1951

Bill Clinton enters Mary Perkins Kindergarten.

1952

At the age of six, with his mother and stepfather, Bill moves to a farm in the country near Hope. He attends first grade at a public elementary school. Korean War ends. Eisenhower elected president.

1953

Truce declared in Korea.

1954

The family moves to Hot Springs where Bill Clinton enters the second grade in a Catholic school. Anti-communist hysteria subsides after Senator Joseph McCarthy's allegations proved to be false.

1956

Bill Clinton enters the fourth grade in a public school.

1957

In September, a mob encouraged by the segregationist stand of Gov. Orval Faubus prevents admission of nine black students at Central High School in Little Rock.

1960

Senator John F. Kennedy defeats Richard Nixon for president and launches Peace Corps.

1962

Kennedy announces said on Feb. 14 that U.S. military advisors in Vietnam would fire if fired upon. Kennedy confronts Khrushchev over missiles in Cuba and puts nuclear forces on alert.

1963

Bill Clinton meets President John F. Kennedy at a Boys Nation American Legion convention in Washington, D.C. in August. JFK is assassinated in November. Lyndon Baines Johnson sworn into office.

1964

Clinton graduates from Hot Springs High School and enters Georgetown School of Foreign Service in the Fall. Gulf of Tonkin resolution approved by Congress. LBJ wins in a landslide over Barry Goldwater and launches Great Society. LBJ also escalates American involvement in Vietnam.

1964

Clinton runs for Freshman Class President and wins. Martin Luther King, Jr. wins Nobel Peace prize for contributions to the civil rights movement.

1964-1966
Clinton works for Senator J. William Fulbright in Washington, D.C.

1965
Clinton runs for Sophomore Class President and wins.

1968
Clinton wins Rhodes Scholarship to Oxford. The assassination of Martin Luther King, Jr., sets off riots in Washington, DC, and in dozens of other cities. Robert F. Kennedy wins California primary and is assassinated in June. Nixon elected president.

1969
Clinton returns to Oxford to complete his second year.

1970
Clinton enters Yale Law School, where he meets Hillary Rodham.

1972
Clinton manages George McGovern's campaign in Texas. Watergate break-in June 17.

1973
Clinton graduates with a degree in Law and moves to Fayetteville to join the Faculty of Law at the University of Arkansas in the Fall of 1973. Israel is attacked by Arab neighbors in October. First OPEC oil price shock triggers inflation in U.S.

1974
Clinton runs for Congress and is defeated. Hillary Rodham moves to Fayetteville and joins the Faculty of Law at the University of Arkansas after Nixon resigns from office August 8.

1975
Bill Clinton and Hillary Rodham are married at their home in Fayetteville.

1976
Clinton runs for Attorney General and wins. Jimmy Carter elected president.

1978
Clinton runs for Governor of Arkansas and wins, becoming the nation's youngest governor. Begins the process of improving education system and other services.

1979
Second OPEC oil price shock and Iranian revolution destabilizes Carter Administration, sends inflation to double-digit levels. Energy crisis.

1980
Clinton is defeated in his bid to be reelected when the country swings to the right and elects Ronald Reagan as president. The Clintons' daughter, Chelsea, is born.

1982

Clinton is reelected to his second term as governor. He launches major education reforms initiative.

1983

Clinton's package of education reforms are successfully implemented in Arkansas.

1984

Clinton is elected to his third term as governor. He launches a successful program of economic development.

1985

Clinton continues to implement economic development programs and is elected Chairman of the Southern Growth Policies Board and is Vice-Chairman of the National Governors Association.

1986

Clinton is named Chairman of the National Governors Association (NGA) and co-chairs the NGA task force on welfare reform. In November, he is elected to his fourth term as governor. Oil prices drop dramatically in February.

1989

Clinton co-chairs the President's National Education Summit.

1990

The Democratic Leadership Council names Clinton as its chairman. That fall, he is reelected to an unprecedented fifth term as governor.

1991
Clinton declares his candidacy for President on October 3rd.

1992
Clinton wins over 2,400 delegates to gain a first- ballot victory at the Democratic National Convention in New York City. Clinton leads Bush in the polls.

Part One

The Higher Patriotism

. . . Some people see things as they are and ask "Why?" I see things that never were, and say "Why not?"

The Serpent speaking to Eve, challenging the conventional wisdom in the Garden of Eden, in a play by George Bernard Shaw

---

Chapter One

A Place Called Hope

Bill Clinton grew up the hard way, experiencing hardship and economic disadvantages as a child. Almost four months before he was born in 1946, his father, William Jefferson Blythe III, blew a tire on Highway 61, just north of the Arkansas border near Sikeston, Missouri. His car skidded off the asphalt and he was thrown from the car and died by the side of the road.

Many years later, as a young man in his early twenties, Bill Clinton visited the spot where the accident occurred. "I was driving North from Arkansas to Chicago," he recalled to Bill Moyers, "and I just was near the town in Missouri and the space of highway where I knew he died, and I had never been there. So I decided to go and check it out. And I did. . . . He was thrown out of a car, face down in the ditch. I was looking at the way the road was and wondering what it might have been like and wishing he'd landed the other way."

Bill Clinton's mother, Virginia Cassidy, had met Bill's father in Shreveport, Louisiana, where she was a nurse trainee at Tri-State Hospital. He was an auto salesman from Sherman, Texas, and she was working at the hospital where he had taken a friend to visit. They fell in love and married. As was the case for many newlyweds, Bill Blythe left Virginia behind when he enlisted to serve in the Second World War in 1942. They were separated by the war for three years.

Following the war, Blythe found a job in Chicago as a traveling heavy equipment salesman. He commuted home as often as he could to be with his young wife. Like many young mothers of her generation, when she got pregnant, Virginia moved back home to live with her parents in Hope where her husband knew she would be cared for while he was away. Virginia's mother, Edith, was a registered nurse. Eventually, the Blythes bought a house in Chicago where they planned to raise a family.

In the Spring of 1946, Bill Blythe drove to Hope to take Virginia, then over five months pregnant, back to Chicago. He never made it home that night. Some of Hope's older residents still remember the power of Virginia's grief.

Almost four months later, on August 19, 1946, Virginia Cassidy Blythe gave birth to a healthy baby boy. She named him William Jefferson Blythe IV, after his late father; not until years later would the young man adopt the name Clinton. The two of them remained with her parents, Eldridge and Edith Cassidy. Mary Baker, who lived next door to the Cassidys, remembered, "They all worked and the three of them including Virginia took turns taking care of him. They loved him dearly. He was the first great-grandchild in the family."

Hope, a rural farming community 32 miles northeast of Texarkana, was coming off an economic boom when Billy was born. During the war, the federal government had built an artillery testing ground just outside of town, bringing in skilled workers to the area and boosting the local economy. Nevertheless, from an early age, he learned from experience what it was like to live in a family that belonged to the working poor: lower-middle class, not chronically broke, but always living from one day to the next. Indoor plumbing was a luxury they couldn't afford; they had to make do with an outhouse.

When Billy was two years old, Virginia Cassidy Blythe left him with her parents in Hope so she could study to become a nurse anesthetist at Charity Hospital in New Orleans. She hoped to earn enough money to support her child.

Billy remained in Hope with his grandparents, who taught him to read and count, and gave him children's books to read when he was three. Although they lacked formal education, they instilled in Billy a love of learning.

Bill Clinton's earliest childhood memories start when he was about three years old. His grandmother took him by train to visit his mother in New Orleans where they stayed in the Young Hotel. It was the first time that Billy had ever been in a building with more than two stories. When he was about to leave for Hope with his grandmother, his mother knelt down at the side of the railroad tracks and cried because her child was leaving her. Only later in life did Bill realize why his mother had to stay behind — so she might get a chance to make a decent living for herself and her son.

When Eldridge Cassidy bought a small country store in a predominantly black neighborhood, the little boy learned by his grandfather's example how to treat all people with kindness and respect. Clinton often speaks of his grandfather's kind-hearted personality and recalled that

Eldridge would extend credit to poor families who did not have enough money to buy food. Eventually, his grandfather extended more credit than his customers could afford to repay. It did not matter to Eldridge Cassidy what color skin his customers had, but whether or not they could put food on the table. And that lesson was not lost on the young boy helping out his grandfather's shop.

Dale Drake, Virginia's cousin and best friend in Hope, told the *Hope Star* that Billy "was loved above all things by his mother and grandparents." She remembers that when Billy went to the store with his grandfather, "he'd go there and play with the children living around the store. His grandfather taught him to never, never be ugly to anyone," she said. "He grew up with a love for people."

Margaret Polk, a relative and neighbor in Hope, remembers that Billy was special and well-behaved. She lived across the street from the Cassidys when Billy was about four years old. Polk told the *Hope Star*, "He always wore a cowboy hat and cowboy boots. He'd ride his tricycle up and down the sidewalk, always wearing that cowboy hat."

Billy also played with Margaret's daughter, Mitzi, who was two years older than him. One event that Margaret observed convinced her that Bill was more mature than other kids his age. "He let Mitzi wear his hat one day when they were playing on the slide," she told the *Hope Star*. Mitzi was about to go down it, when the string on the cowboy hat got hung up on the slide. Before we could get to her, Bill climbed up the slide and pushed her feet up in order to free the string. He was such a little thing then, and I think that showed he was thinking beyond his age. He just seemed to accept responsibility early."

One childhood friend who remembers Billy Blythe at this time is Joseph Purvis. They attended kindergarten together in the early 1950s.

My mother, Martha Houston Purvis, and Bill's mother, were very good friends. I have seen pictures of our mothers with Bill and me in our respective strollers.

Hope, Arkansas, in the late 40's and early 50's was not a place of great financial wealth, and the result was that everyone was pretty much in the same social strata. On reflecting over some 40 years, however, I can see that we were all rich beyond our wildest imaginations in that Hope was a town with a great community spirit and a great deal of love. For nearly all of us, it meant that you grew up with both parents and also had your grandparents, cousins and others there around you. Everyone in the town knew everyone else and everyone there seemed to look out for everyone else's children. Thus, in many ways, the town was like one large neighborhood.

I remember quite vividly that in the 1951-52 school year we went to Miss Mary's kindergarten. This kindergarten was run by two old maid sisters, Mary and Nannie Perkins. Their kindergarten was run in a small white clapboard school house with a mini steeple and bell that was located in their backyard on East Second Street in Hope.

This school had a large open room for classes and something of a cloakroom in the back. I also remember that everyone had to bring their own "pallet" as it was called then because after lunch recess, we were all required to come in and lie down on our pallets to take a nap. How I hated those naps!

Purvis vividly recalled a painful event in Clinton's early life:

"At any rate, one day I recall that we were all playing high jump with a jump rope in the yard around the school house during the lunch recess. This was played by two boys each grabbing an end of the rope, stretching it straight across and everyone taking turns high jumping over the rope. As you cleared a particular height, the rope was raised to whatever level the holders thought appropriate.

The general attire for boys at that time was a t-shirt, blue jeans and either army boots or cowboy boots. On this one particular occasion, I remember Bill was wearing cowboy boots because when it came his turn to jump over the rope, his heel caught on the rope and he fell hard to the ground. I remember Bill wouldn't stop crying, and Miss Mary or Miss Nannie had to call his grandparents to come pick him up and take him home from kindergarten.

Imagine my shock when I got home from school and found out the reason Bill had been crying was that the fall broke his leg in three places".

Billy's grandfather took him to the hospital where he was put in a cast up to his hip and his leg was suspended in the air. Mrs. Henry Haynes, his Sunday School teacher at First Baptist Church, went with a group from the church to visit Billy in the hospital. "He was in my four-year old class," she recalled. "I remember him as a bright child who adjusted well. He was a handsome little boy with curly hair."

George Wright, Jr., now an industrial relations coordinator for Medical Park Hospital in Hope, was another of

Billy's kindergarten playmates. He recollects that Billy wanted to be everyone's friend. "And he was! He never forgets names! I remember him, even when he was younger, as an extrovert, fun-loving, and having a good sense of humor."

Billy developed a deep and lasting affection for his hometown because of these childhood years. "We're all just poor folks — his family," said Margaret Polk. "He doesn't forget his roots. He still comes here to attend funerals and reunions. Bill hasn't forgotten us."

Chapter Two

Home Fires

When Billy was four, Virginia Blythe married Roger Clinton, a car salesman. There were frequent arguments between Virginia and Roger, who was an alcoholic. After drinking, he occasionally beat Virginia. He was usually calm but when he drank, he became angry. During one episode, he fired a gun into a wall of the living room and was put in jail.

Roger had operated a Buick dealership in Hope, but there had not been enough business to run it successfully. He bought a farm outside of Hot Springs, a well-known health and tourist resort noted for its mineral baths and horse races, and joined his brother's Buick dealership.

Billy had one of his most vivid childhood experiences at the farm. "When I was seven or eight, a ram butted me and cut my head open," Clinton told the *Arkansas Gazette*, pulling his hair back to expose a scar on his forehead. "I was too young, fat, and slow to run, even after he knocked me down the second time. He must have butted me ten times. It was the awfullest beating I ever took and I had to go to the hospital for stitches." The pain of the injury was temporary and he learned to be more careful in his new surroundings.

When Billy was seven, the family left the farm for the town of Hot Springs, where Virginia enrolled Billy in the second grade at St. John's Catholic School. The family belonged to the Baptist Church, but Virginia believed that St. John's would give Billy a better preparation for the town's public school system. At this time, the young boy became known as Billy Clinton, even though he did not legally change his name until later.

Billy received good grades at St. John's, except that he got a low mark in conduct on his report card. His teacher, a nun, explained to Virginia that Billy was so intelligent and alert that he answered questions before the other children could raise their hands. The teacher could not restrain him from this over-enthusiastic behavior. She thought that giving Bill his low grade might get his attention. Bill got the message and learned to give his classmates an equal chance.

Early in his life, Bill recognized the benefits of education. "When I was a small boy, I was taught, as so many of my generation were, that I had to get a good education and work hard so that I could do better than my parents and grandparents had done. Citizens of that time took the overall health and strength of America for granted and worked to make sure their children could benefit from it more than they had." An avid reader, Bill was reading the newspaper every day by the time he was eight years old and soon developed a strong interest in current events.

In 1955, Bill's family bought their first black-and-white television set and he became fascinated with politics as he watched the 1956 Democratic National Convention on television. The fight between John F. Kennedy and Estes Kefauver for the vice-presidential nomination and the excitement of politics left a lasting impression on him.

Bill went to fourth grade at Ramble School, the public elementary school in Hot Springs. David Leopoulos, a classmate, lived a block away from Bill and the two soon became good friends:

Ramble school was a red brick school with wooden floors. It had two stories and had great rolls for lunch. From the first week Bill attended Ramble school most kids knew who he was and wanted to be around him. Bill used a catch phrase, *Hot Dog*. Every time he would get excited about something he would use that phrase. In less than a week most everyone in the school was saying, *Hot Dog*. I never knew anyone who did not like Bill, for he treated everyone with respect.

During the summers and on many weekends I would go to Bill's house and spend most of the day and some nights. A typical day would consist of playing touch football. These games were very competitive. We would argue most every time we played. I was skinny and fast and Bill was large and sometimes slow. He made up for his slowness with pure desire.

We spent many hours playing Monopoly and listening to Elvis records. We had most of Elvis' records memorized and would hum them during our dog eat dog touch football games. We also spent time together in total silence. He would be there in person, but his mind was somewhere else. At first it was frustrating, but I soon got used to it. He still does it today.

Even in grade school, Bill was a peacemaker, stopping

playground fights wherever he could. Whenever he saw someone in need, Bill tried to help—David Leopoulos remembers one Thanksgiving, when Bill went above and beyond the call of duty.

Virginia sent him to the grocery store down the street from his house to get something. There was a young boy sitting at the bus stop. This person had a bag of potato chips in his hand. Bill noticed that he didn't seem very happy, so he went up and introduced himself to the boy. A few minutes later the two boys walked into Virginia's back door.

Virginia said, "Bill, who is your friend?"

Bill said, "Mom I met Johnny at the bus stop and he told me he wasn't going to have any Thanksgiving dinner today. So I asked him to eat with us — you don't want him to just have potato chips for Thanksgiving dinner, do you?"

One day, David and Bill were waiting for a bus, when several older boys decided to pick a fight with David.

I was sitting on the bench at the bus stop. Bill was talking with some other kids a short distance away. I was outnumbered and I was a skinny runt. While these hoods (as we called them) were talking to me Bill saw what was going on and walked up behind them and just stood there. He looked at me and said, "David, how are you doing?" These guys walked away. He never looked at them. I never remember Bill having a fight with anyone, but I knew he would stand up for what was right.

When Bill was ten, his mother and stepfather had a son, whom they named Roger, Jr. Virginia was very close to her two sons, and wanted to spend as much time with them as she could. As a nurse anesthetist, however, she was often on 24-hour call for surgery. She hired a sitter to watch the two boys when she was working. Bill also took on the responsibility, when he was older, of babysitting little Roger.

His stepfather's alcoholism continued to be a problem. There had been many episodes of violence that bothered Bill in Hot Springs. One day, Bill had enough. "One of the most difficult things for me was being fourteen and putting an end to the violence," he later recalled. "I just broke down the door of their room one night when they were having an encounter and told him that I was bigger than him now, and there would never be any more of this while I was there." He took his mother and younger half-brother by the hand and issued a warning to his stepfather: "You will never hit either of them again. If you want them, you'll have to go through me."

Roger's drinking led to a divorce when Bill was 14. In a deposition, Virginia said, "He has continually tried to do bodily harm to myself and my son Billy." The next year, though, Roger convinced Virginia that he could sober up. Bill tried to persuade his mother not to remarry him, arguing that his stepfather could not be reformed. Virginia still loved Roger and according to Bill, "she was old-fashioned in some way and she felt that Roger, Jr., needed a father." When his mother remarried Roger Clinton, Bill made the best of it: to make his mother happy, he changed his last name from Blythe to Clinton.

Despite the domestic violence, Bill really cared for his stepfather. "He was a wonderful person, but he didn't like himself very much," Bill later said. "He had a prolonged bout with cancer. And I think in the course of fighting it through somehow, he gained some peace with himself that enabled him to reconcile with all the rest of us. He was a marvelous person and he was very good to me. And his family was good to me. It really was a painful experience to see someone you love, that you think a lot of, that you care about, just in the grip of a demon."

This painful experience provided insights into the problems of addiction. "I think most people who are alcoholics, or who are drug addicts, or who have some other compulsion suffer from at least bouts of low self-image, self-esteem," he said. "There's some fear, some demon they can't get rid of."

Looking back, Clinton still remembers some happy times in his childhood. "Overall I was a pretty happy kid. . . . When my stepfather married my mother they moved to Hot Springs, they both worked, we had a comfortable living. I had a little brother when I was ten. I had a normal childhood. I had friends, I did things, I was absorbed in the life of a child in a beautiful place where people were good to me and I learned a lot in school. I had a good normal life. But at times it was really tough. I had to learn to live with the darker side of life at a fairly early period. But I wouldn't say it was a tormented childhood. I had a good life and I've still got a lot of the friends of that childhood."

Chapter Three

The Turning Point

Bill's high school years were very significant to his character and development. He became a student leader and gained valuable skills that would help him greatly in life and in politics. During this time he met many lifelong friends who would play a role in his early career.

Perhaps the most important influence on his values was his mother Virginia, who often engaged him on the pressing moral issues of the day. Dave Leopoulos recalled:

In the afternoons when Virginia would come home from St. Joseph's hospital, we had a very interesting ritual. She would drive up to the back of the house at breakneck speed, get out of the car, wave to us and go in the back door. No matter what we were doing we would stop, go into the house, and then it would start. Virginia would toss her purse with a shoulder length strap onto the kitchen counter and most always say, "I just can't believe it."

Bill would say, "What can't you believe?"

Then we would get our lesson on what was right - wrong, good - bad or fair - unfair about many different experiences she was having or news she had read in the newspaper. (That was back in the days when news was news.)

During our earlier years, when we were between eight to twelve years of age Bill and I would listen a lot to Virginia. In high school, however, he would debate her tooth and nail. Neither would give an inch on their side. There were some red faces and bulging veins in the neck during those debates. I was never sure who won, I was afraid to ask. I am quite sure these conversations were the beginnings of molding Bill into a caring, compassionate, concerned, thinking individual.

Bill met Carolyn Yeldell Staley in high school, when she lived around the corner from his house. She, too, remembers the animated conversations between mother and son:

Almost without exception the subject would center on some injustice she had witnessed, some denial of fairness, and she would tell us about the situation. We would gather around in the kitchen and discuss the issue and possible solutions. Often we would understand that, for now, there were no immediate solutions but that they needed to be sought as soon as possible.

Virginia treated Bill as a full adult from the first time I met them. She respected him, discussed issues with him, and trusted him with a great deal more freedom than most of us had. She recognized, I believe, that Bill was a strong and uniquely gifted young man and wanted to help him have the fullest range of opportunities possible in life.

Carolyn spent a lot of time at the Clintons' home on 213 Scully Street.

The yard was pretty with many roses and flowers which were Virginia's joy. She would often come home from work in the spring and summer months, change into shorts and a tube top for sunning and work for hours in the yard.

Connected to the house was a carport which housed two Buicks driven by the Clintons. The Clintons also owned an old 'Henry J' car which was a small to mid-size creamy yellow convertible. Bill took this car out often in high school for jaunts on sunny summer days. Above the carport was a basketball goal which Bill spent many hours enjoying. He loved to shoot baskets with friends or by himself.

The neighborhood itself was quiet and kind of secluded, although houses began to be built there in greater numbers after we left high school. One of the loveliest sights from Bill's picture windows and my home was a field of peonies which bloomed in late April and May each year. This was a stunningly beautiful sight to have a full city block of pink, rose and deep purple blossoms across the street each Spring.

Two large houses were across from mine on Wheatley Street. One was the home of Hill Wheatley who was the major real estate owner in downtown Hot Springs. Behind his house was a pond where neighborhood kids could go and fish. This was a popular spot for Roger Clinton, Jr., to spend many hours fishing with friends his age in the neighborhood. Also connecting to the pond was a lovely little brook or 'creek' as the kids called it and it provided many happy times of walking and exploring for the neighborhood gang.

Through the high school years, Bill and I spent a lot of time together and our friendship deepened into one which is still very special today. Other friends have remained close also since these early years, notably David Leopoulos and Joe Newman. In fact, we still have lunch together once a month.

The time we spent together was often at either my house or Bill's, listening to music, playing and singing at the piano, and reading. David and Joe and others would some times come to Bill's and play touch football in the back yard, and then we'd wind up in one of our houses to visit. Some mornings Bill would call and ask me to come over and bring my crossword puzzle out of the *Hot Springs Sentinel Record* newspaper and we would see who could finish first.

Bill was always reading something, and David's joke to me was, 'Hey, you want to go over to Bill's and watch him read?'

Lots of the time we spent together was simply in being together, not always even talking, but just bonding through the hours. Sometimes Bill would drop over to my house and say he was going to run some errands around town and ask if I would like to come along. We'd drive around Hot Springs in the Buick convertible and enjoy the beautiful weather as we stopped here and there — the post office, the music store, school, wherever the errands would take us.

We spent a lot of time doing things together as a group.

Hardly ever did anyone actually have a date; rather, we just spent time together as a group. We watched many old movies on television (Bill is still an expert on movie classics and stars), played miniature golf or went bowling, typically. Everyone had dates, of course, for special events like the prom, but by-and-large we just spent time together.

In the tenth grade, Bill started Hot Springs High School. He enrolled in a World History class taught by a young man named Paul Root. In that classroom, Bill began a journey which would take him far beyond the simple life he knew.

I first met Bill Clinton when he was 15 years old. I was 28 years old and in my fourth year as a teacher. This was a small class and every student enrolled was very good academically and displayed much interest in the subject matter. Most of the students in this class were taking Latin and other advanced courses. This, of course, was true of young Bill Clinton. At fifteen, Bill was already looking down on me. (I am 5'8".) He was a tall, gangly kid with an ever present smile and an intense interest in everything.

Young Bill Clinton was one of those students that history teachers pray to have in their class. He understood that the study of the peoples of Europe and the other parts of the world was related to American history and that the past was somehow related to the present, and possibly even the future. He wanted to understand the relationships among peoples and the relationship between the geography of a nation and political decisions of that nation. Why democracy grew in nations that had a strong navy as opposed to a strong army was of interest to him.

When outside reading assignments were chosen Bill chose as one of his readings *Animal Farm*. Some of my students thought *Animal Farm* was a cartoon but Bill understood it as a commentary on the continuing phases of the Russian revolution.

Root did not know it then, but their paths would cross again. He recalled, "As I followed Bill's career, it became obvious that he was pursuing depth in the study of the relationships of people worldwide." When two decades later, Governor Clinton would need a special assistant in the Governor's Office to develop working relationships on education policy, Root would be there to help.

Bill's high school friends remember him as a caring, supportive person. Dave Leopoulos recalled that — he would especially help those who wanted to help themselves:

In high school I was not a great student. I was failing an Algebra course and needed at least a "B" on my final test to pass the course with a "D". Bill found out about my troubles and told me I was coming over to his house to study the night before the test. Well, I went over to Bill's house, but I wasn't in a serious mood. I was joking and laughing during most of the evening. Bill finally had enough and let me have it. He said, "If you don't care enough to help yourself then I can't help you." I had never seen him that mad at me before. Needless to say I studied the rest of the night. The next day, I failed the test. Bill was disappointed - more than I.

Our senior year I needed to pass the typing course in order to graduate with the Class of 1964. I needed to pass the typing test by typing 60 WPM with few mistakes. I was allowed to take the test as many times as I had time to take it. This process started about two weeks before school ended. It came down to the last day of school. I could take the test one more time that morning. If I passed it I graduated, if not it was summer school for me. The night before the last day of school I was sitting at home scared to death, knowing I couldn't pass the test. After all I hadn't passed it yet. There was a knock on the door. My Mom answered.

"It's Western Union," she called. "He has a telegram for you." I could not believe my ears. After all, telegrams are for important people. The telegram was from Bill Clinton.

"Good Luck on your typing test tomorrow," it read. "I know you will pass it. Your Friend, Bill." Yes, I did pass the test. My friend was with me, as usual.

Much of our time was spent talking, playing cards, (he counts cards and knows who played which card and which card you would likely have in your hand) eating ice cream at Cook's Ice Cream, singing songs at Carolyn's house, playing touch football in his back yard or next to a nearby cemetery. When Bill was alone he read lots of books. His band activities took up a lot of time — he really got into his music.

Bill took a leadership role in many different musical activities during high school. He played in the Marching Band, Concert Band, Stage Band, Pep Band, Band Key Club, and combos. He was a band officer, emcee of the band variety show, and many solo-ensemble events. Bill also helped to organize and schedule the many events for the annual Arkansas Band and Orchestra Festival.

Already a talented player at this time, Bill became First

Chair Tenor Saxophone in the All-State First Band, the highest honor a high school musician could earn. He emceed the annual band variety show, and won various trophies and awards, both as a soloist and as part of the group, in the *Stardusters* stage band for his region and state. He earned many First Division solo and ensemble medals and citations. Bill was the top band officer as "Band Major" and worked as the Assistant Band Director as a student officer.

Bill Clinton and Carolyn Yeldell Staley became closer friends because of their shared interest in music.

He knew that I was a talented pianist because he had heard me accompany the large Hot Springs High School chorus and ensembles. One day he asked me if I would be his accompanist for the solo competition during the state band festival. I agreed and we began meeting several times each week at my house to perfect his solo. These rehearsals were intense times of hard work. We never just sat around and talked. Bill was always very serious about his performance at the solo competition and we worked hard to win a first place rating.

At the state band festival, Bill always performed very well and received first place ratings as often as I can remember. He was always eager to know how he had been judged and to read the comments, so he waited around until they were posted. I usually played a piano solo too and he liked to watch and see my rating and read the judge's comments.

Music forged a real friendship between us. As our friendship developed Bill would often come over to my house simply to pass time and visit and we would often play the piano. He would sit on the piano bench at the upper end of the keyboard and we would name songs and try to play them by ear. Bill also liked to sing and one of his favorite songs was *The Green, Green Grass of Home*. Sometimes other friends would drop by and we'd all sing. We also liked Peter, Paul and Mary and other folk songs. Another favorite singer was and still is Judy Collins.

Bill would sometimes walk into the living room of my home and be seated without my knowledge while I was playing the piano. When I finished the piece he would applaud.

Bill and I spent a great deal of time listening to records when we were high school friends. Our favorites were Ray Charles, Nancy Wilson and Dionne Warwick, but we also listened often to jazz recordings by Dave Brubeck and Stan Getz. Sometimes when we played the piano together we tried to play the Brubeck pieces, especially *Take Five*. Bill also liked recordings of symphonic band music. One of his favorite compositions for band was *Chant and Jubilo* and he often said he wished our band could play this for our high school graduation processional.

Through music and band, Bill amassed a large network of friends and acquaintances throughout the state. He was selected to be first-chair tenor saxophone for the All-State Band, the highest honor attainable for a band member. Bill attended band camps in the summer and found great joy in music, both for the discipline it required and for the beauty of it. He was offered at least one music scholarship for college, but government had already gotten his bid for a career choice.

One of Bill's favorite teachers at Hot Springs High

School was Virgil Spurlin, the Band Director. Everyone has a teacher in high school to whom they felt closer to than any other. Virgil Spurlin was like a father to Bill. The emotional bond between them is evident in Spurlin's recollections.

Even though I did not know Bill in his very early age back in Hope, Arkansas, as Billy Blythe, I think that those days had an impact on the teen-age Bill, the present-day Governor Bill, and the Democrat Presidential Candidate Bill. All these earlier days were hard for him to deal with, yet they became a part of making Bill a more "mature" teen-ager than most of his peers.

I first knew Bill when he was in Junior High — when his interest in music and in other related subjects became evident — at least, to me. I felt at that time he had more talent — and not just musical talent — than was "par for the course." He was permitted to participate in regional High School events, even while he was a junior high school student at the time. He always seemed to come across as a young man older than his chronological age. Because of this, he could compete with more advanced challenges.

One of the things that will always stand out about Bill is his unique combination of abilities, ambitions, and talents. Even since high school, he has used his musical talents to good advantage on many occasions. While attending Georgetown University during a time of racial unrest, he would often use his saxophone to break the ice with new people. He organized an integrated group to play in the K-Mart parking lot in his hometown when others would not have tried such a move.

He has been able to combine his humanitarian, political, and public relations skills with his god-given talent of music and it has worked very well in each case. Bill has always let his Christian character and beliefs take priority in his dealings with others.

Someone asked me what I thought about the idea that if Bill had met Elvis Presley at the time that he actually met and talked with JFK, would he have chosen music as a career instead of trying politics? I really don't think so, because he has always used his great talent in music to further his deeper desire to bring about other more important results among his fellow human beings — a more "politically motivated" end result — more than a mere pleasant air or melody to be enjoyed just as entertainment.

Randy Goodrum first met Bill Clinton in 1963 and was one of his best friends. Goodrum recalled:

Bill and Joe Newman were one year ahead of me in school and called me to participate in the formation of an instrumental trio called *The Three Kings*. He was an All-State saxophone player and Joe, All-State drums. Both were heavily involved in the band program and well known to be great musicians . . . I was flattered. We hit it off and for two years, had a very fun and creative time performing around town mostly for community events and variety shows.

That was a pivotal time for me because during that time I was trying to decide between medicine and music. I decided to pursue music as a career. That little trio was an important time for all three of us.

Bill had a tremendous passion for music as well as expert knowledge of the instrument. He worked, studied, and practiced hard to get to be "All-State" and I know that Bill contemplated being a professional musician, which was a very unusual and risky business to consider in Hot Springs, Arkansas. The trio afforded us the opportunity to experiment, expand, and see if we could play in front of people and get a positive response.

At the time Stan Getz was popularizing the *bossa nova* and we did a number of songs from his records and a potpourri of pop, jazz, and blues tunes. We rehearsed until we could play a given piece of music backwards and forwards; however, we always left plenty of room for spontaneous improvisation. We rehearsed wherever we could gather around a piano: the band room, my house, Bill's house, or at friends' houses. My mother remembers serving gallons of iced tea to us and I remember Virginia Clinton with her ever present smile doing likewise.

During that two year period I got to know Bill quite well. He had the extraordinary ability to give you 100 percent of his attention when you talked or worked with him. He had an amazing memory, was a great listener, and even though he was the leader of the band, he would take any and all suggestions and use them if they made sense, sometimes while we were on stage. He had a natural rapport with the audience wherever we played and a great sense of humor. From where I sit, he is still fundamentally the same.

I have known many people who have gone from obscurity to fame in my life, mostly in my business, and almost always they are affected and changed. Bill hasn't. We have kept up with each other over the years and each time we see each other or talk on the phone we simply take up where we left off.

The Three Kings changed Goodrum's life. He went on to earn a degree in piano and become a professional musician. In 1981 he was honored as ASCAP's Country Songwriter of the Year and also earned a Grammy nomination. "I have played with hundreds of bands and with thousands of musicians in the subsequent years," he said. "In some ways *The Three Kings* was one of the most ideal musical experiences I ever have had."

We became friends because Bill gave his friendship to me. He was never shy. Recently another friend of ours described her own children to me as follows: "They are at the age where they're sure everybody else is cool and they're not." Most of us remember that, but I don't think Bill had to deal with that self doubt. At least not when we were young. He was able to make friends with a lot of us. He has worked at keeping his old friendships alive when they could have slid away because of the course of his life.

Bill was an excellent student. He always got high grades. But he wasn't perfect. In the eleventh grade we were required to do a project for a science fair. Everyone had a partner. My partner was Bill. He told me he'd take care of everything. That was good since I sure had no idea what we'd do. Finally the day before the fair he came up with a curved, shiny piece of sheet metal and put a hot dog on it. Our project was a solar hot dog cooker. Great. I think we got the "D" we deserved. Since the solar hot dog cooker, Bill has had better ideas.

Newman recalled that he and Bill always had fun together — on and off the stage.

We did the things kids do. His family had an old car built by Henry Kaiser - a Henry J. It had no top. I believe it had been wrecked and the top cut off. He loved that car. We shared lots of miles in it together. He was the student director of the pep band that traveled to out of town football games. He always wore this big sombrero when he traveled. It must have been four feet across. I believe Bill wouldn't mind wearing that sombrero and riding that Henry J. again. He has a great sense of humor. He's always ready with a joke and he smiles easily. He is comfortable to be around. It is not in his nature to turn into a self-consumed person who will forget why he chose the life he did.

Bill's interest in the arts extended to the theater, where he played leading roles in *Arsenic and Old Lace* and other plays. He also excelled in his academic subjects and was a National Merit Semifinalist. Bill was President of the Beta Club (for outstanding academic achievements) and participated in the Calculus Club, Mu Alpha Theta (the math club for advanced students), Junior Classical League (for advanced Latin students), and the Bio-Chem-Phy Club.

The principal of Hot Springs High School, Johnnie Mae Mackey, was a forceful influence on Bill and his classmates. Carolyn Yeldell Staley remembers how she instilled in them a sense of patriotism and civic pride:

The seeds of a life in public service were planted early in Bill's life, and really in all of our lives. We attended high school at a time when we had enormous respect for our teachers, for their service to us and for education in general. We had an amazing high school principal,

Johnnie Mae Mackey, who was a strong woman and a proud American. Her husband had died in World War II and she had devoted much of her extracurricular time to the activities of the American Legion Auxiliary and its programs. She held a Flag Day assembly each year and taught us to revere our flag and the freedom it stands for. She taught us flag etiquette and that we should always stand when the flag passes by. Her voice boomed out her admonition to patriotism and love for America, and the importance of service to our country.

Mackey was unafraid to step in when she thought Bill Clinton was getting too distracted from his studies. At one point, she had to place a limit on the number of organizations any one student could belong to — or Bill would have been president of them all. Nevertheless, he managed to win election to the student council. Glenda Johnson Cooper enjoyed casting her first vote for Bill Clinton.

My generation was influenced and in many ways shaped by the Presidency of John Kennedy. I was a shy girl who moved every year so I never was involved in politics but I admired kids who were. Bill Clinton stands out in my memory because he was so friendly, self-confident and kind.

I first met Bill when he was running for student council in the 10th grade. He came up to me and shook my hand introducing himself. He was always generous with his time, helping newcomers to Hot Springs High. I was struck by his positive attitude, his intelligence, and his sincerity. He seemed so comfortable with himself, his abilities and so optimistic about his future. I remember thinking that he was a great campaigner, so

energetic, compassionate, funny, talented, and involved.
Remember, this was a time when public service was
something honorable — a great opportunity to make our
country a better place for all.

In class, he was very studious and competitive with
a deeper understanding of current political issues as are
most gifted students. We weren't far from the Little
Rock of 1957 and we attended an all white school but
Bill despised racial intolerance as well as the negative
stereotyping of Arkansas. His feeling was that we were
as good as anyone else in this country and that education was the key to fundamental change in our poor
state.

Carolyn Yeldell Staley also sensed that Bill had a
promising future in public service. "Bill would walk into
my house when we had relatives or friends visiting from
out-of-town," she recalled, "and by the time he left they
were marveling at this young man. He had such a natural
gift for conversation, was impressive and charismatic, and
made a lasting impression."

Bill also displayed leadership skills at the time by
involving himself in many community projects and services. He was a member of the Kiwanis Key Club, and the
Hot Springs High School faculty selected him as a *Civitan*
Junior Businessman. He received the Elks Youth Leadership Award for Arkansas. As a result of his accomplishments, Bill was often sought after by organizations seeking his unique talents, and by local civic clubs, which
wanted him to speak to their organizations and to chair
drives and campaigns in the community.

Edith Irons, Bill's high school counselor, recalled that
Miss Mackey soon had not only to limit Bill's ability to

join organizations, but she had to stop the organizations from recruiting him.

The principal of the high school, Miss Johnnie Mae Mackey, had discussed with me that the civic clubs were asking him to do so much he was missing too much school. At that time, the phone rang. It was the chairman of the annual Heart Association drive, asking for Bill to head the heart fund drive.

She said, "No. Bill's mother said that he is missing too much school."

Miss Mackey hung up the phone and said, "Now, I have to call Virginia and tell her I lied," which she did. Of course, Virginia agreed with her — for *no one* disagreed with Miss Mackey.

Carolyn, Bill, David, and their friends and schoolmates learned to regard their nation with love and honor. Aspiring to elected office — aspiring to be a statesman — was a lofty and well-respected ambition. Young men and women learned that the duties of citizenship were not to be ignored.

The early 1960s were filled with American idealism, in large part due to the zest and the youthful spirit of the New Frontier. Bill was caught up in the mood of the times. John F. Kennedy's vision, in 1962, of landing a man on the moon before the end of the decade, perhaps best exemplifies the sense of can-do idealism which inspired the young Bill Clinton. Kennedy's speeches electrified the nation: "We choose to go to the moon in this decade," Kennedy said, "and do the other things not because they are easy but because they are hard, because that goal will serve to organize and measure the best of our energies and skills, because that challenge is one that we are willing to accept, one we are unwilling to postpone, and one which we intend to win." The sense of urgency — of vital importance — which characterized the President's speech resonated with Bill's own sense of optimism that problems in Arkansas could be solved.

Many young Americans in Bill's generation also learned from President Kennedy about the importance of investments for the future, of making sacrifices now and reaping long-term rewards. "I decided to be a Democrat," Clinton later recalled, "starting in the presidential election of 1960, when John Kennedy excited me with a promise to get the country moving again. I think he gave people the sense that they could make a difference. And he did it without ever promising that all the problems could be solved — just that tomorrow would be better than today. He [also] convinced me that he and Lyndon Johnson wanted to do something about civil rights problems, particularly in the South, my own region."

In 1963, when he was sixteen years old, Bill was invited to participate in Boys' State, a civics program run by the American Legion to teach young leaders about government and politics. He was elected as one of Arkansas' delegates to the national convention of Boys' Nation in Washington, DC. There he ate lunch in the Senate Dining Room with Arkansas Senator J. William Fulbright. Fulbright had years of experience in foreign affairs matched by very few public servants before or since. At that time, his long service with the House and Senate Foreign Relations committees had already spanned the terms of office of five presidents, from Roosevelt to Johnson. Fulbright had been involved with almost every important foreign policy issue since the early 1940s. Over lunch, Bill and his friends asked questions about the issues and about Fulbright's ideas and listened carefully to each answer.

Carolyn Staley was selected to go to Washington for Girls' Nation, the counterpart to Boys' Nation. She recalled the moment Bill Clinton decided to go into public service: when he shook hands with President John Kennedy in the White House Rose Garden. "This was both a tremendous honor and opportunity for us, she said. "Virginia said she could see in Bill's eyes upon his return home that he was clearly on a path to public service through elected office."

The shock of John Kennedy's assassination left its mark on Bill's generation of young Americans. Most of them still remember exactly where they were and how they felt when they first heard the news of his death on November 22, 1963. Millions of young men and women had felt a warm personal connection to Jack Kennedy, admiring his vitality, his enchanting personality, and his courage. Bill and his generation felt a profound loss at his death. The principal of Hot Springs High School, ordered the flag at school lowered to half mast that day and for a week of mourning thereafter. David Leopoulos described how they all grieved when John Kennedy was felled by an assassin's bullet not four months after Bill and Carolyn had met him in the Rose Garden.

Jack Kennedy was young and stood for basic rights. He seemed to care about every American's situation. Bill's view of government was full of optimism and positive images. Serving people was paramount. Empathy for people, helping people help themselves was the course to take. Then they took our leader away. The day Kennedy was killed was the day that optimism started its turn to pessimism, and the day our country will always regret. We were all crushed when we lost our leader.

As early as his junior year in high school, knew that he wanted to achieve an elected office in government. He told *Georgetown Magazine*: "By the time I was seventeen, I knew I wanted to be what I'm doing now...and I knew that if I was in school in Washington I would have many opportunities to learn a lot about foreign affairs, domestic politics, and economics. . . . I just started asking people, including staff members of our congressional delegation, what was the most appropriate place. The consensus was that the School of Foreign Service at Georgetown was the most appropriate and the most academically respected and rigorous."

Edith Irons offered advice to him that year which changed the course of his life forever. She could not have known at the time that she was advising a future Governor and a possible president. There are turning points in each of our lives, when we make crucial life choices. Edith Irons was there at Bill's.

I remember Bill Clinton as an All-American young man who set his goals and *never* deviated from them. His fine sense of humor (which included the ability to laugh at himself), his feeling for fair play, his generosity and integrity in dealing with his peers and other members of the community, stand out vividly in my mind. He loved knowledge, books, and people. He was always a gentleman, showing respect and good manners, but at the same time he was a regular fellow who was loved by his peers, teachers, and *yes*, even the civic leaders. He kept his feet on the ground but his eyes on the stars and refused to accept defeat.

At the beginning of his sophomore year, . . . he came into my office and said, "Mrs. Irons, where would you go to school if you wanted to be a foreign diplomat?"

"Off the top of my head, "I replied, "I'd say Georgetown University."

"Why Georgetown?" he continued. I told him because they had a good Foreign Relations program and also the proximity to Washington was advantageous.

"Why proximity to Washington?" he asked. He had a keen interest in civics, politics, and history. I told him he would probably learn as much watching how the government worked as he did in school.

I gave him the catalogue for Georgetown and told him I would order more catalogues and send them to him as they came in. I explained that it was *most difficult* for a Southerner to get into the Ivy League schools and that I would explain to him the steps he had to take at a later conference.

"Could you tell me now?" he persisted.

"Yes, if you have the time," I said. I told him he would have to take the College Board, American College Tests, and Achievement Tests at the end of his 10th grade year to get an idea about them and then test again at the beginning of his Junior year and apply at that time. Because of the great difficulty in getting accepted into Georgetown, I suggested he also apply at a couple of others. He did everything he was told but did not apply to any other college.

He graduated from high school and we had not received any communication as to his acceptance at

Georgetown. Sometime in June he was notified that he was accepted and I breathed a sigh of relief. This was typical of the confidence Bill had in himself. He had set his goal, investigated what needed to be done to accomplish it, did what was necessary, and never considered defeat. If he had considered defeat a possibility, he would have applied to other schools — but not Bill, this was the one he wanted.

Bill's determination, one of his strongest character traits, would serve him well in later years. He was looking forward to going away to college, enjoying some real independence, and finding out what he wanted to do with his life. He knew he would eventually work in public service and politics, and a sense of optimism, pride in his heritage, and easy self-confidence gave him the feeling that he could achieve just about anything he set his mind to. But he knew he hadn't reached this milestone alone. Virgil Spurlin still remembers the words Bill wrote to him in his senior yearbook, the 1964 *Old Gold Book*: "I honestly tried to do a good job for you — now, it's time for me to leave and make the best I can of myself. I know that I'll be better because of my association with . . . one of the greatest Christian men I have known. . . . God bless you. (signed) Bill Clinton."

Chapter Four

Years of Study

Politically, it was an interesting summer. President Johnson was taking the opportunity to press for passage of civil rights legislation which had been planned by the Kennedy Administration. On June 29, shortly after Bill's acceptance to Georgetown, Congress approved an omnibus Civil Rights Bill of 1964 which banned discrimination in voting, jobs and public accommodations. On August 7, Congress passed the Gulf of Tonkin resolution, authorizing President Johnson to take action in Vietnam after North Vietnamese boats reputedly attacked two U.S. destroyers. At that point, there were over 15,000 troops in Vietnam and aid to South Vietnam was running at an annualized rate of over $500 million. Four days later, Congress approved the War on Poverty. Beatlemania was sweeping the nation and signaled the birth of the counterculture. Bill Clinton, with his hair cut short, packed a conservative wardrobe to match the climate of a Jesuit-run University in Washington, D.C.

Early in the Fall, Bill drove with Virginia to Georgetown to register for his freshman year. Edith Irons recalled that his first days at Georgetown required a bit of adjusting.

Bill and his mother went to Georgetown for his orientation. A Jesuit priest had shown them around the school and they came back to his office. He said, "What foreign languages do you speak?"

Bill answered, "None, sir."

The priest exclaimed, "What in the name of the Holy Father is a Southern Baptist who can't speak a foreign language doing in the *Mother* of all Jesuit schools?!" As Bill and his mother headed back toward the car, not a word had been spoken for quite a distance when Bill walked over to her, put his arms around her shoulders, and said, "Don't you worry, Mother. They will know what I'm doing here when I've been here awhile."

Bill didn't waste any time. He moved into his dormitory and became friends with the other young men in his building, including a Texan named Christopher Ashby:

I remembered the gathering of the Loyola Hall freshmen on my first night at Georgetown. It was my first night really away from home, following my first airplane flight and my first time east of the Mississippi. I was scared. I met this tall, friendly kid, who somehow seemed less scared than the rest of us. I was immediately drawn to him when I heard his accent and learned he was from Arkansas. I was from Texas, and Hot Springs had a familiar ring that Bayonne and Pittsfield did not. He was as comfortable to me as the others were disquieting.

That was the first time I met Bill Clinton. From the very beginning, his most memorable and attractive characteristic was his friendliness. He was able, in a way I was not, to overcome the trauma of an uncertain moment, and make those around him feel welcome and at ease. He and I shared the moments of freshman year, the proms, the girlfriends, the Quigley exam cram sessions. Through all of this I never imagined that I would be watching his nomination at Madison Square Garden, I was only struck by what a nice guy he was and how much I enjoyed his company. I was too young to project beyond the moment, but he had an inner quality which I simply enjoyed being around.

Bill was still concerned about his ability to pay for school. His mother had little money to spare — not enough to pay tuition, room, board, and other essential expenses. Bill needed a job. Bill thought about a job working "on the Hill." He had only one real meeting with a U.S. Senator, Senator Fulbright, whom he had met at the Boys Nation convention. But he had to think of the right approach. Bill had worked the previous summer on a campaign for Arkansas Chief Justice Jack Holt. He called him to ask for a favor. Justice Holt called Fulbright's administrative assistant, Lee Williams, and recommended the young man for his first paid position in government.

Williams told Bill that he had two choices: a part-time position for $5,000 per year or a part-time position for $3,500 per year. Bill didn't hesitate; he asked for two part-time jobs.

"You're just the guy I'm looking for," Williams replied. "Be here Monday." And so Bill started as an administrative and research assistant for the Chairman of the Senate Foreign Relations Committee of Congress.

Early in the school year, Bill ran for president — of the Freshman Class. As at other universities, student politics at Georgetown dealt with issues of various degrees of weightiness, such as organizing student directories, planning homecoming dances, lobbying for changes in food service and dealing with other issues which are about as exciting to the average collegian as reading the World Book Encyclopedia on a Saturday night.

Neil Grimaldi remembers first meeting Bill during the first weeks of classes. Bill knocked on his door and said, "Hello. I'm Bill Clinton. I'm running for president of our class." Grimaldi recalled that he was surprised by Bill's sense of focus and direction — most other first year students were still adjusting to college. Stephanie Weldon was one of those impressed by Bill's well-planned campaign.

When he said he was running for freshman class president and described his ideas and plans, I somehow knew that this was the most natural and correct thing that he could do. I later would describe this to friends as the sense that when you met Bill you wanted to say to him, "I want to vote for you; what office are you running for?" For me, that sense has never abated.

Bill won over even his competitors for office. Helen Henry dropped out after listening to him describe his agenda and vision for the University student body:

When I found myself running against him for Freshman Class President, he took the time to sit down with me and outline his platform. By the end of our conversation, he had impressed me so much that I decided not to run. I simply had to admit that he was perfect for the job: high-minded, yet practical.

Even though few Georgetown students paid much attention to campus politics, none of them ever looked down on Bill or resented him because he enjoyed running for office. Fairly soon, he made a name for himself on campus. Dru Bachman was a friend who had heard the name Bill Clinton long before she met the man.

Everyone at Georgetown knew of Bill Clinton: he was the campus *politico*, a self-confessed over-achiever in a school, cradled in the heart of the most political city in America, with a student body almost totally indifferent to politics. In those days, it was *not* stylish to run for class office. It was even less stylish to openly court every friendly face with a handshake in search of a vote. But that's exactly what Bill Clinton did with a sunny naiveté that knew no different. It *was* very stylish to attend polo games and embassy parties and to treat academics as a minor inconvenience, particularly for those of us in the School of Foreign Service. And that was *not* what Bill Clinton did. Somehow, he just never bought into the pseudo-sophisticated pose assumed by so many. He openly admitted to being a small town boy who had come to the big city to soak up every ounce of information and experience he could find and he proceeded to do just that with a hunger and gusto bewildering to those with far less self-assurance.

Following his victory, Bill reminded readers of the *Georgetown Courier,* a student-run magazine that "the freshman year is not the time for crusading, but for building a strong unit for the future. You must know the rules before you can change them."

Bill studied hard his first year, achieving Honors on the Spring Dean's Dean's List in 1965, with a 3.57 GPA. He enrolled in a class for non-Catholics about world religions. Father Joseph Sebes, the dean of the School of Foreign Service, taught the class, which students had playfully named *Buddhism for Baptists*. Sebes greatly influenced Bill's religious development. "I got a feel from Father Sebes for what I believe is the innate religious nature of human beings," he said. "We went through all these cultures and all their religions and no matter how different they were, it was obvious they all had a hunger to find some meaning in their lives beyond the temporal things that consume most of us through most of our days. I really developed an immense appreciation for that."

Bill learned a great deal from Father Sebes, but he also challenged the Jesuit in a good-natured and tactful way. Christopher Ashby recalled the story:

Because the Catholic students in those days had to take theology, the non-Catholics got to take other courses, including *Comparative Cultures,* taught by Father Sebes. The course was really a course in comparative religions. Father Sebes was a stern but brilliant Hungarian Jesuit who had spent most of his life in China. He was morally rigid but intellectually inclusive, which made for an interesting course. During a student-faculty reception, Bill approached Father Sebes to discuss the course. During the conversation, Bill stated that the course was "not fair" because a number of the non-Catholics in the class were Moslems or Hindu, so of course they would do better on the portion of the test that pertained to their religions. We Christians, who were being newly introduced to all of the subject matter, could not compete. Father Sebes was not used to being told he was "not fair." He reacted predictably. He stated that Bill was totally wrong, that any student who studied hard had as good a chance of making an "A" as any other. By the end of the semester, Bill had left Father Sebes two alternatives, to give Bill a B and prove that Bill was right, or to give Bill an "A" and show that the course was indeed "fair." The Father really had no choice. Bill studied hard and Father Sebes gave him an "A."

As about the only Southern Protestants at Georgetown that fall, Bill and I would kick our way through the fallen leaves strewn on the cobblestone streets to attend the Georgetown Presbyterian Church. I was Presbyterian, and there was no good Baptist church close by. The church had been a hospital during the Civil War. After church we would buy Sunday dinner, which consisted of a massive submarine sandwich for 55 cents, at a local food stand. We would talk about the civil rights movement that was swirling in the country at the time and about how we had grown up with good and decent folks who were so wrong about something so important. He influenced me greatly in those discussions, because in those days I was still caught up in the arguments about States' rights versus Federal rights that were so prevalent in Texas. He showed me that the place to start is with the individual, decide what is right for them, and then worry about how the legal system should fit.

Though far from home, Bill never forgot his roots.

He took every opportunity Georgetown's academic resources had to offer in order to learn more about the issues facing his home state. One of his favorite books while at Georgetown was *Let Us Now Praise Famous Men*, by James Agee. The book was about poor Southern sharecroppers and tenant farmers, and it provided him with a deeper understanding of the serious problems facing poor farmers in his home state.

Bill kept in close touch with his friends from Hot Springs. His high school friend Carolyn Staley recalled the time they spent together during Christmas vacation in 1964, when they had lengthy discussions about important political and social issues. Bill was especially enthusiastic about the importance of equal educational opportunity.

> I remember Bill remarking that . . . surely babies born anywhere in the USA are the same and that what matters is what opportunities they have along the way as they grow and develop. He maintained that education was a major difference across the country and that he wanted to help make sure that all Arkansas young people had the very best education possible, if he ever had the opportunity to do something about it. I could see that the seeds had been planted early for what was to later become the centerpiece of his service as Governor of Arkansas — education reform.

Bill's sophomore year found him once again President of his class. As such Bill was actively involved in orientation programs for first year students. One student had a unique need: Harold Snider was blind. He recalled how Bill, undaunted by the challenge, helped him adjust to his new surroundings.

In 1965, I was accepted as the first blind student to attend the prestigious Georgetown University School of Foreign Service. I was thrilled with the idea of studying at Georgetown and living in Washington D.C. My parents were not quite so thrilled. Money was not the problem. They were worried about how I would manage on my own, living in a dormitory and studying at Georgetown. They were more worried about my blindness than they were about my ability to do the work for a degree.

On September 18, 1965, my parents and I arrived at Loyola Hall on the campus of Georgetown University with a car full of my belongings. The first person we met when we entered the building was Bill Clinton. Bill was head of the freshman orientation for students in the School of Foreign Service. He was accompanied by his friend, John Dagnon, a student in the School of Business Administration.

Bill immediately put my parents at ease, totally charming my mother and father with a disarming smile and Southern courtesy. He told us that he had approached several local agencies for the blind in the Washington area, but none of them were willing to provide someone to get me acclimated to the campus. He told us that he had taken it upon himself to do the job. He assured us that with a little common sense, I would be travelling the campus by myself in no time.

This was hardly the approach one would expect from a total stranger who freely admitted that he knew nothing about blindness. But this was no ordinary person, it was Bill Clinton.

After my parents got me settled, and we got through the obligatory freshman reception, my parents departed and Bill and I got to work. For the next three weeks, Bill and I were practically inseparable. First of all, he had to learn how I got around by myself. He had to learn how I used the long white cane and my hearing to get from one place to another. He had to learn how I conceptualized spatial relationships, that is, how I understood how far one thing or place is from another. I explained that I first learned to travel independently following prescribed routes and, after mastering those routes, I could vary the route and go anywhere. We decided to use the same approach at Georgetown.

My first week at Georgetown was spent in orientation and registration. Bill and I walked the campus, going from one building to another. Fortunately, part of the campus leading to the School of Foreign Service was down O Street and right on 36th Street one block to the Walsh Building. That part was easy.

The main part of the campus at Georgetown was daunting. Bill and I together had to discover landmarks which I could use to know whether I was going in the right direction, left to New South and the cafeteria or right to White-Gravenor and further on up the steps and over the small hill to the girls' dorm, a very important place to go! Together, Bill and I found sound cues for which I could listen in order to determine where I was going. After about the first ten days, my confidence increased and I could find my way to most of the major buildings on campus.

After I registered and got my class schedule, we were faced with a whole new problem. I had to learn to get from class to class, sometimes with only ten minutes to get from one end of the campus to the other. Since I learned to travel independently using routes and landmarks, we quickly learned where I had to go and exactly how much time it took to get there. When Bill wasn't available to walk with me, one of our friends, John Dagnon or Sue Mooney, went along. They had both become interested in what Bill had been doing.

After almost three weeks, I could travel to most parts of the campus by myself. I had graduated from the Bill Clinton School of Independent Travel, at least for the time being. Along the way I had acquired a whole bunch of new friends, thanks to Bill. During our time at Georgetown, Bill and I saw each other sporadically. Occasionally, we would double date or just meet for a hamburger at the Tombs.

During the year, Bill took on a more vocal role in the chambers of the Student Council. Bill's efforts on behalf of consumers, which would later highlight his first gubernatorial term, manifested themselves early in his career. In November 1965, with his Vice President, Terry Modglin, he took action to counter the high food prices students were paying on campus.

"If the food service is to be a service to the students its prices should be below or at least equal to competitive prices in the area," he explained to the Georgetown's student newspaper, the *Hoya*. "Some students just cannot afford the service the way it is now . . . . [They] are being done an injustice." Bill's efforts paid off; by the following month, the food service had lowered the prices to his satisfaction.

One of Bill's most influential instructors was Professor Carroll Quigley. He believed America's uniqueness stemmed from a trait he called *future preference*. By that, he meant that Americans, over the years, have have believed in and acted on two simple ideas that the future can be better than the present, and that everyone has a personal, moral responsibility to make it so. Harold Snider shared Bill's respect for the professor.

The toughest freshman course in the School of Foreign Service was *Development of Civilization*, taught by Professor Carroll Quigley. Dr. Quigley had a charismatic personality, a dynamic lecture style, eccentric habits, and a notorious grading style. For instance, after teaching Plato's *Dialogues*, he would typically heave the book out the window of his second-floor classroom in the White-Gravenor building.

Bill and I found him fascinating, electrifying, and brilliant. He inspired in both of us a sense of personal responsibility and an eagerness to enter public service. Dr. Quigley encouraged us both to go to England to do graduate work. I know that he wrote letters of recommendation for both of us and was very proud and pleased that we both went on to study at Oxford. Dr. Quigley was our mentor and friend. He left an indelible impression on our lives.

At the end of their sophomore year, Bill and his friends Tom Campbell and Chris Ashby joined the Alpha Phi Omega fraternity. The fraternity had traditionally been responsible for running student elections and coordinating orientation on campus, and the three friends took an active role in those activities.

During his junior year, Bill continued to speak out on student government issues. Writing in the November issue of the *Georgetown Courier*, he sounded what would become a familiar call for him: "If elected representative government is to have any meaning at all," he wrote, "it must make a deep commitment to meet [issues] head-on. . . . We cannot adopt a policy of isolation or inaction, or our politics will be without substance. We, as a student body, must urge our representatives to enter and support them in those fields where they are most needed — to plant the seeds of improvement, to reap the harvest of beneficial change. The times demand it."

Bill's commitment to politics did not go unnoticed by his classmates. Dru Bachman Francis still remembers that he had a focus unique among his peers:

Many of us worked in the popular saloons on M Street, or better still, didn't work at all. Bill toiled away on the Hill for Senator Fulbright and probably visited every white-columned building and monument that the city had to offer. Typical adolescents that we were, most of us had no sense of time or urgency, much less an agenda. Bill exhibited all the signs of someone who was on the way to somewhere else and in a hurry to get there. If he had not been so totally amiable, genuinely kind, open, and friendly, he would have been heartily disliked by one and all, but he had absolutely no pretense about him and that, of course, made him irresistible.

In early March 1967, he ran for President of the Student Council. Bill's opponent was the former sophomore class Vice President, Terry Modglin. Bill, labeled the "establishment candidate" by the Georgetown *Hoya*, called for greater visibility and financial support for the Student Council, improvement of student advising, and a cost-efficient food service. Modglin campaigned to reassert the role of students as central to the function of the

University, and criticized the Student Council for fiscal and administrative excess. Hyperbole was triumphant.

In his first-ever electoral defeat, Bill lost to Terry Modglin by 147 out of the 1320 votes cast. His classmate Neil Grimaldi recalled that though Bill might have lost the election, "he never lost who he was." Public image does not always reflect the truth.

During their senior year, Bill, Tom Caplan, Tom Campbell, Christopher Ashby, and Jim Moore lived together in a house at 4513 Potomac Avenue. All five men were extremely busy that year, and rarely spent time together. About the only time they spent as a group was around the dinner table. Ashby considered their supper time debates one of the most valuable aspects of his college experience.

The most intellectually stimulating and exciting and educational part of my Georgetown experience was dinner. Bill worked for Senator Fulbright, and I worked for Senator Henry "Scoop" Jackson of Washington state. Senator Fulbright was against the war in Vietnam, and Senator Jackson was a supporter. Bill was smart and insightful, and so were the others. We talked nightly, and sometimes into the night, about what was going on in the city and in the world. Bill and I did not agree about Vietnam, but I preferred to discuss the situation with him than with most others because he made me think and he sharpened my abilities. He was a big part of my education.

Bill is not only impressive, he is fun. We have not always agreed, but we have always found the other an interesting counterpoint. Talking to Bill, sparring with him and being around him had always been one of those really joyful experiences that one seldom has, and only with true friends.

Every weekend, Bill drove over two hundred miles to be with his stepfather, Roger Clinton, Sr., who was dying of cancer. He was being treated at the Duke University medical center in North Carolina. As he grew older, Bill had begun to understand the roots of his stepfather's alcoholic addiction and had developed a sympathy and love for Roger. One Easter weekend, he and his stepfather went to a service at the Duke Chapel. "It was beautiful," he recalled. "I think he knew that I was coming down there just because I loved him. There was nothing else to fight over, nothing else to run from. It was a wonderful time in my life, and I think his."

Bill's ability to reconcile with his stepfather was testament to the strength and depth of his personal faith and religious convictions. "I really believe in . . . the constancy of sin, the possibility of forgiveness, the reality of redemption," he later told *US News & World Report*.

Carolyn Yeldell Staley, who has remained close to Bill Clinton since high school, sees religion as an important — but intensely personal — part of his life.

Bill is a Christian and his personal faith is very important part of his daily life. His faith has grown and deepened through his adult years. He is a faithful member of Immanuel Baptist Church and sings in the choir regularly. Bill told me not long ago that the book *Mere Christianity* by C.S. Lewis is one of the most important volumes he has read in recent years. The book chronicles Lewis' personal struggle with faith and intellect and his arrival at Christianity as his personal statement of belief. Bill is private about his faith and does not trivialize it by overly publicizing his church attendance. Rather, his faith is very personal and real.

Roger Clinton died later that year. Bill mourned his passing, and the university chaplains showed their sympathy by posting an announcement of Bill's loss throughout the campus. At the time, Bill was taking rigorous courses in International Studies, his major, and was trying to carry on a normal life. He was also preparing for the Rhodes Scholarship competition. He volunteered as a counselor in a student-led clinic to help alcoholics. Additionally, he chaired the Student Athletic Commission, and was elected to Phi Beta Kappa for his high grades. Bill's friends gave him comfort and support, and continued to include him in their social life by inviting him to their parties. Sometimes Bill brought interesting foreign guests home with him: Danes, Germans, and others he had befriended through his work on the staff of Senator William Fulbright's. Kenneth Fuchs, who had covered Bill's student council activities for the Georgetown *Hoya,* recalled that he encouraged his friend to apply for the Rhodes Scholarship:

In late 1966 I had been one of two Rhodes Scholarship finalists from Texas, my home state. Some at Georgetown had allowed that they thought it rather presumptuous of a student in the School of Foreign Service to apply for this prestigious award. Indeed the assistant Dean in the College of Arts and Sciences who kept a supply of the requisite applications tried to persuade me that completing the forms would be a waste of time.

Not long after submitting the materials, I was called for an interview in Houston by a committee of distinguished former Rhodes Scholars and was honored to be selected as a finalist. In the last round of interviews, in New Orleans, I met another group of former Rhodes Scholars, each a representative from one of the states comprising the region that included Texas and Arkansas. Unhappily, though, the committee's final list of candidates did not include my name.

I recounted these events to Bill upon my return to Georgetown and suggested that he was just the sort of person the regional committee was looking for.

Bill had asked his boss, Senator Fulbright, to recommend him for the Rhodes Scholarship. Fulbright himself had been a Rhodes Scholar many years earlier, and Bill still believes that Fulbright's support was crucial to his acceptance for the honor. At the time, he thought that he did not have "a chance in the world," but his friends urged him on.

Before his final interview, Clinton found a copy of *Time* magazine at the airport and read an article about the world's first heart transplant. One of his interview questions, coincidentally, concerned the same subject as the article. Bill later reflected that finding the magazine was the "luckiest thing in the world."

Bill's mother sat by the phone all day, waiting for him to call with the news of the Rhodes Committee's decision. "I never refused to do an anesthetic before in my life," she said. "But this was on Saturday, and they had an emergency, and the doctor called me, and . . . I said, 'I'm sorry. You'll have to call someone else. . . . It was around five o'clock in the afternoon, and he called and he said, 'Well, Mother, how do you think I'll look in English tweed?' "

Bill was only the second Georgetown student ever to receive a Rhodes Scholarship. The award was especially meaningful to Bill since he had come from a disadvantaged background. He had earned both recognition and opportunity based upon his own merit. Part of that merit, of course, involved recognition from a prominent political connection, Senator Fulbright. It was a connection, though, which he had made on his own, without any family influence. "They gave me that job when I was . . . nobody from nowhere," Bill later recalled. "My family had no money, no political influence — nothing." Bill was self-made.

While Bill was at Georgetown the country was becoming divided over the Vietnam war. 1967 was the year that some Americans began to organize their opposition to the Vietnam war, which had been raging since mid-1965. He considered himself "inside the system" because he was working on Capitol Hill for Senator Fulbright. But the system itself could not be insulated from the war — each day at work, Bill noted on the wire service printer the names, ages and home towns of hundreds of Americans killed in Vietnam. He identified those from Arkansas so that Senator Fulbright would send a personal letter of condolence to each family.

Tom Campbell recalled that the war was not much of an issue at Georgetown until after the Tet Offensive of January 1968, when United States servicemen in Vietnam suffered many casualties. During the spring of their senior year, not many Georgetown students were sympathetic to the U.S. government's policies in Southeast Asia, but all four of Bill's roommates committed to joining one of the armed forces. Although the war would become a source of emotional turmoil for Bill, another event closer to home was much more disturbing.

Martin Luther King's assassination by James Earl Ray in Memphis, Tennessee on April 4, 1968, triggered an eruption of deep anger and the worst race riots in U.S. history. For Bill Clinton and his peers, the 39-year-old Martin Luther King, Jr., had been both their hero and their conscience. Bill despised segregation and admired King's leadership, moral courage, and idealism in his struggle for civil rights. Many leading Americans admired King's principle of non-violent social change and his belief that education and economic development should be the instruments for achieving social justice and economic progress.

In early 1968, King had begun work on the Poor People's Movement, a nationwide nonviolent mass movement to campaign for economic justice. King wanted to promote investment in depressed areas, equal opportunity for jobs, low-income housing, and education.

The weekend after King's assassination, northwest Washington, D.C., was in flames. By chance, Bill's high school friend Carolyn Yeldell Staley had planned a visit for the same weekend. She recalled flying over the nation's capital and seeing the smoke and fire downtown.

At the airport Bill told her that they were going to do some volunteer work at a relief agency in the city. The student relief effort was organized by the Georgetown University Community Action Program (GUCAP) and Bill had already signed up when Carolyn arrived. Carolyn found herself among a small band of courageous young volunteers. She recalled:

They put a red cross on the doors of Bill's white Buick, filled the trunk with the supplies we were to deliver, and gave us each a hat to wear to help cover our face. . . . We delivered our boxes of supplies to the basement of a church where people were staying who were home-less because of the fires and damage.

Afterward, they parked the car and walked around the areas which had been most severely burned and looted, near 14th and U streets, Northwest.

It was as if Bill wanted to get as close as he could to this moment in time, this page of our nation's history. We knew that a major peacemaker had died, and that the future of our nation's civil rights progress was hanging in the balance.

Neither of us said anything as we walked around. We were both numb and shocked at what had happened and what we were seeing. I had recently taken up 35mm black and white photography and I broke the silence by remarking to Bill that I wished I had my camera to record the amazing scenes I was seeing. Bill was a little impatient with me for saying that, thinking, I guess, that photography would somehow trivialize the moment, but I knew that my motives were good. He asked me why I needed a camera, would I ever forget what I was seeing?

We turned the corner and looked up to see four or five young Black men walking in our direction down the middle of the street. We calmly turned around, walked back to the car, and left the area.

Back at Bill's house, I recall how quiet we were and how Bill was very melancholy. He had learned long passages of King's *I Have a Dream* speech and I heard him saying them under his breath sometimes. This was another of our heroes who had great dreams for America who was gone, killed—first John Kennedy, and now

58

Martin Luther King. Perhaps we realized that these great leaders were now gone and were concerned about how the gap would be filled, how America would recover.

King's speech had been about our nation's democratic values — about the Constitution's sacred guarantee to all men and women, of all colors, that they possess certain inalienable rights. The speech found words for many of Bill's strong emotions about the need to unite the American people without regard to race or creed.

Kenneth Fuchs also recalled spending time with Bill during this tragic event in the nation's history.

Our small talk quickly turned to the events of the moment, specifically the assassination of the Reverend Martin Luther King, Jr.; I think, just the day before. Bill and I went to the roof terrace of a student dormitory, a vantage point from which we could see smoke billowing from various locations along what we guessed to be Washington's 14th Street. Here were two Southerners, both witnesses to the civil rights marches and demonstrations of the mid-sixties, asking each other what Dr. King's death would mean for the civil rights movement he had led.

Would the looting and arson result in a backlash that would make further progress more difficult?

Would Dr. King's studied civil disobedience be given up for illegality and violence?

Bill reflected on the tragedy which we found still hard to believe. He was deeply saddened. I could see that his feelings were profound and sincere. And I was moved by that.

A few weeks later, on June 6, 1968, Senator Robert F. Kennedy was assassinated after making his victory speech following the California primary. Bill Clinton, like most Americans across the country, was once again shocked and deeply saddened. In Kennedy, Bill had seen a political leader with the courage to stand up for what he believed, to fight for racial unity and social justice.

Many years later, Bill Clinton would still remember the words Kennedy had spoken to a frightened nation during the tense weeks following the assassination of Martin Luther King, Jr.: "What we need in the United States," Kennedy had said, "is not division. What we need in the United States is not hatred. What we need in the United States is not violence or lawlessness; but love and wisdom and compassion toward one another; and the feeling of justice toward those who still suffer in our country, whether they be white or they be black. Let us dedicate ourselves to what the Greeks wrote so many years ago: to tame the savageness of man and make gentle the life of this world. Let us dedicate ourselves to that," he said, "and say a prayer for our country and for our people."

"Bobby" Kennedy had entered the race for president late in March 1968 after Eugene McCarthy had already won the New Hampshire primary. Both were already vocal opponents of the Vietnam War. He had been Attorney General in his brother's administration and remained in the cabinet for the balance of the four-year term after Vice-President Johnson inherited the presidency. When Johnson ran for president in 1964 and defeated Senator Barry Goldwater in a landslide, Robert Kennedy ran for the United States Senate in New York and won. The next year, when Bill Clinton was president of his sophomore class, Georgetown University had invited Robert Kennedy to

1968

speak to the student body.

Newspaper editorialists and political leaders reflected on what might have been had Kennedy lived. Senator George McGovern remarked, "He was the most sentimental, the most thoughtful, and the most idealistic member of that remarkable family that gave him to the nation." Two of his biographers, Lester and Irene David, wrote: ". . . Robert emerges as the Kennedy who felt the deepest, cared the most, and fought the hardest for humanity — crying out against America's involvement in the Vietnam War, championing the cause of blacks, Hispanics, and Mexican-Americans, and crusading against the suffering of children, the elderly, and anyone else hurt and bypassed by social and economic progress."

For young Americans, the Kennedys symbolized the best in American idealism. When Robert Kennedy was killed, millions of Americans felt a loss of hope and faith in the future. 1968 was the line of demarcation for many young Americans between a hopeful, constructive attitude toward "the system" and a period of despair, alienation and rejection of mainstream values. The women's movement was on the rise along with the sexual revolution. The anti-establishment, non-conformist, Hippy culture, which indulged in promiscuous behavior, soft and hard drugs and rock and roll, offered an escape from the violence, racial tension, and social unrest of the late 1960's. Georgetown students were conservative compared with students at Berkeley and Columbia, but very few American students were unaffected by the social and political turmoil of that time. Coast-to-coast, there was a sea-change in the mentality of the youth culture as the generation gap grew wider and wider over such issues as the Vietnam War, taste in music, hair length, "recreational" drug use, and couples living together before marriage. Although he shared the anti-Vietnam War views of his former employer, Senator Fulbright, Bill Clinton remained a pro-establishment moderate by the standards of the counter-culture of 1968. Bill defied the stereotypes: he was neither an anti-establishment Hippy nor what would become known in the 1980's as a shallow, materialistic Yuppie. Instead, he approached the end of his college years having extracted the wisdom of the best minds at Georgetown and remained solidly in the mainstream of American political and moral values. He never lost hope.

After graduating from Georgetown, Bill returned home to Hot Springs. He watched on television as the Democratic National Convention met in Chicago, in the midst of violent anti-war protests and brutal police reprisals, and nominated Vice-President Hubert Humphrey to be the Democratic candidate for president. Racism and the Vietnam War were dividing the nation and preventing progress; Arkansas was no exception.

That summer, an Arkansas couple running for governor and senator were avid supporters of segregationist Presidential candidate George Wallace. They actively sought to capitalize on the racist connection, asking Arkansans to vote for "Jim, Virginia, and George."

Bill was deeply concerned about the impact the racist candidates would have on Arkansas. He and his friend Tom Campbell went to listen to one of their rallies. After it was over, Bill went up to the man and said, "You make me ashamed to be from Arkansas." For him, these candidates were demagogues who embodied the intolerance that divided American society.

Even though Bill questioned him passionately, the man did not lose his temper; he simply replied, "If you don't like what I stand for, write me a letter." Bill was impressed by the man's even-tempered response to his challenge, Campbell recalled. He learned that the way to deal with heckling and angry dissent is with calm confidence and respect — even if it not given in return. The incident further strengthened Bill's resolve to work for his home state.

Sometimes, one has to leave home before one can come back with the focus perspective and judgement to make a difference. Georgetown gave Bill Clinton that chance. It was not enough that he studied political science, history and international relations. He had grown and had witnessed momentous changes in American society. Now he was about to embark on yet another important journey--to Oxford, England.

Chapter Five

The Innocents Abroad

In the fall of 1968, the *S.S. United States* set sail for England on its traditional voyage carrying America's top students to a year of study at Britain's finest schools. Rhodes Scholars, Fulbright Scholars, Marshall Scholars, and Rotary Scholars all met up at Manhattan's 46th Street dock and boarded for the long voyage. Among this august group was a Foreign Service graduate from Georgetown named Bill Clinton.

Clinton immediately set out to make friends with everyone aboard. When squalls struck, he brought chicken noodle soup to the seasick. When boredom set in, he brought out his saxophone and cheered up his compatriots. Douglas Eakeley was among those Clinton befriended on the voyage.

Even among that over-achieving, self-selected group, Bill's potential for leadership was apparent. My first impression was: "Is this guy for real?" It didn't take long to find out. He was (and remains) one of the more naturally gregarious persons I have ever met.

Bill's interest in others conveyed a sense of understanding and sympathy that gave him an ability to relate to people of all walks of life. It was matched by intellectual curiosity and a fascination with public affairs.

Clinton's world view was broadened by his peers as well as by his studies at Oxford. Stephen Oxman, a fellow Rhodes Scholar who is one of Clinton's top foreign policy advisors today, remembers him as deeply interested in others, and anxious to seek out different perspectives on important issues.

I remember from the first moment we met how interested he was in talking with people and how much he enjoyed it. He displayed an unusual ability to engage people from many different backgrounds in friendly, substantive conversation. I think this skill arises from Bill's inherent liking for people. He finds in others a great source of life's richness and potential, and he gives of himself so that others find this in him as well.

Tom Williamson, who was one of the 32 Rhodes Scholars on the ship, was at first wary of the outgoing Southerner.

As the ship pulled away from the dock on New York's west side, Bill approached me with a warm smile and his hand extended. He looked me squarely in the eye and introduced himself, speaking in his distinctive Arkansas drawl.

I feigned a cordial response, but I was wary of this new acquaintance. I was the only African-American in the Rhodes Scholar group that year, and I smugly assumed that Bill was a self-conscious Southerner seeking to assuage some of his guilt about the disgraceful racial legacy of his region of the country. I thought I knew his type well — white people who think they are doing blacks a special favor by reaching out to be friends — but I was mistaken.

During the journey across the Atlantic, I discovered how very wrong I was about Bill. He had seen through my initial diffidence; yet he persisted in wanting us to be good friends. Even though Bill realized that I had dismissed him on first impression, based on my racial stereotype of white Southerners, he was generous in sharing his own unique brand of homespun wit and political idealism — a combination that I shortly found irresistible. I simply could not sustain any dislike for a man who believed that Governor Faubus's demagogic resistance to desegregation at Central High School in 1957 was the most shameful event in the history of Arkansas, who had full command of the lyrics to all the great Motown hits of our time, and who insisted that playing the saxophone was a workable substitute for *bona fide* charm and urbanity in trying to engage a young woman's attention.

Clinton was enrolled in Oxford's University College, where he studied for a graduate degree, a Bachelor of Philosophy (B. Phil) in politics. He also attended many lectures outside his field of study. John Isaacson still has vivid memories of their two years together in England:

There were four Americans in our class who landed at University College: Bob Reich, Doug Eakeley, myself, and Bill. Eakeley and I looked vaguely conventional, as conventional as American undergraduates in that period were likely to get. Reich was just as outlandish then as he is now, at the center of every eclectic gathering, a force in the theater, an American gremlin, a gargoyle popped live off an Oxford tower, articulate and charming, to amuse modern Brits.

Bill was a stunning contrast. He towered over Oxford undergraduates. He greeted every reluctant, shy, perfectly-mannered English schoolboy with a big grin, a hearty handshake, and a serious dose of down-home Americana. Some of them have never recovered.

Early on in our two year stay at University, Bill took up a kind of semi-permanent residence in the Porter's Lodge of the College. University College is a lovely, 17th century building, with high walls and one gate. You got in through the gate, under the glaring eyes of Douglas the Porter, a former Sergeant-Major in the British Army and a pillar of English society, as it was best understood, before the Second World War. Bill Clinton was the only person I ever saw Douglas befriend. They sat in the Porter's Lodge, feet by the fire, and turned it into some bizarre version of an Arkansas country store. They were both huge, courageous, very funny, boisterous men, and they harassed literally every undergraduate — Yank or Brit — to come through the door.

I knew then, as we all did, that he'd run for office. He had gifts the rest of us couldn't apprehend. The rest of us, Reich excepted, could have talked to Douglas until we were blue in the face and he wouldn't have so much as remembered our names; but Bill was his partner, his confidant. He shared the eminence of his office readily with Bill; felt, I think, that Bill's gifts for charm and irreverence enhanced the sheer august weight of the Porter's Lodge.

Because of his Rhodes Scholarship award, Clinton's Oxford experience was the only time during his academic career when he did not have to work to pay his bills. Consequently, he was able to spend many spare hours reading and exploring his new horizons. In April 1970, Clinton got word that his Georgetown friend Harold Snider was accepted to study at Oxford for a doctorate in Modern History. He offered to help Snider familiarize himself with the city's unfamiliar twists and turns. Snider gratefully accepted his offer.

I didn't have any other friends at Oxford, and I only knew the British academics who had interviewed me. Also, the use of the long white cane among blind people in England was in its infancy. Although British blind students had been studying at Oxford for over a century, they had been totally dependent on help from sighted people getting around on a daily basis. I wanted to be as independent at Oxford as I had been at Georgetown, and the same fine teacher was eager and available.

Oxford has been a center of learning since medieval times. Bill really had his work cut out for him this time. The blend of ancient and modern in Oxford is readily apparent to any visitor. Oxford colleges are spread out all over the city. Streets do not run perpendicular or parallel to each other. They run into each

other at odd angles. Bill showed me New College
Lane, Holywell Street, Broad Street, High Street, the
Cornmarket, and Catte Street. Between April and July
1970, Bill and I worked together on learning Oxford. I
took the train from London and arrived at Oxford as
early as possible. We usually had as near a Southern
breakfast as you could at a "greasy spoon" in the
Covered Market. British bacon, fried eggs, tomatoes
and mushrooms are even better when they are a little
greasy. After breakfast, Bill and I would set forth to
learn a different part of Oxford. It took no more than
eight or ten trips to Oxford for me to learn the city and
its colleges, streets and stores. In the afternoon, we
would sometimes end up at Bill's favorite pub, the Turf
Tavern, for one beer. Neither Bill nor I are big drink-
ers. Bill was living in a house in North Oxford along
with other students. In July, he introduced me to his
landlady, Diana Marx, who was a nurse at the Radcliffe
Infirmary and who shared the house with her tenants.
My wife and I moved to Oxford in early September,
and she was due to give birth to our first child in mid-
October. Diana became our friend and was very helpful.

I was a much better and more confident cane travel-
ler when I learned Oxford with Bill than when we had
learned Georgetown. . . . Bill was even a better teacher
the second time around.

Harold Snider went on to a distinguished career fighting for the rights of the handicapped. In 1989 then Republican National Committee Chairman Lee Atwater asked
him to be the party's first Director of Outreach for People
with Disabilities. He now serves as Deputy Director of the

National Council on Disability.

Clinton also spent time hitchhiking with Tom Williamson around the rolling green countryside outside of Oxford. Since Oxford students did not have the luxury of telephones in their living quarters, most made plans by leaving notes in the porter's office where their friends were staying. Williamson remembers:

> Somehow this nineteenth century mode of communication seemed to suffice for Bill and me to arrange a wide variety of activities together. We would rendezvous at Chinese or Indian restaurants from time to time in search of relief from the dismal meals that were standard fare at our college dining halls. We would hitchhike to London on weekends to sample English theater. (We could have taken the train, but we were trying to save money for travel to the Continent during the comparatively lengthy winter and spring vacations that were gratefully part of the Oxford tradition.) We showed up for basketball practice with the Oxford University team since even mediocre players by American standards, as we were, contended for starting roles on the Oxford team. We joined with several of our other friends and colleagues in organizing an international student protest in London against the war in Vietnam. And we engaged in interminable discussions about the remoteness of our prospects for finding dates at a university where coeducation was still very much a tokenist phenomenon.

Clinton and Williamson found free lodging in London at The London School of Economics, where Clinton's Georgetown friend Dru Bachman was doing graduate work.

She recalled:

> Our flat became a stopping place for Bill and his friends from Oxford. When they came to London, we provided the odd meal and a free spot on the floor. Again, the contrast was apparent; Bill and the Rhodes Scholars were engrossed in endless debates about The War and every other topical issue imaginable while the rest of us were far more intent on pursuing the self discovery which only living far and away can bring. One could see that the issues they struggled with were intensely personal, not only for themselves, but for all those who thought that their involvement could make a difference. In fact, I don't think that Bill Clinton has an indifferent bone in his body. Impersonal is beyond his understanding. I suppose that has been embarrassing at times, even a political detriment. I know that it has been misunderstood and misconstrued as insincere, but that fundamental concern, that social conscience, is and always has been very genuine.

Tom Williamson believes that Clinton was the most popular Rhodes Scholar in the class of 1968. Clinton made lasting friendships with students from all over the United States, of all backgrounds. Clinton and his friends talked and listened to Motown records. Williamson remembers:

> There are many admirable qualities that explain the breadth and depth of Bill's popularity at Oxford, but one strikes me as most salient for appreciating his character. Bill is genuinely enthusiastic about learning from his friends and associates. Unlike many exceptionally intelligent people who are preoccupied with

showcasing their intellectual acuity, Bill relishes the opportunity to have his own knowledge expanded and his insight refined by others. Make no mistake — he enjoyed formulating and forcefully expressing his own views, especially in the areas of race and the war in Vietnam but he remained remarkably receptive to the diverse thinking of the people he had embraced in his wide circle of friends. This self- effacing openness graciously flattered the intellectual pretensions of many of Bill's associates in the Oxford community while enhancing his own knowledge and understanding.

Stephen Oxman recalled that Clinton actively sought new opportunities for study whenever they arose. At one point, he learned that renowned foreign policy expert George F. Kennan would be spending a season at the university. Clinton arranged for Kennan to teach a seminar on American foreign affairs to interested Rhodes Scholars. Even today, Oxman remembers that his fellow Scholars "were impressed by how important the understanding of foreign policy was to Bill."

Intellectual inquiry did not stop at the classroom door. Clinton and his friends stayed up late at night debating important issues of the day. Clinton's roommate, Doug Eakeley, recalled his lively dinner conversations with Clinton, Isaacson, and fellow Scholar Bob Reich.

One of my most lasting impressions of our first years at University College was of dinner at the great hall. Almost invariably, Bill and Bob would be the leading participants in an animated table discussion, ranging over a wide variety of subjects, involving any number of English and foreign students, exploring problems and seeking solutions and lasting far beyond normal dining hours.

One of the recurrent subjects of those dinner conversations was the Vietnam War. Like many of our generation, Bill's opposition to the War was passionate and principled. It collided with his equally passionate and principled commitment to his country and to a career of public service. His anguished decision to give up his ROTC deferment and subject himself to the draft reflects a combination of courage, integrity, and sense of calling so typical of him.

His anguished decision to give up his ROTC deferment and subject himself to the draft reflects a combination of courage, integrity, and sense of calling so typical of him.

Douglas Eakeley

Each American student at Oxford was treated by the British as an unofficial ambassador from the United States. Clinton and his colleagues were constantly questioned about their attitudes toward American foreign policy, particularly the Vietnam war.

In order to better understand the political context of the difficult decisions that Bill Clinton faced at Oxford, it is important to remember the lessons of history and how the United States became involved in a civil war in Southeast Asia. The Vietnam War found its roots in the development of the U.S.-Soviet relationship after World War II. In 1946, George Kennan, while a diplomat at the American Embassy in Moscow, had written an 8,000 word memorandum to the State Department which articulated a new policy called containment. The thesis of the memorandum, later published under the pen name "X" in the July 1947 issue of *Foreign Affairs*, was predicated on the need to demonstrate American strength to the Soviets by setting up "situations of strength" in the form of viable non-communist societies on the periphery of the Soviet sphere of influence. The goal was to stop Soviet expansion through the continued presence of the U.S. Army, the development of what would come to be known as the Marshall Plan, and the construction of American military bases in friendly countries.

Kennan made a clear distinction between Soviet imperialism, which he saw as the real enemy, and international communism, which he argued should be confronted only when it was clearly used as "the instrument of the Kremlin." American foreign policy during the 1950s, however, did not distinguish between the two: it viewed communist activity anywhere as a threat to America's vital global interests.

With China falling under Mao's communist rule in 1949, the U.S. became increasingly apprehensive about communist expansion. John Foster Dulles, foreign policy adviser to General Dwight Eisenhower and later his Secretary of State, advocated a policy which went beyond containment and sought the "liberation of captive peoples."

After North Korea invaded South Korea, the U.S. government began to view the ongoing French war in Indochina — Vietnam — as a direct parallel to the war in Korea. American policy makers, however, ignored crucial differences between the two. Unlike their counterparts in Korea, communist leaders in North Vietnam were allied with nationalist anti-colonialists in South Vietnam. This inaccurate comparison to the aggression of North Korea was reinforced by the McCarthy era's anti-communist hysteria, which portrayed communism as a hegemonistic monolith bent on the destruction of the United States. Ho Chi Minh, the leader of the anti-colonialist movement in Vietnam, combined communism with a powerful and popular nationalism, and thus forced a cruel dilemma on the U.S.: the choice between opposing communism and supporting a genuine nationalist revolution.

The U.S. sent 35 military advisors to South Vietnam on June 27, 1950, and agreed to provide military and economic aid to the French-supported anti-communist government. In July, 1954, the Geneva agreements called for United Nations-supervised elections in Vietnam by July 1956 and prohibited the introduction of additional military forces. In the agreements, the U.S. government implicitly recognized the conflict as a civil war by stating explicitly that the 17th parallel was a line of demarcation between North and South but was only "provisional and should not in any way be interpreted as constituting a political or territorial boundary." This fact was overlooked by those who suggested that North Vietnam was involved in aggression against a *foreign* country rather than supporting a war for national unification more akin to the American Civil War than to the Korean War.

Despite the warnings of General Matthew Ridgeway that American intervention with ground forces would be "disastrous," the U.S. gradually assumed the role of the French commitment to South Vietnam after the French defeat at Diem Bien Phu in 1954 and its subsequent withdrawal. The American government under Dwight Eisenhower, John Kennedy, and Lyndon Johnson was committed to the South Vietnamese regime. Eisenhower increased the number of advisors to 685 and assumed control of training South Vietnamese troops; Kennedy increased the number of advisors and troops to 15,000, and aid to South Vietnam exceeded $500 million by the end of 1963. The Gulf of Tonkin Resolution in August 1964 gave Johnson a pretext to escalate the war. Johnson ordered the continuous bombing of North Vietnam in February 1965, and by year-end, U.S. forces in Vietnam totaled 184,300. Johnson and his generals escalated the war to the extent that by the end of his administration, over 500,000 troops were "in country" in Vietnam.

As the sufferings of the Vietnamese people and the horrors of war played out on television screens all over the world, and as increasing numbers of body bags arrived home in the United States with no tangible gains to justify the mounting death count, many Americans began to question the moral basis of the war. By December, 1967, protesters were staging large-scale demonstrations against the war. Bill Clinton was strongly influenced by his employer, Senator J. William Fulbright, who as chairman of the Senate Foreign Relations Committee had held hearings investigating the war. Fulbright had written a book, *The Arrogance of Power*, a powerful analysis and critique of the Vietnam war. Initially uneasy with the protest movement, Clinton had been reluctant to join anti-war protests. But Fulbright described the student protest movement as "an expression of the national conscience and a manifestation of traditional American idealism," and made a strong case for differentiating between just and unjust wars.

"From the time of Grotius to the drafting of the United Nations Charter," Fulbright wrote, "international lawyers have tried to distinguish between 'just wars' and 'unjust wars.' It is a difficult distinction of law and even more difficult one of morality, but it is certainly a valid problem and, far from warranting contempt, those who try to make that most pertinent distinction deserve our sympathy and respect."

While a student at Georgetown, according to his housemate Tom Campbell, Clinton had not actively participated in anti-war efforts. This was in part due to Clinton's job with Senator Fulbright, but it also reflected the Georgetown students' general disinterest in the war — until the Tet Offensive in January 1968 turned many undergraduates bitterly against the war.

The Tet Offensive had shown the ability of the North Vietnamese to stage a major assault on provincial capitals and major cities in the South, including an attack on the American embassy in Saigon. American retaliation for the attack led to massive air strikes against strategic targets in which many innocent civilians were killed. As the bloodshed continued, most Americans began to question the country's involvement, and Senators Eugene McCarthy and Robert F. Kennedy launched anti-war presidential campaigns against the incumbent of their own party. By the end of 1968, the war had lost the support of a majority of Americans.

By the time he arrived at Oxford, Clinton had begun to take part in the anti-war movement — even helping to organize rallies and protests. David Mixner, a prominent Los Angeles activist, noted Clinton's increasing involvement.

Coming out of the 1968 Kennedy and McCarthy campaigns for president, many of the young and talented students who participated in politics for the first time were looking for a way to continue our involvement against the war in Vietnam and to work in the system to create change. John Gardner of the Urban Coalition (later the founder of Common Cause) organized a weekend retreat in Martha's Vineyard for about forty young leaders, to explore ways that we could continue the important work started in the campaigns. Among those attending the retreat were . . . Larry Rockefeller, Strobe Talbott, ... and Bill Clinton.

Three others of us, including myself, went on to create an organization called the Vietnam Moratorium Committee which organized nationwide protests against the war in 1969. In hundreds of cities and towns around the country, we had protests against the war on October 15, 1969. We followed that with a massive march on Washington on November 15, 1969. Bill Clinton, during the summer of 1969, had volunteered his time and efforts to assist us in preparing for these important events.

In 1970, I briefly went to Europe and saw Clinton at Oxford. It was there that he and I began our friendship. It consisted of intense public conversations about public service, struggles about the draft and our moral obligations to our country, our personal beliefs, where we would be in twenty years and our ability to help change the world for the better. We all believed, at that time, that the most noble direction we could take was to serve in elective or appointive office. He really deeply believed that government could feed people, that we could end war, that poverty did not have to be a permanent condition, that we could make our country great and prosperous and that our generation would be the one to do it. There never was any doubt in his mind that he would return to Arkansas. He felt a deep personal obligation to return to his home state and to help the poor that he saw on a daily basis as a child.

What struck me most about Bill was his warmth. His ability to make you feel important, to feel loved and to enable you to dream his dreams. While we would talk late into the night, one would find ones self suddenly a part of his dream, his vision and his path.

The issue of the draft was a pressing moral dilemma for Clinton and his colleagues. When Clinton received a draft notice, he acknowledged it and contacted his local draft board in Arkansas, which told him he could finish his term at Oxford before going to boot camp.

During the summer of 1969, Clinton considered the options available to him. Although he opposed the war, he felt obligated to serve his country in some way. He rejected outright the choice which many of his generation had made — draft resistance and evasion, because while he opposed military intervention in Vietnam, he was not anti-military *per se*.

Clinton concluded that the Reserve Officer Training Corps (ROTC) was an option which would allow him to "possibly, but not positively, avoid both Vietnam and resistance." He applied for an ROTC scholarship at the University of Arkansas Law School in Fayetteville. He regretted that he would not be able to join his Oxford friends at Yale or another Ivy League university, but he knew that ROTC at Fayetteville was the only way he could serve his country with honor and yet avoid a head-on confrontation with his deeply felt moral concerns about the Vietnam War. Still, there was no guarantee that the conflict in Southeast Asia would be over before Clinton graduated, nor that Clinton's ROTC unit would not be called up at any moment.

Strobe Talbott, senior editor at *Time* magazine, was a

Rhodes Scholar with Clinton. He recently devoted a column to reliving the anguish they all endured in 1969. "As the summer went on," Talbott wrote in a March 1992 *Time* article, "Clinton was increasingly unsure about the course he had chosen. . . . He was troubled that while he would be earning an officer's commission and a law degree, some other, less privileged kid would have to go in his place to trade bullets with the Viet Cong."

But Talbott understood Clinton's desire to keep his options open. "In the autumn of '69, no one who was at the mercy of the draft knew for sure who would be called up when and according to what procedures. The Administration's policy was constantly shifting, and its pronouncements were, from the standpoint of an antiwar 23-year-old, far from trustworthy."

Clinton was so unsure of his immediate future that he didn't even make living arrangements for his second year at Oxford. Finally he found a spare room with Talbott and Frank Aller, a young man from Washington State who was studying Chinese history and culture.

Talbott, Aller, and Clinton spent a great deal of time talking about the war, the draft, and their moral dilemmas. "The hell of it was, there was no right answer. If you obeyed your country, as Bill had concluded he should do, you'd be contributing to its greatest folly. If you followed your conscience and defied the law — Frank's choice — you would be causing pain, even disgrace, to your family and outrage in your community back home."

William A. Fletcher, now a professor of law at the University of California at Berkeley, reflected on the toll the Vietnam War was taking on his friends Frank Aller and Bill Clinton at Oxford.

Frank Aller was my closest friend among the Rhodes Scholars; we had met in Portland, Oregon, during the regional interviews. The Rhodes scholarship was premised on our ability to serve the public interest, in Cecil Rhodes' now somewhat quaint words, to "fight the world's fight." The idea of public service was not a narrow or confined matter, but rather a broad and encompassing idea — it was public service as we were given the freedom, and the duty, to define it, according to our own conscience.

Bill was a large, friendly presence. Maybe something approaching charisma, but it was more like magnetism. We all were drawn to Bill. He had the politician's gift of an easy open manner, and an instinctive understanding and sympathy. But he was not the sort of person one thinks of as a "born politician." He was not a back-slapper, manipulator. He was a genuine person, and we liked him.

The central issue in our lives was the War. When we were awarded our scholarships over Christmas vacation of our senior year in college, graduate school deferments would have allowed us to compete the scholarships before we became vulnerable to the draft. But in February, President Johnson revoked graduate school deferments. We were all vulnerable as soon as we graduated from college, before we took one step toward England.

Frank received his draft notice during our first year at Oxford, and decided that he would not go. There was a party for Frank at Bill's room at University. All of us were deeply conflicted. A few, like me, were already committed to serve. But I began to think that Frank was right, and that I was wrong — that my higher duty was to resist the war we all thought was wrong. Most of us, including Bill, had not yet had to face the decision. All of us admired Frank for his courage, and sympathized with him for the decision that he had to face sooner than most.

We were all deeply patriotic. You could not have found anywhere a group of young men more genuinely wanting to serve their country. But the question was not the morally simple question our fathers had faced. Fighting in World War II had been hard; deciding whether one ought to fight had not been. For us the decision itself was hard.

We sought advice and counsel as best we could. Mostly we sought it by talking to one another. We did not judge one another harshly based on the different choices we made — we knew that none of the choices was easy. Bill and Frank were particularly close, and talked about it repeatedly. This was especially true during their second year at Oxford, when they lived together in the same house, at some distance from the University. Strobe Talbott, one of their housemates, has written movingly about this in an issue of *Time* magazine published in the spring of 1992.

At the end of our two-year scholarship, Frank stayed in England, a draft resister. I went into the Navy. Bill, along with many classmates who had drawn high numbers, stayed in school. We did not resent those who had drawn high numbers. Had I had the option, I would have done the same thing.

I first learned of Frank's suicide from a note sent around to Frank's class of Rhodes Scholars, a year and a half after we had left from Oxford, Frank had eventually returned to Spokane, and had spiraled into a depression brought on by his deep inner division over his duty and the war. My first response was to call Bill. We tried to comfort each other over the telephone, tried to bring back Frank, with all his goodness and humanity.

This was a community agony. We may have looked to the outside like three young men who went different ways. We may have looked to the outside like a draft resister, a Navy officer, and a high-lottery-number law student. But we knew that we were in it together. There were many choices, all of them difficult, none of them wrong. There were many ways to be moral, patriotic, even right.

The dilemma was painful to Clinton, but he finally came to the conclusion that he could not shun his obligation to serve his country. In October 1969, he called long-distance to his new stepfather, Jeff Dwire, whom Virginia had recently married. Bill Clinton asked Dwire to have the local draft board put his name back into the draft. Clinton was put back into the draft pool in October 1969, and was ranked 1-A, completely qualified to serve.

All that remained between Clinton and the jungles of Vietnam was the draft lottery. Each eligible young man was to be assigned a random number. The lower the number, the greater the chance of being drafted.

On December 1, 1969, Clinton received his lottery number: 311. It was high enough to assure him that he would never be called up. The following day, he sent off his application to Yale Law School. On December 3, Clinton wrote a letter to his ROTC supervisor at the University of Arkansas, Colonel Eugene Holmes, explaining his choice to accept the decision of the draft board.

Several months after he wrote the letter, Clinton was still uncertain of his future. In the spring of 1970 Talbott recalled that "the Rhodes administrators circulated a questionnaire to determine which scholars were planning to return for a third year at Oxford. Clinton's answer: 'Perhaps. If not, will be entering Yale Law School, or getting drafted.'" Clinton received a scholarship to Yale Law School for the fall of 1970.

The Vietnam War cast a shadow over Bill Clinton's two years at Oxford. Clinton would look back at this time as one of painful soul searching, a time of emotional decisions which had a major effect over the direction of his life. Sadly, these questions also had an divisive impact on the life of this nation. The current generation of baby-boomers who are now becoming national leaders all went through the Vietnam era and faced similar choices. For Clinton, who supported Operation Desert Storm in 1991 and in retrospect, supported the Korean War and World War II, it was a time which called for a moral choice reflecting a higher patriotism. In no way did that choice in 1969 diminish his potential to be an effective Commander-in-Chief in 1993 any more than did Dick Cheney's legal deferment during the Vietnam War diminish his capacity to be an effective Secretary of Defense in Desert Storm. As Clinton told the *Washington Post*, "My antiwar feelings were particularly painful to me at first, because I never really was anti-military in the sense that a lot of people were." In an interview with *Nightline*'s Ted Koppel, Clinton recalled, "One of the most precious memories of my childhood is my mother trying to get me to me to know my dead father, showing me a presidential citation he'd received for good duty in the war. I was proud of that. I wanted to be part of my country's defense and my country's service."

Chapter Six

New Beginnings

Clinton moved to New Haven in the late summer of 1970. His scholarship did not cover his living expenses, so he took on a number of part time jobs. At various times during his law school career, he taught for a law enforcement program at a local community college, worked for a city councilman in Hartford, and assisted a lawyer in New Haven.

His first semester, though, was taken up by Joe Duffy's Senate campaign. Duffy was the antiwar candidate in a three-way race. Clinton was in charge of Duffy's efforts in Connecticut's Third District, of which Yale was a part, but in geography only: most of the district was blue-collar and ethnic. Clinton worked the phones from morning until night and talked with people across the region. It was an old-fashioned campaign, with precinct walkings and town meetings, and Clinton loved every minute of it. Duffy lost his Senate campaign to Lowell Weicker. He won the Third District.

Clinton then lived in a beach house on Trumbull Beach, in Milford, Connecticut, with Don Pogue and his old Oxford roommate, Doug Eakeley. Pogue discussed Clinton's life at this time:

Even in 1970, when we first met, Bill's warmth for people always seemed to help him maintain a balance in difficult times. And they were difficult times. No sooner had the civil rights movement lifted the burden of slavery from the American psyche, then that psyche was dashed into turmoil again by the war in Vietnam. Our generation — inspired by John Kennedy to believe in public service — faced public service that had gone very wrong.

Many of us had families who were split and friends who died during that time. When we met, Bill had recently lost a close friend from Oxford. It was a confusing time, and it hurt. One of my earliest memories, though, was my amazement at how well Bill maintained his balance during those events. Bill was certainly influenced by, and had the advantage of the mentoring of Arkansas' Senator Fulbright, who, while an internationalist, was also a non- interventionist opposed to the war. But Bill brought his own strengths to the discussion. He talked with people; he listened; he read — he seemed to be reading a new book each week. And he always had time to help out with whatever political campaign needed his talents, and to talk with people — whether they were serving in the dining hall or walking on a picket line. He seemed to have a reserve of decency towards everybody he met that just kept him going.

I had first heard of Bill from a friend of mine who

was a Rhodes Scholar with Bill at Oxford. John Isaacson
called me in the spring of 1970, before I left England to
come back to law school in New Haven. He told me I
would like this guy, and he was right. I think everybody liked Bill.

Bill worked hard, too. He wasn't part of the silver
spoon brigade. And he wasn't satisfied with just being
smart. He would always take his papers back and re-
write them one last time. I remember being frustrated as
he noticed shades of grey in what appeared black and
white to me, and being impressed by how well he
expressed the different hues.

During the first semester, Bill joined in a "counter-
course," a study group trying to uncover points of view
which weren't reflected in the mandated curriculum.
Bill voiced his views in this group, openly and with
ease. It always seemed that he had just read something
which gave a new or different way to look at an issue.
Sometimes the discussion was intense — it was law
school, and we were all young — but Bill seemed to
keep it in balance, reminding us of Arkansas watermelons — the "biggest and best" — or telling us the
thoughts and feelings of the voters in one of the campaigns he was working on.

Susan Bucknell was Don Pogue's girlfriend at the time.
They are now married and still live in Connecticut:

My early recollection of Bill is of a studious, bright,
energetic, warm, and friendly person, who welcomed
me into their student community. He and Don argued
foreign policy and debated the themes of their papers.
Bill and I shared nostalgic memories of Oxford, where I

had been an undergraduate and he had been a Rhodes
Scholar. Life on the beach was fun; but it was also
earnest. All of us shared a sense that we wanted to play
roles in public service. Bill was clear about his commitment to politics, and political discussions were an important aspect of the community dialogue.

 Bill's sense of the importance of family, and community relationships was evident in his close ties with
his mother and with his constant desire to make sure
that no one was left out. He was always broadening
relationships and ties. When Bill's mother came to
visit, she took our small student community out to a
dinner at an Italian restaurant in New Haven. It was an
event marked by sharing and celebration — a clear
affirmation of Bill's affection and respect for his mother,
his desire to introduce her to his friends, and the
importance of his Arkansas roots. Much of the conversation centered on his mother and her struggle to
become an anesthesiology nurse in order to support the
family. Bill's appreciation and their closeness was evident.

Clinton's life at Yale Law School was a combination of
working hard and spending time with close friends. He
played touch football, listened to Carole King on the
stereo, and helped out by cooking for his roommates. As
Don Pogue recalled, Clinton's cuisine was somewhat one-
dimensional.

There really isn't much to be said for Bill's cooking.
Basically, Bill was a frier. He fried everything. And he
did it in one continuous motion — from frying pan to
plate and into the mouth. All while he was standing

there holding the frying pan. But at least he washed the frying pan. That was part of the continuous motion — ending up in the sink. It all flowed. I can see him there, metal sponge in hand, still talking, smiling.

William Thaddeus Coleman III, the son of President Richard Nixon's Transportation Secretary and a leading Detroit lawyer in his own right, became Clinton's roommate in his second year at law school.

I was one of ten African-Americans in a class of 125 students. From the first day of law school, the African-American students gravitated to each other, and almost immediately began to form close bonds and relationships. By the second week of class there was a "black table" in the cafeteria. This self-segregation was readily acknowledged and accepted by the majority student body, with one notable exception. There was a tall, robust, friendly guy with a thick Southern accent and a cherubic face who would unceremoniously violate the unspoken taboo by plopping himself at the "black table." At first, his presence at the table would cause discomfort; many of the black students would stare at him with an expression suggesting the question, "Man, don't you know whose table this is?"

The tall guy with the thick Southern accent would be oblivious to the stare, and would simply become engaged in the conversation. He was immensely curious about people. He had an ability, in a non-obtrusive manner, to get people to talk about themselves. He was fun and funny; on occasion even raucous. He had the gift of the true story teller, in which he could take the simplest event, and in retelling it, turn it into a saga complete with a plot and a moral. At the same time he was serious, and would discuss social and moral issues with concern, depth of knowledge, and insight. By simply being himself, the Southerner dissipated the unspoken taboo and became a regular and welcomed member of our table. The person of whom I speak is Bill Clinton.

During our second year in law school, Bill and I were roommates, sharing a house off campus with two other students [these were Don Pogue and Doug Eakeley, Clinton's old Oxford roommates]. As his roommate, I learned more about Bill's background and developed an intimate acquaintance with Bill's priorities and concerns. . . . Bill always expressed gratitude to his grandparents, who, though poor and uneducated, felt that the opposition to integration was simply wrong. Bill could not accept or understand the fact the children whom he played with every day could not attend school with him. As a child, Bill had to deal with these issues, not as a matter of abstract principle, but as the emotional reality of a child who perceives he is arbitrarily separated from his friends. Dealing with these issues at an early age had a fundamental impact on Bill which has led him to reject racism with a personal passion, which, frankly, I find rare in individuals who are not themselves victims of racism.

Bill's childhood experiences also created another characteristic which is unusual and special. Because the roots of racism are deep, the heart often does not keep pace with what the mind wishes to believe. Consequently, some of the most ardent advocates of equal rights, nonetheless unintentionally treat African-Americans in a condescending or patronizing manner. In matters of race and racism, the heart will usually prevail over the head, and, in this regard, there simply is no question about Bill's heart.

Clinton was very proud of his Arkansas roots, and he spent hours in the student lounge regaling his friends with tales from his home towns of Hope and Hot Springs. One day, a young woman was passing through the lounge with some classmates when she heard a loud voice declare, "And not only that, we have the largest watermelons in the world!" She asked her companions who the speaker was. They replied, "Oh, that's Bill Clinton, and all he ever talks about is Arkansas." The young woman was intrigued. She resolved to get to know this outgoing and handsome fellow. Jeffrey Glekel was an eyewitness to the her next encounter with Bill Clinton:

One evening in the Yale Law School Library I spotted Bill studying and attempted to convey to him the advantages of joining the Yale Law Journal. As I described to Bill the various attractions of serving on the Law Journal, he listened with his usual courtesy and asked me a number of questions about the operation of the Journal.

Nevertheless, I somehow sensed that Bill was far from convinced that the Law Journal was the place where he should be concentrating his energies. I decided to dangle before Bill the various attractions of Law Journal membership, such as prestigious judicial clerkships and appointments to law school faculties.

Little by little, though, I noticed Bill's concentration begin to slacken and his interest to wane. It was becoming clear to me that Bill's focus was somewhere other than the Law Journal. As I continued to talk,

Bill's eyes seemed to wander; he appeared to be glanc-
ing over my shoulder with increasing frequency, while
we continued to discuss whether or not he should participate in Journal activities.

I managed to sneak what I hoped was an inconspicu-
ous glance to see what was attracting Bill's attention.
There seated at a nearby desk with a stack of books and
notepads was my classmate Hillary Rodham. After a
while, Hillary walked over to us and said to Bill,
"Look, if you're going to keep staring at me and I'm
going to keep staring back, we should at least introduce
ourselves".

At that moment, Bill Clinton was at a loss for words and
momentarily forgot his own name. Jeffrey Glekel, watching
the chemistry develop from the sidelines, decided to throw in
the towel.

I realized that I was fighting a losing battle on behalf
of the Law Journal and excused myself — little suspect-
ing that Bill had found an asset that evening far more
valuable than Law Journal membership.

Clinton recalled years later, "I was so embarrassed. It
turned out she knew who I was. But I didn't know that at
the time either. But I was real impressed that she did that.
And we've been together, more or less, ever since."

Hillary Rodham was born in Chicago on October 26,
1947, the daughter of Dorothy Rodham and her husband
Hugh, a textile manufacturer. She grew up with her two
brothers in the suburb of Park Ridge. She attended Wellesley
College, the academically prestigious Massachusetts
women's college, where she was elected student body

92

president during her senior year and graduated with high honors in 1969. She entered Yale Law School in 1970.

Clinton knew from the start that Hillary Rodham was going to be an important part of his life. Soon, Clinton and Rodham began spending time together at school and at the beach. Susan Bucknell recalled the time they all spent together:

> Before the first semester ended, Hillary became a frequent visitor to Fort Trumbull Beach. When I first met her, I was impressed by her directness, her own commitment to public policy, her intelligence, and also her affection for Bill. It was fun to be with them as a couple. They enjoyed and respected each other and recognized each other's potential. As women grappling with the Women's Movement, and as young women trained for professional careers, we were searching for men who would support and respect our potential. I always felt that Bill and Hillary had a solid foundation for an equal partnership and that this was a value which Don and I shared with them. There was also a delightful sense in which they complemented each other. I can still hear Hillary's humorous and fond admonition of Bill when he would wax a little too eloquent on some idealistic vision. I always had a sense that this was a couple who would have made it across the West in a covered wagon.

Don Pogue, Clinton's roommate, saw something in common between Clinton's favorite professor and his new girlfriend:

> I think Bill's favorite professor may well have been

J.W. Moore. Moore taught Procedure. More than that. Moore was Procedure. There was a national law of procedure to a large part because Moore wrote it. Crusty and cigar-chomping, Moore had a dominating grasp of the subject. He was an awesome intellect. Bill was attracted to such people — which brings us to Hillary.

People who think Hillary is smart are like people who think Shakespeare is a good writer. They are right, but they've missed the point. There is a difference between being good and being very good. Hillary was very good.

Bill and Hillary really were a good match. She was more Midwestern, schooled in straight, analytical thinking. He noticed subtle differences. They shared an open, warm approach to people — it seemed a good harmony.

During the summer and fall of 1972, Bill Clinton and Hillary Rodham moved to Texas to work for the Democratic presidential campaign. Rodham worked in San Antonio to register Hispanic voters for the Democratic National Committee. Clinton, along with Betsey Wright and Taylor Branch, headed up Senator George McGovern's state campaign headquarters in Austin.

Working on the McGovern campaign gave Clinton valuable experience in vote getting. Judy Trabulsi worked with Clinton in Austin, Texas. She recalled:

I watched this 25-year-old from Arkansas mobilize this very diverse state of ours. Building consensus by bringing together South Texas Hispanics, West Texas judges, East Texas Blacks, and North Texas conservatives. And building friendships with the staff by sharing work, music, Mexican food, and touch football. Bill Clinton embraced everyone he met and made them feel special, and his energy and enthusiasm were contagious. I recognized then his very special qualities — leadership, commitment, passion, and compassion — and I knew he could make a difference in this country.

Taylor Branch shared an apartment with Clinton, and was impressed by his natural talent for politics. He told *The Washington Post*, "Bill was way ahead of me in seeing that a lot of politics had to do with how people got along and understanding how individuals worked: who is lazy, who you could depend on. He knew how to reach people, how to play to their strengths and weakness. Politics is love of the people and the process. Bill was naturally good at that." Branch went on to earn a Pultizer Prize for *Parting of the Waters: America in the King Years*, a history of the civil rights movement.

In October 1972, Sarah Erhman, who was on the staff of Senator George McGovern and later served as a Director of Issues and Research for the McGovern campaign, went to work in South Texas where she met Clinton:

I arrived in San Antonio on a Thursday in time to help plan a rally for Senator McGovern in front of the Alamo. In connection with that event, I went to the airport to meet the McGovern plane. We walked down to the tarmac and saw a tall young fellow dressed in a white linen suit and he was standing at the foot of the stairway. I asked who he was and someone said he was the state coordinator for McGovern. He looked to be about 23 or 24 years old and I was quite impressed with his youth. I went over to speak with him before he went over to brief Senator McGovern on the events and I thought to myself after a few minutes, "That kid is really going somewhere...I'll bet he'll be the president of the United States someday."

I didn't see Bill Clinton again for quite some time but I did meet a friend of his who was in San Antonio some days later to work on voter registration. Her name was Hillary Rodham, she had come down from Yale University Law School and she was in the campaign headquarters. I was profoundly impressed with her intelligence and grasp of the issues, and her strength and toughness. We were together only for a week but we became fast friends.

Clinton and Rodham spent the entire semester working in Texas, and then returned to Yale in time to ace their finals. They had not attended a single class. As Betsey Wright remembers, "they were breathtaking."

One year, Clinton and Rodham were partners in Yale's annual moot court competition. Douglas Eakeley recalled how Hillary's legal skills perfectly complemented her partner's.

Hillary has the same wonderful personal warmth and commitment to public service that Bill has. But coming from the Middle West, she was more direct and outspoken than Bill, the gentle Southerner. They made a wonderful team, as evidenced when they became the finalists together in the mock trial competition sponsored by the Yale Law School Barrister's Union. A former U.S. Supreme Court Justice presided, and I vividly recall seeing Bill and Hillary interrogating witnesses in a splendid (and coordinated) display of forensic skill.

The fast-paced intellectual atmosphere at Yale lent itself to fierce debates over the issues of the day, debates which honed the skills of aspiring political leaders such as Bill Clinton. On January 22, 1973, the Supreme Court's landmark *Roe v. Wade* decision, which guaranteed abortion rights during the first trimester of pregnancy, invalidated anti-abortion laws in Texas and Georgia and overturned similar laws in 44 other states. The same month, Henry Kissinger concluded the four-party Vietnam peace agreements in Paris and the last American troops evacuated Saigon on March 29. Each of these crucial events, and others, provided grist for mealtime discussions.

Bill Clinton's years at Yale changed his view of the world as he developed an appreciation of the importance of law in society. Clinton had mastered skills in writing legal briefs, negotiating, identifying significant points in massive volumes of case law, and persuading others to accept his point of view. Perhaps more importantly, Yale was renowned for teaching its students not only what the law *is*, but how to decide what it *should be* — excellent instruction for those, such as Clinton, who would go on to write the law.

Many of Clinton's classmates looked forward to lucrative appointments to corporate law firms — but not Bill Clinton. He could have sought them out if he had wanted to, but long before he applied to study law at Yale, he had decided that he would respond to a higher calling — to serve the people of his poor home state and to do what he could do to turn their lives around. Clinton packed his bags and boxes, got in his car, and headed home for Arkansas. He was almost 27 years old.

Chapter Seven

A Higher Calling

Upon graduating from Yale Law School in 1973, Bill Clinton intended to establish a small-town law practice in Arkansas. One of his professors, however, had told him of two openings at the University of Arkansas Law School in Fayetteville. During his drive home to Hot Springs, Clinton stopped at a telephone booth and called Dean Wylie Davis to inquire about the job. "I don't have anything set to do," he told Davis, "but I'm coming home to Arkansas, and you might want me to come teach up there a year because I'll teach anything, and I don't mind working, and I don't believe in tenure [for myself], so you can get rid of me anytime you want."

Clinton was offered an appointment to teach Constitutional Law, Criminal Procedure, and Admiralty Law. Admiralty Law was not one of the law school's most important courses, given that Arkansas is a land-locked state; so it fell to the school's youngest professor who accepted the assignment without hesitation. Wylie Davis recalled why he decided to hire a twenty-seven year-old, fresh out of law school, whose only teaching experience was a brief stint in a New Haven community college: "I thought he was a good risk to be a first-class, brilliant law teacher. I think he would have been tenured if he had not gone the other route [into politics]." Davis knew that Clinton had leadership potential. "I wish we could have kept him," he said. "He was a damned good teacher."

Clinton made lasting acquaintances with some of his law students, including David Matthews, whom he met in the summer of 1973. Matthews, who later was elected to the Arkansas House of Representatives recalled:

In the summer of 1973, I was working as a sales clerk in Perry's Jewelry Store in Fayetteville, Arkansas, and waiting to begin my first year of law school in the fall. Bill had just moved to Fayetteville to become a law school professor that fall. One evening, Bill came into the jewelry store to browse. He and I struck up a conversation. I sensed immediately that he was an interesting and intelligent man. During the course of the conversation, he, of course, learned that I would be starting law school and I learned he would be a professor there. We talked some about the Watergate mess, and he shared with me his concerns that the country was in a real crisis situation.

Luther Hardin, a former student now in the Arkansas State Senate, remembers Clinton's commitment to befriend his students.

Bill Clinton was my teacher in Criminal Procedure in

the Spring of 1974 and was a good professor. While his teaching tended to be sympathetic to some of the 1960's Warren Court holdings on criminal procedure, he was very fair and very tolerant of more conservative views. He encouraged discussion, kept the class directed and while he digressed at times the discussion remained relevant. It was one of my favorite classes of my freshman year.

My memory of Bill Clinton is that of a teacher who was comfortable in the classroom setting and enjoyed teaching. As a teacher Bill Clinton showed a great deal of compassion and understanding. Clinton was never condescending and while showing displeasure he never humiliated any student for being unprepared as some professors did. At the time I certainly felt like that was a virtue. Clinton, who was not a bad ball player, would play half-court basketball with us occasionally at Barnhill Arena on the University of Arkansas at Fayetteville Campus. He was always very friendly.

The life of a law school professor had its own challenges. Nevertheless, Clinton did not lose sight of his goal to be more actively involved in public service. While Clinton had studied law in Connecticut, one of the wealthiest states in the entire country, he was about to embark upon a political career in one of the poorest.

To better understand the situation Clinton confronted as a young political leader in Arkansas, it is necessary to understand the forces which contributed to the political culture of the poor, rural state in America's heartland. It is one of the poorest states in the nation, with a per capita income fluctuating between 47th and 49th, sometimes competing for last place with Mississippi and West Virginia.

As the popular saying among the state's opinion leaders goes, "Thank God for Mississippi!" Many people have two images in mind when they consider Arkansas: Sam Walton, the richest man in America during most of the 1980s as the founder and chief executive of Wal-Mart, Inc.; and the widespread, intense poverty of the Ozarks. Arkansas, the smallest state in the South, is indeed a land of contradictions.

Discovered in the 16th century by the Spanish explorer Hernando de Soto, the region which later became known as Arkansas was claimed by the French in 1682 when La Salle claimed the entire Mississippi Valley for France. In 1803 it was sold as part of the Louisiana territory to the United States. At the time, the population of Arkansas totaled around 500 people.

In 1819, the United States Congress granted Arkansas its own territorial status, and admitted it to the Union in 1836. While slavery had existed in Arkansas long before the United States had acquired it from France, there were very few slaves until the 1830s. The total population of the state was 14,000 in 1820, and increased over 30 times, to 435,000, by 1860; in that year, 111,259 slaves — just over 25 percent of the total population — lived and worked in Arkansas.

By the end of the 1820s, the federal government had killed or expelled most of the Native American tribes in the area, including the Choctaws, Osages, and Cherokees, among others. Frontier Arkansas was a rough place: crime, violence, and backwardness tarnished the image of the state for generations. The three major institutions in Arkansas frontier society were religion, unrestrained capitalism, and a conservative press led by the *Arkansas Gazette*. Plantation owners gained power during the 1830s when they borrowed money from Eastern bankers to finance their purchases of land and slaves. When according to the terms of the Missouri Compromise of 1820, Michigan was admitted in 1836 as a state free from slavery, a slave state was required to be created to maintain the uneasy balance of power. In the name of "Southern patriotism," the plantation owners pressed successfully for Arkansas statehood.

Eastern capital continued to finance the importation of slaves from other states during the 1830s. Real estate speculation, encouraged by easy credit, led to an economic boom in the same decade. The New York banking crisis of 1837, followed by a collapse in cotton prices, resulted in one of the most severe depressions in America's brief history. Hundreds of financial institutions nationwide collapsed, and Arkansas defaulted on its public debt in 1841. Land prices dropped 90 percent and slave prices, 75 percent. The approximately 500 members of the plantation elite who had committed Arkansas to the evils of slavery were wiped out. Only the Civil War would end the depression.

Arkansas was the only state in the Union which did not invest in children through public education and was the only state which never voted to allocate taxes on property, income, or commerce to finance schools. Those who wished to educate their children had to pay for it themselves. For only four months of each year, Arkansas students attended 836 one-room, one-teacher schools and 109 academies averaging one or two teachers apiece. Arkansans traditionally have been fiercely independent, wary of big government, and loyal to their families and communities. They preferred to take care of their own.

As civil war approached, the Arkansas legislature voted against secession. But in the spring of 1861, after ships

102

from South Carolina fired on Fort Sumter, President Abraham Lincoln called up the Arkansas militia to join the battle on the side of the Union. On May 6, 1861, the planter-politician faction of the assembly forced the state to refuse Lincoln's demands and to join its neighbors in the Confederacy. After four years of a violent war, devastation, and broken families, Arkansas finally outlawed slavery in 1865, two years after the Emancipation Proclamation. As long as equality and civil rights were enforced under the Reconstruction, black men had the freedom to vote and to hold public office.

Following the end of Reconstruction, it took only four years for white leaders to manipulate the polity and to institute discrimination and segregation. As the economy declined, white farmers and townspeople began to ventilate their political and economic frustration through racism. The early 1890s witnessed the worst years of interracial violence in Arkansas and throughout the South. In Arkansas alone, in 1892, 20 black men were murdered in lynching and mob violence which the *Arkansas Gazette* argued was "useless . . . to deplore." The mob respected no one — not even Governor James Eagle himself, who tried to stop a lynching but was pushed down and had to be saved by his companions. Black men, women, and children across the South were terrorized and intimidated, and lived in constant fear of bullets and sticks of dynamite.

Economic divisions amongst whites widened, as railroad owners, cotton merchants, and lawyers built huge Victorian mansions in Little Rock while farmers and sharecroppers suffered in abject poverty. Arkansas farmers joined with their Southern and Midwestern counterparts to give life to the Populist movement of the 1890s and brought to the fore one of the state's most formidable political leaders,

Jeff Davis, who campaigned for Arkansas against Eastern bankers, and for rural areas against the political elite in Little Rock. A magnificent showman, Davis portrayed himself as a rural hillbilly battling for the small farmer against the moneyed interests arrayed against him. He quickly advanced from the attorney general's office to the governor's mansion, but when the proud voters of Arkansas sent him to represent them in the United State Senate, his country ways invited ridicule. When the progressive movement — which stood for reform of government — reached Arkansas in the 1910s, voters rejected Davis's candidate for governor and elected in succession a businessman and a professor who brought needed progressive reforms to the state, including a tax for higher education and commissions to encourage economic growth.

In the 1920s the leadership of Arkansas sought to counter its backward image with a public relations campaign about the "Wonder State", the sixth largest producer of crude oil in America. Arkansas boasted that it had the largest diamond mine in the country and that it produced 92 percent of U.S. aluminum ore.

The Great Depression amid the Dust Bowl of the 1930s hit Arkansas hard, and 128,000 "Arkies" moved west seeking work. Over a third of the state's farming population left agriculture and two-thirds of Arkansas's farms disappeared. World War II brought federal money and wartime industry: new military installations were constructed, as well as two relocation centers for Japanese-Americans uprooted from the West Coast.

Although it had become known as one of the more progressive Southern states, Arkansas shocked the nation in 1957, when Governor Orval Faubus called out the National Guard to Little Rock's Central High School in an attempt to prevent integration. President Dwight Eisenhower was forced to send in federal troops to protect the "Little Rock Nine" from white mob violence and to enforce the law. Ironically, Faubus was a progressive on most issues other than race: he invested in education, health care, and infrastructure, and remained concerned about Arkansas's future.

Traditional Arkansas progressivism expanded to include racial equality during the 1960s, as black men and women were finally made full partners in the social, economic, and political life of the state. Little Rock, once the subject of international scorn, was acclaimed for its progress in race relations.

Arkansas elected its first Republican governor since Reconstruction, the moderate Winthrop Rockefeller. He accomplished a number of important reforms, but was in turn defeated by the even more progressive Democrat Dale Bumpers in 1970. Bumpers further revitalized the progressive tradition, but powerful conservative forces in Arkansas continued to resist meeting the basic needs of the people. There was thus much work to be done, and Bill Clinton knew he had to be a part of it.

Thus in early 1974, just six months out of law school, Clinton decided to run for Congress against John Paul Hammerschmidt, the popular Republican incumbent in Arkansas' Third Congressional District.

Clinton knew it would be an uphill battle and he did not expect to win. "The only reason I ran for Congress is they couldn't get anybody else to do it," Clinton said. " . . . I [hadn't planned] to get into politics that early. I was sort of easing into my life, and I loved Fayetteville." Clinton made an agreement with the Arkansas Law School that he would not resign from the faculty, but would only be paid for the time he was actually teaching.

Jim Crawford, an Oxford classmate, was in Hot Springs when Clinton announced his candidacy. He remembers the young candidate as a "gregarious, thoughtful, intellectually committed person."

In the spring of 1974, having finished my tour in the Navy and a short stint with a small company in St. Louis, I joined the consulting firm of McKinsey & Company in Chicago. My first assignment took me to Hot Springs, Arkansas, and I think it was on my first day there that I returned to my hotel, the Velda Rose, kicked off my shoes, and turned on the local TV news. To my surprise, there was a live report from Hot Springs of Bill announcing his first run for Congress. The hotel in which he was speaking, I noticed, was just down the street from the Velda Rose.

I jumped up and went over to the other hotel, just in time to greet Bill coming out from his news conference. I only expected a short exchange with him, but to my surprise he asked if I had dinner plans, then asked me to join him when he heard I had none. We spent a wonderful evening shooting the breeze, catching up on mutual friends, and talking about our careers. What struck me about our time together was that he had even extended the offer. I'm sure Bill's schedule at that time was hectic, and that his announcement day had been stressful. All he probably wanted to do was have a quiet evening with his mother . . . and unwind. Instead, he was out with me, exuding energy and genuine friendship.

While Clinton was campaigning, Hillary left her staff attorney position with the Children's Defense Fund and moved down to Washington to take a job with the House Judiciary Committee staff responsible for planning impeachment proceedings against President Richard Nixon.

President Nixon had denied any involvement in the June 17, 1972, burglary of the Democratic National Committee headquarters in the Watergate office complex. The truth was that Nixon's staff had orchestrated a cover-up. The task fell to the House Judiciary Committee to draw up the three articles of impeachment charging the president with obstruction of justice, abuse of power, and contempt of Congress. Rodham moved to Washington, DC, to assist, and stayed with Sarah Ehrman, her old friend from the McGovern campaign in Texas. According to Ehrman, the two women led busy lives but "occasionally met at the refrigerator where there was yogurt and diet soda — about all there ever was."

Back in Arkansas, many of Bill Clinton's friends and colleagues in Fayetteville joined his campaign. David Matthews read about Clinton's political ambitions in the newspaper, and quickly jumped on the bandwagon.

I immediately went to Bill's office at the law school and volunteered to help in the campaign. I ended up being one of his drivers and traveling with him some. The only criteria for being a driver in that campaign was to own your own car and have a tank of gasoline.

Equally enthusiastic was Ann Rainwater Henry, a college professor from Fayetteville active in Democratic politics, along with her husband, State Senator Morriss Henry. When Bill ran for Congress in 1974 his boundless energy and enthusiasm were contagious. He inspired us all and we became involved with his campaign in fund-raising, phone calling, working at headquarters: whatever our schedules would allow us to do. Unfailingly generous with his thanks, Bill's own energy and commitment to the task helped keep up all the campaign workers' enthusiasm. . . . We were joined together for a cause and enjoyed the campaign and created bonds among each other that are still present. You can always bring a smile to a face to recall that first congressional race and the thousands of miles Bill put on his little car going all over the Third District.

Important to Clinton's chances was the backing of several organizations. The Political Education Committee of the Arkansas State AFL-CIO endorsed Clinton early. George Ellison, a union leader, commented that Clinton possessed "the brightest future of anyone who has been before this convention in a long, long time." The Arkansas Education Association (AEA) also endorsed Clinton, praising his position that the decision as to how to spend federal aid to education in Arkansas must be the responsibility of local school districts. The AEA also cited his support of teacher improvement and supplementary programs that contribute to improving educational excellence.

During his congressional campaign, Clinton advocated a number of plans that showed early in his political career a concern for economic and social justice: a fairer tax system, a national health insurance program, public funding of presidential elections, anti-inflation protections, an excess profits tax for the oil industry, and a strengthening of antitrust laws against the oil industry.

Clinton was not afraid to criticize Congress as well as President Nixon. "I think Congress has been too weak for too long," Clinton told the *Arkansas Gazette*. "They have not been willing to take care of their own house, nor to watch the other people enough." The "other people" Clinton referred to were the officials of the executive branch and in particular, President Nixon, who had been implicated in the Watergate scandal.

The American people," Clinton said, "have a general feeling of helplessness about the federal bureaucracy, which is unyielding, distant, and not responsible." He criticized his Republican opponent, Hammerschmidt, for his support of Nixon. "I think it's plain that the President should resign," Clinton said, "and spare the country the agony of this impeachment and removal proceedings."

"The American people have a general feeling of helplessness about the federal bureaucracy, which is unyielding, distant, and not responsible."

Bill Clinton, 1974

One night, all the Democratic candidates in Arkansas gathered in Russellville for a pre-election dinner. Clinton was allowed three minutes to speak, and was scheduled to speak after everyone else, at 11:00 PM. By that time, the crowd was weary and anxious to go home. Then Clinton took the podium. David Pryor, then a Congressman and now U.S. Senator, recalled: "He got up in those three minutes and immediately mesmerized the audience of several hundred people in a very brilliant three-minute political presentation. He brought the crowd to its feet." The Russellville speech marked his political debut. His words caused many long-standing politicians to take note of this newcomer. The Bill Clinton sounded like someone they wanted to see in office — and everyone knew it.

After winning the Democratic primary in a runoff race,

Clinton focused on beating Hammerschmidt and on advocating a more responsible and effective Congress. He promised to make the House "stand up and do what it [is] supposed to do." Clinton promised to "just stick to the issues," and said he would not run a negative campaign. By contrast, Hammerschmidt assailed Clinton with false accusations. He called the 27-year-old Democratic nominee "immature" and accused him of having a "radical left-wing philosophy." He criticized Clinton for working for George McGovern's 1972 presidential campaign, and claimed that Clinton's campaign was financed largely by "labor money."

Billy Burton Hathorn notes in *The Republican Party in Arkansas: 1920-1982* that Hammerschmidt had a strong reputation as a "conservative, colorless representative who is more interested in answering constituents' letters than in making angry speeches." Clinton once got so frustrated with hearing about his opponent's "friendly, down-home style" that he burst out, "I get sick and tired of hearing how nice Hammerschmidt is!"

Clinton also condemned Hammerschmidt's voting record on education. The Republican had voted against education funding and had fought the creation of the National Education Association. Clinton called for the creation of an independent federal Department of Education (at the time, the Office of Education was administered under the Department of Health, Education, and Welfare). An investment in young people, he believed, would be economically productive for America. Better educated citizens "get good jobs and pay more taxes over a lifetime than the money invested in their education."

Clinton made a strong case for economic austerity. "We need a congressman," he said during the campaign, "who's not afraid to say no to the unnecessary government spending that has hurt the economy of the country."

During the summer of the election, the Nixon administration collapsed over the White House-orchestrated cover-up of the Watergate break-in. President Nixon resigned from office on August 9, 1974, rather than face almost certain impeachment and conviction. Vice-President Gerald Ford was sworn in as the 38th president, and one month later, on September 8, granted an unconditional pardon for all federal crimes Nixon "committed or may have committed" while President. In a speech on September 13, 1974, to the Arkansas State Democratic Convention in Hot Springs, Clinton reacted strongly to the unprecedented turn of events and articulated a powerful message, one which he had not abandoned to this day.

"The question before us, my friends, is not what they have done, but what we can do for our people. How can we return to the people the prosperity and stability which they have earned by their efforts and their loyalty to our way of life?

"We ought to go back to the roots of our Democracy: the people. They have some ideas of their own about what the politicians ought to do.

"We ought to go back to the roots of our Democracy: the people. They have some ideas of their own about what the politicians ought to do."

Bill Clinton, 1974

"We know that in every system of laws, because men are frail and fall short of glory, justice must be tempered with mercy. But we want it remembered that — even for the favored few — mercy must be tempered with justice.

"We do not mind showing generosity to foreign countries but we know that foreign friends cannot be bought. We want America's needs to be met first. Charity begins at home.

"We do not want the federal government to give up its attempts to protect our national security and promote domestic well-being. But we do want to cut back on wasteful spending and bloated bureaucracies. These middlemen of government meddle with our lives without increasing the common good.

"In short, in the words of a friend of mine who works on the Scott County Road Crew: "The people want a hand up, not a hand out.""

"The people want a hand up, not a hand out."
Bill Clinton, 1974

"As we meet today, the purpose of our party must be to restore justice and fairness — not just to the courtrooms and the halls of government. We must bring it back to the farms and factories, the streets and stores, the homes and hearts of all Americans.

"The good government we love has too often been made use of for private and selfish purposes. Those who have abused it have forgotten the people.

"Today, we must deliberate. Tomorrow, we must take out of this hall the will to set things right. Let us begin."

As the campaign drew to a close, Clinton ran low on funds. As David Matthews told *The Washington Post*, "The fact is we could have had the money. There were overtures to Bill about funding him that last week, but the implication was that there would be strings attached." Clinton's answer made his views clear. "Let's just go with what we've got," he said. They finished the campaign

$45,000 in the red — and their conscience in the clear.

Clinton came closer to defeating John Paul Hammerschmidt than anyone ever has. He earned 48.2 percent of the vote and won thirteen of twenty-one counties. Despite his loss, the National Committee for an Effective Congress called Clinton's campaign "the most impressive grass roots effort in the country." Although he lost the election, he impressed many voters. The *Arkansas Gazette* commented, "It is regrettable that Arkansas did not quite add its own extra momentum to the national Democratic landslide. . . . In any event Bill Clinton very nearly made it to Congress and surely he will be back in 1976 . . . ." Clinton still calls his effort "the best campaign I ever ran, . . . just a lost cause that almost won." He told the *New York Times Magazine*, "I just got in my little car and drove and had a hell of a time. . . . I was still in my 1970 Gremlin, and later I had a little Chevelle truck with Astroturf in the back. It's what I like about politics. You learn something. You hear another life story. It's like being able to peel another layer off an unlimited onion every day."

Bill Clinton's foray into politics at the state level had taught him much about the political landscape of Arkansas. He made new friends across the 21 counties he campaigned in, and impressed many more throughout the state. The congressional race focused his energies into important social and political issues which he would vigorously support throughout his career.

Chapter Eight

Promises to Keep

When President Nixon resigned in August 1974, Hillary Rodham's work for the Congressional impeachment committee came to an end. She decided to move down to Arkansas to be with Bill Clinton and to teach at Fayetteville.

The decision was not an easy one to make. Susan Bucknell-Pogue, Clinton and Rodham's friend from Yale, recalled that Rodham faced difficult choices.

Caught between her own career aspirations and a partnership, Hillary struggled with the decision to move to Arkansas. She was fearful that it might prove less than a satisfying environment for her. However, she made the decision to go, fully determined to embrace both her partnership with Bill and Arkansas. One of Hillary's great strengths is indeed her ability to be practical and focus on what really matters.

Sarah Ehrman remembers how she felt when Rodham told her of her decision.

In August 1974, Hillary told me that she was going to
Arkansas to take a job teaching as an assistant professor
of law at the University of Arkansas Law School in
Fayetteville. And there was much consternation in my
face, I'm sure, when I heard the news because this
young woman had a tremendously bright future in law
in the Northeast and could really have done anything
she wanted.

But she decided that she was going to go down to
teach law in Fayetteville and just see whether she and
Bill Clinton could make a life together down the road.
She had a lot of stuff with her — books and paper and
clothing and all sorts of things including a bicycle and
she couldn't figure how she was going to ship it down
to Fayetteville.

I offered to drive her to Fayetteville from Washington, DC, which was about a two-and-a-half to three-day
drive. We had an absolutely marvelous time. We would
drive for 20 miles and I would stop the car and I'd say,
"Hillary are you crazy, are you sure you want to go to
Fayetteville, Arkansas?"

And it went that way all the way down the way
through the Blue Ridge mountains, the Great Smoky
mountains, into Tennessee and across the Mississippi
to Arkansas. And we spent that wonderful time together
talking, gossiping and exchanging ideas and getting to
be fast lifelong friends.

When we arrived, in Fayetteville it was the day of
the Texas-Arkansas football game and the entire town
was full of screaming college kids yelling: "Soui,
Soui, pig, pig, pig!" It was just an astonishing sight. I
said to Hillary, "For God's sake, Hillary, are you
crazy? You're not going to stay in this town. *Why* are

you doing this?"

"I love him," she said. And that was enough for me.

Rodham taught Criminal Law, a seminar in children's rights, and Civil Procedure. Dean Wylie Davis recalled, "I didn't anticipate that Hillary would be coming on, either. That was serendipity — enormous — she was really great, too. She was great in criminal law — she was great in everything she did."

Time magazine relates that when Rodham first arrived in Arkansas, Clinton took nine hours to travel the one-hour's distance from the Little Rock airport to his family home in Hot Springs. He was so proud of his state, and so proud to show it to Hillary, that he took her everywhere from scenic vistas to restaurants that served fried pies, an Arkansas specialty.

Ann Henry became one of Hillary's closest friends in Fayetteville:

> Bill and Hillary were guests at both large and small parties because Bill, especially, loved kicking ideas around and talking politics and history. Occasionally Hillary would join me and Diane Divers Blair for poolside visits about political, social, and personal issues. Through our normal interactions and personal affinity, we became good friends.

One day in August, 1975, a year after arriving in Fayetteville, Hillary returned from an out of town trip. "Bill picked me up," she recalled, "but instead of driving me to my apartment, he drove me up to this house, and he said, 'I've bought that house you like.'

"'What house I like?'

"'You know. Remember when we were driving around the day before you left and there was a "For Sale" sign and you said, 'Gee, that's a nice house'?'

"'Bill, that's all I said. I've never been inside it.'

"'Well, I thought you liked it, so I bought it. So I guess we'll have to get married now.'"

The prairie-style house was a bungalow, with beamed ceilings and a bay window. But it was unpainted, so Clinton and his friends rushed to paint the house, inside and out, in time for their wedding. Hillary Rodham asked Ann Henry to plan their wedding reception. She still remembers the festive event as if it were much more recent than nearly two decades ago.

Hillary's mother, Dorothy Rodham, came to visit Fayetteville around Labor Day of 1975 and came to our home for lunch. October 11 was set for Bill and Hillary's wedding date. They had decided they wanted a private family ceremony at the house on California Drive they had bought and a larger celebration afterward. Our home seemed a natural place to hold a large informal reception following the private ceremony.

Hillary delegated all details to me. So we washed windows, ordered food, and got the yard in shape for the big party. My memory is that Chuck's Bakery created a beautiful three-tiered cake, decorated only with icing in cream and pale yellow roses. There was no bride and groom on top — just the flowers. I borrowed my mother's white handmade cutwork tablecloth which was used in both our home receptions to use on the main table. We had a champagne fountain out on the porch where ferns and hanging baskets were hung for color. We probably also had another table with small smoked

meat and cheese sandwiches and other assorted finger
foods available for the hundreds of guests who filled
our home and side yard to celebrate. Someone played
our grand piano during the whole evening; I don't
remember who it was.

Law school faculty, university, local, and state dignitaries, politically active businessmen and their spouses,
and law students came from all over the Third District.
At 7 PM that Saturday evening, the weather was perfect: balmy, low 70s temperature with a cool breeze.
People wandered inside and out and visited, visited,
visited. I wonder how many of us ever dreamed we
were attending a party for a future presidential candidate.

Clinton and Rodham continued to teach law at the
University of Arkansas at Fayetteville. Dr. Charles Chastain,
the chairman of the department of Criminal Justice at the
University of Arkansas at Little Rock, heard about Clinton
and hired him to teach a course to undergraduates, in
addition to his Law School course load.

In the fall of 1975, Clinton taught a course called *Law
and Society,* an "introduction to the law" class in which he
analyzed how civil and criminal law was applied to various
segments of society. His students loved him and gave him
rave reviews.

Chastain asked Clinton to teach the Arkansas Criminal
Code during the 1976 spring term. The Arkansas Bar
Association had entirely rewritten the State's Criminal
Code in 1974 and 1975. Bill Clinton tackled the topic
head-on, and made the detailed new code comprehensible
to his students. Topics ranged from victim's rights to
interpreting rules of evidence and the insanity defense.

Over 25 police officers took his course, driving in from all over the state to hear this brilliant and engaging professor. For Clinton, too, the course was highly rewarding: it prepared him for his next job — the Attorney General of Arkansas.

Attorney General Jim Guy Tucker, who was leaving the post to run for Congress, had convinced Clinton to run for Attorney General. Clinton officially filed as a candidate on April 1, 1976. He supported a number of significant legal reform issues during the campaign, including work-release opportunities for Arkansas prisoners, laws to compensate crime victims, the appointment of an ombudsman to settle complaints about state government, and stronger consumer and antitrust efforts.

Clinton supported compensating crime victims for their losses, telling voters that governments "house, clothe, and feed the convict, while we forget about the victim. Nothing is done to replace the property or pay the medical expenses of the innocent citizens who are victimized by criminals."

After Clinton's announcement address, a reporter posed a question which would become an issue four years later: "Will the fact that your wife has retained her maiden name hurt you politically?"

"I hope not," Clinton replied. He was right — for the time being. Hillary Rodham was a becoming a prominent lawyer in Arkansas and was increasingly recognized nationwide as an expert on children's rights. The *Arkansas Gazette* noted, "It was important for her to maintain the recognition she had built as Hillary Rodham."

Professor Chastain suggested to the 29-year old law professor that since he was running for Attorney General, it would be a good idea to meet more police officers. He arranged for Clinton to visit the police headquarters in Little Rock.

When he met Clinton at the headquarters, Chastain could not find any officers that he knew, so Clinton introduced himself to one of the officers, a hard-nosed, surly, tough-looking detective.

"Hi," he said, "I'm Bill Clinton. I'm running for Attorney General." The man was unmoved and was not terribly interested to know who he was.

"So what *is* your position on the death penalty?" the grumpy officer asked in a demanding tone of voice.

Clinton replied: "Well, I don't like it, and I think it should be used only very cautiously for extremely heinous crimes, like the murder of a police officer." The officer lightened up. He happily shook Clinton's hand and took him for a tour of the police station, introducing him to everyone.

During the campaign, Clinton reminded his audiences that politics is a high calling. "I am committed to the proposition that politics can be an honorable and important work," he said. "Without good politicians, we cannot have the kind of society that we want and need."

In November 1976, Clinton triumphed over his two opponents in the Democratic primary with more than 55 percent of the vote. Since no Republican had filed for the position, Clinton was unopposed in the general election and therefore won unanimously.

When Clinton arrived at the Attorney General's office, he discovered his kindergarten classmate Joseph Purvis working there as a deputy attorney general. Purvis has never regretted his decision to continue to work with his old friend, who ran an extremely efficient, yet still intellectually rewarding operation.

Bill quickly instilled a feeling among everyone who

worked in the office that we were on a mission to work for the public. Part of it was heightened by the atmosphere created by a young public official who was only 30 years of age with an equally young staff. Part of it was a reaction to the Nixon era politics which had just ended in Washington. The ten of us working in the criminal division were putting in an average of 60-75 hours per week.

I remember particularly one late Friday afternoon when most other people involved in state government had long since gone home, being literally up to my eyeballs in work and two steps away from blowing my brains out. There was so much stuff piled on my desk that I could barely see someone sitting across from it in a chair. Just at the moment I was going to scream, Bill walked in and sat down in the chair across from my desk. He peered through the stacks of briefs and research and gave me that warm smile of his, handed me a stick of gum and asked me very softly, with a grin, "Joe boy, are you having fun?"

"What in the hell did you say?" I shot back.

"I asked you if you were having fun," Bill replied, "because if you are not having fun, you better put this down and move to something else. When this becomes work instead of fun, it is time to move on."

Clinton is one of the most brilliant thinkers I have ever been around. He can quickly and incisively analyze a situation and formulate a solution to whatever the question or problem might be. He has an uncanny ability, when looking at a problem or question, to be able to see and focus not only on the immediate answer to that problem but also to see it as part of a bigger picture.

During his two years as Attorney General, Clinton became noted for his pro-consumer and anti-utility views. He pushed for a tougher ethics law, one which would apply to elected and appointed officials alike, and which would place more stringent reporting standards on lobbyists. He also fulfilled his campaign promise to expand work-release programs for prisoners in order to reduce prison over-crowding. An August 1977 editorial in the *Arkansas Gazette* praised Clinton for being "a stout champion of the Arkansas consumer, but, even more importantly, . . . a champion of individual rights against arbitrary government."

For some time now, Clinton had his sights set on the governorship, a position in which he could implement progressive reforms in his home state. He felt it imperative to improve economic and social conditions in Arkansas, a state which ranked among the neediest in the nation in critical areas. David Matthews recalled Clinton's decision to run for Governor in 1978:

I vividly remember a meeting we had at the Holiday Inn in Rogers, Arkansas, while he was Attorney General. We were discussing whether he should run for the United States Senate or for governor. The Senate seat was open due to the death of Senator John McClellan. I was encouraging him to run for the Senate and assured him I was confident he could win. He told me that day that, indeed, he had poll results which indicated that he could win the Senate nomination.

"But I believe I can do more good for the people of Arkansas as Governor," he said. I knew then he would run for Governor and not the Senate.

Although he was criticized for being "liberal" on gun restriction laws, marijuana use, capital punishment, and women's rights, Clinton was victorious in 71 of 75 counties in the primary. Against four opponents, he took 59.4 percent of the primary vote.

During the campaign, Clinton stressed that Arkansas's economic problems could be remedied only by improving the quality of education in the state. It was extremely difficult to do so, he noted, in a state which paid teachers less than anywhere else in the United States.

Clinton faced GOP State Chairman A. Lynn Lowe of Texarkana in the general election. Lowe's only asset in the campaign was the presence on the ballot of a referendum which called for the elimination of sales taxes on groceries and prescription drugs. Clinton opposed the referendum on fiscal grounds, citing the $60 million it would cost the state. Lowe countered that the budget already had a surplus.

The Arkadelphia *Southern Standard* candidly assessed Clinton's chances: "He cannot lose unless he stumbles badly or is caught molesting a nun in the process of robbing the church widows' and orphans' funds." Lowe's bid for the governorship failed along with the referendum. On election day, 1978, Clinton received 338,684 votes, 63.4 percent of the total. After his election, Clinton told the Georgetown *Voice* that his support of the Equal Rights Amendment cost him as much as 10-15 percent of the vote. "I thought the issue was important enough not to back away from," he said. "I thought it was necessary to combat the irrational statements about the impact of the legislation that simply couldn't be true. It is an important issue that shouldn't be neglected."

The 32-year-old Clinton had come a long way. But now he faced his most difficult challenge — improving the quality of life of the people of Arkansas. He was the second youngest governor in the history of the United States.

Chapter Nine

A Man in a Hurry

Even before he was elected governor, Clinton was touted as "far and away the most attractive candidate material the Democratic Party has going right now," in the words of the Searcy, Arkansas, *Daily Citizen*. Political pundits heaped praise upon this socially liberal and fiscally conservative rising star. Some mentioned him as a Vice Presidential prospect in 1980 for either Jimmy Carter or his challenger, Senator Edward Kennedy. There was only one hitch — Clinton was only 32 years old in 1978, and would not reach the constitutionally required minimum age of 35 until August, 1981.

Clinton's political star was rising fast — indeed, Senator Sam Nunn of Georgia would later describe him as a "rising star in each of three decades" — but he never compromised his values in the pursuit of votes. His successes came as a pleasant surprise to some of his more skeptical friends from Oxford, one of whom was Tom Williamson.

I would often engage Bill in debate, and I frequently found myself won over by his ability to make me feel that he was sincerely willing to reconsider or modify his own thinking based on the viewpoints that I had advanced. However, there was one abiding point of disagreement between us during our Oxford days. Bill was committed to returning to his native Arkansas and dedicating himself to a career of public service as an elected official. His motive was to play a leadership role in reshaping Arkansas into a state where there would be equal opportunity, quality education, and meaningful jobs for people of all races. Bill was convinced that Orval Faubus' constituency was a small, unrepresentative minority that had besmirched the basic decency and fairness of the great majority of Arkansans.

I repeatedly scoffed at what seemed to me the political naivete reflected in his lofty aspirations. I told him that I would be pleasantly surprised if he were right, but that my expectation was that winning elective office in Arkansas would require that he compromise substantially the political ideals that he and I so fervently espoused at Oxford.

Once again I proved to be quite wrong about Bill. . . . I have had a chance to bear personal witness to his pursuit of a progressive racial and social agenda. I have not been disappointed. In retrospect, I should have known better than to underestimate Bill's commitment to political idealism and his determination to make his dream a reality.

Clinton later reflected that his first gubernatorial campaign was "a little bit like running for class president. . . .

We live in a state which has too long viewed politics as a sport rather than a pathway to tomorrow." *Arkansas Democrat* editor Starr later wrote that "the foundation was laid for Camelot at the Capitol."

Clinton asked his old friend Randy Goodrum to perform at his inaugural ball. Goodrum remembers that Clinton had not changed much since their days together at Hot Springs High School.

My songwriting career had just started taking off and I was starting to have numerous pop and country hits when Bill called me to go to Little Rock to perform in a show called "Diamonds and Denim" to help commemorate his first term in office as Governor of Arkansas. I wouldn't have missed it for the world. Later, I went to the Mansion and there was a large party going on with dozens of people I didn't know. Bill spotted me and introduced me to Hillary and a few others. Then he said, "Come here — I've got something to show you." We went downstairs to an unfurnished recreation room where over against the wall was a superb pinball machine. We proceeded to play a couple of games before rejoining the crowd. The time I spent one-on-one with my old friend was the nicest thank you I could ever have received. Our friendship had remained the same through all the changes in both our lives.

Bill could talk about any subject from saxophone reeds to world affairs without dominating the conversation and turning it into a lecture. He was idealistic and always thought things could be better. It was obvious to all his friends that he always held a "greater vision" and believed that changes could be made to benefit the lives of all people everywhere.

Bill Clinton was sworn in as the fortieth governor of the State of Arkansas on January 9, 1979, succeeding the former governor, David Pryor, who had left for the United States Senate. In his inaugural address to the Arkansas Legislature, Clinton presented his vision for the future of his state:

Like anyone else I will tend to make decisions that reflect the values and principles I have come to cherish over the years of living and struggling to grasp what understanding I can of the human condition.

For as long as I can remember, I have believed passionately in the cause of equal opportunity, and I will do what I can to advance it.

For as long as I can remember, I have deplored the arbitrary and abusive exercise of power by those in authority, and I will do what I can to prevent it.

For as long as I can remember, I have rued the waste, and lack of order and discipline that are too often in evidence in government operations, and I will do what I can to diminish them.

For as long as I can remember, I have wished to ease the burdens of life for those who, through no fault of their own, are old or weak or needy, and I will do what I can to help them.

For as long as I can remember, I have been saddened by the sight of so many of our independent, industrial people working too hard for too little because of inadequate economic opportunities, and I will do what I can to enhance them.

Today, we begin anew the people's business in a time that is confusing, uncertain and sometimes difficult to comprehend. In the recent past, we have learned

again the hard lessons that there are limits to what
government can do — indeed, limits to what people can
do. We live in a world in which limited resources, limit
knowledge and limited wisdom must grapple with problems of staggering complexity and confront strong
sources of power, wealth, conflict and even destruction, over which we have no control and little influence.

Let us not learn too much of this lesson, however,
lest caught in the thrall or what we cannot do, we forget
what we can and should do. We are a people of pride
and hope, of vision and will, of vast capacities for
work. We have the prospect, for which we have waited
so long, of economic growth, which does not require us
to ravage our land and so reject our heritage. We have
the immeasurable benefit of living in a state in which
the population is sufficiently small and widely dis-
persed for people of all kinds still to know and trust
each other, still to believe in and work together for the
common good.

We have an opportunity to forge a future that is
more remarkable, rich and fulfilling to all Arkansans
than our proud past. We must not squander it.

There is much to be done.

In education, we have lingered too long on or near
the bottom of the heap in spending per student and in
teacher salaries. We must try to reverse that. However,
we must be mindful that higher quality education will
not come from money alone. The money must be but
part of a plan which includes better accountability and
assessment of students and teachers, a fairer distribution of aid, more efficient organization of school districts, and recognition of work still to be done in

programs for kindergarten, special education and gifted and talented children.

Clinton went on to advocate an agenda which included environmental protection, ethics in government, equal opportunity and economic development, and tax relief for the elderly.

As governor, Clinton made major improvements in the area he cared most about: education. In 1978, Dr. Kern Alexander, of the Educational Finance and Research Institute at the University of Florida, had performed a comprehensive study of education in Arkansas. His report was dismal: "By almost any standard, the Arkansas system of education must be regarded as inadequate," he wrote. "Children of the state are not being offered the same opportunity to develop their individual capacities as children in other states. . . . From an educational standpoint, the average child in Arkansas would be much better off attending the public schools of almost any other state in the country."

Keeping his campaign promise, Clinton set out zealously to improve his state's education system. Governor Clinton dedicated a large portion of the 72nd Session of the State legislature in trying to move Arkansas from its ranking of 50th among the 50 states in education. His budget provided for Arkansas's largest-ever increase in financial support for public elementary and secondary education.

Clinton made it clear that while he strongly supported increased funding for education, he did not believe that "just throwing dollars at the schools would guarantee quality education." Hence, he linked his increases in the education budget with legislation that established procedures for measuring both the programs designed to im-

prove the quality of education and the performance of
public schools in Arkansas. Nevertheless, a massive infu-
sion of public funds made the crucial difference: Clinton's
budget included a 40.5 percent increase in elementary and
secondary school funds, a $1,200 salary increase for teach-
ers, and increased funds to meet rising overhead costs.
Arkansas teachers' 1978 salaries, at only $10,000 in 1992
dollars, were the lowest in the country and only two-thirds
the national average.

Phyllis Finton Johnston, writing in *Bill Clinton's Public Policy for Arkansas: 1979-1980*, cited Clinton's successes in achieving his education policy goals. In his 1979-
1980 budget, Clinton called for a more equitable distribution of state aid to school districts. There was a fierce
debate over how to distribute almost $900 million in state
aid over two years to the public schools, which included a
significant $80 million increase that Clinton proposed and
the legislature adopted. The eventual compromise distributed half of the new money over two years on a per-student
basis, benefiting districts growing in population, and another half to help equalize higher and lower income districts, with the poorest schools getting an increase four
times greater than the richest schools.

Clinton won approval for a statewide educational testing program for measuring performance in the basic subjects, which Clinton believed was an important diagnostic
tool for individual teachers and students. The first tests
were given to students in April, 1980. Some 51,000
elementary and junior high school students took the standardized tests. The scores reflected a glaring need for
improvement in the educational system.

When Clinton took office in 1979, only a few school
districts had established programs for gifted and talented

children, and little money had been appropriated by the state to assist in funding local programs. Under the Governor's leadership, grants totaling $398,797 were made to sixty-five local districts for gifted and talented children. Clinton was also instrumental in setting up the Governor's School for Gifted and Talented Children, a summer program at Hendrix College for over 250 outstanding Arkansas students from across the state. It offered advanced study in English, mathematics, natural sciences, social sciences, art, drama, choral music, and instrumental music. Classes continue to be taught by Arkansas teachers and guest lecturers, including Bill and Hillary Clinton.

Clinton also implemented other important education reforms. Legislation was enacted to require all teachers to take the National Teacher's Examination before they could be initially certified to teach in Arkansas or before they could teach a new subject. Clinton signed the Fair Dismissal Act of 1979 which protected Arkansas teachers from arbitrary, capricious or discriminatory firing by a school board. He also enabled all state children to go to kindergarten by increasing funding for transportation and teaching materials.

Clinton set up a Vocational Education and Training Task Force to study the long-range needs of the state's vocational training programs and to make recommendations. Historically, the state's vocational-technical training programs had lacked adequate funding. Clinton was convinced that an effective program was possible, and from October 1980 through January 1981, 184 high schools received reimbursement for vocational education.

The Governor appointed Dr. Don Roberts to direct the State Education Department. Roberts had achieved much success as a Virginia superintendent in the areas of accountability, standardized testing, school reorganization, and special programs. Clinton announced that Roberts had "done the kind of thing we should be doing" in education. Clinton and Roberts assumed a very strong leadership role in carrying forward the administration's commitment to education. They shifted the emphasis from centralized control at the state level to assistance to local school boards and providing better service.

In her book, Johnston concluded that Clinton's education plan was a "policy which resulted in substantial, positive improvements," and in 1990, when Dr. Alexander reevaluated the quality of Arkansas' education, he reported that the system had dramatically improved: "I can tell you that as of today, I would much rather have my children in school in Arkansas than in Tennessee, Alabama, and Georgia. Arkansas has made strides in these 12 or 13 years through the efforts of the governor, the Legislature, and school people. It has surprised me that you have moved as quickly as you have." Since the Governor had led the fight for education reform, credit for this success was due largely to one man: Bill Clinton.

Clinton had successfully campaigned for Governor on the promise to raise money for state highways after a state-commissioned report concluded that 8,154 miles of the state highway needed various improvements to meet the needs of the citizens of Arkansas. Some of the roads were badly deteriorated — they had not been substantially repaired for fifteen years. Clinton and the state legislators were caught in what the press characterized as a "no-win" situation. The Governor had the option of either letting the damaged roads remain as they were, or increasing taxes to generate revenue needed to repair the roads. It was a serious dilemma from a political point of view, since neither option would be politically popular.

Clinton was under intense pressure from the Highway Department and Commissioners, as well as from dozens of city and county officials to raise highway funds, but he wanted to generate revenue without taking it away from public schools, health services, human services and other programs that he considered essential. Clinton's original proposal to raise $45 million annually for road repair relied as much as possible on existing revenue sources. He supported raising user fees — registration and title-transfer fees — and raising taxes on tires and gasoline. Clinton's original plan was to switch from a fee system based on the car's weight to one based on its value. This would have saved most motorists money since about one-half of the cars registered in Arkansas were at least five years old.

Nevertheless, organized interests opposed to other aspects of Clinton's plan forced the governor to revert to the old weight-based system of fee payments. Unfortunately, much of the revenues were to be raised from the many Arkansans who owned cheaper but heavier used cars. Newer, more expensive cars were lighter than the older cars to get better mileage.

Of the $53.9 million received by the Arkansas State Highway and Transportation Department during Clinton's administration, $46.1 million was used to match federal-aid highway funds of $256 million. About 1,130 highway construction and repair projects were started during this time.

In the end, registration fees nevertheless doubled, and Arkansans, especially the poor and the fixed-income retirees who bought heavier used cars and therefore had to pay higher title-transfer bills, reacted in fury. "I know that it enabled us to have the best street system in the cities we've had in a long time," Clinton later remarked. "It helped maintain the system they had, and it certainly helped a lot of state projects get finished. In that sense it was a great success, but it was a failure because the people objected to the form in which the money was raised. I think the title-transfer tax was raised too much, and the car-license tax on older cars was raised too much."

Bill Clinton had entered office committed to achieve certain policy objectives and set out to accomplish them, but his spirit and determination was frustrated by public resistance to drastic change. The auto registration issue was only one of a number of controversies which Clinton had to address. David Matthews, who has known Clinton since 1973, reflected on his urgent impulse to effect change in his state:

When he began his administration in 1979, Bill was like a man in a hurry to accomplish many things in a short time. Like many native Arkansans, Bill was frustrated with the reputation Arkansas had always had for being a backwater state. Those of our generation were all scarred by the 1957 Little Rock desegregation crisis. I think somehow Bill felt that, through his sheer energy, he could change our state overnight. His commitment and dedication to fundamental change in our state was viewed by some as arrogance. He had surrounded himself in his first administration with equally bright and sincere young men and women who only furthered the notion that his administration was arrogant.

The young governor's staff was brilliant, young, re-form-minded, and from out-of-state. Clinton's aides were convinced that they knew what was best for the state. The

Governor learned the hard way that having the wisdom and political courage to stand up to special interests, in order to advance change in the public's best interests, did not necessarily assure political success. Many improvements he sought were resisted by entrenched interests, and furthermore, Clinton's staff was not able to win widespread support for Clinton's initiatives. Years later, Clinton reflected on his choices to researcher and author Diane Blair. "In assembling an effective staff," she wrote in *Arkansas Politics and Government: Do the People Rule?*, "he learned it was most important to find people 'who are not only good at government, but good at making people feel good.'"

Time after time, Clinton took on the powerful special interests of his state head-on. The Chamber of Commerce was upset when he changed the name of the Arkansas Industrial Development Commission to the Department of Economic Development, and altered its focus from industrial recruitment to small business development. Similarly, Clinton's vision was blunted in the area of conservation. To bring conservationists together with their opponents, who favored logging rights, the Governor held hearings on the wholesale clear-cutting of forests. Naturally, this angered the Arkansas timber industry.

Attempts by Clinton to improve his state's health care system also ran into trouble. Following a nation-wide search early in the Clinton administration, the Governor appointed Dr. Robert W. Young as Director of the State Health Department, based on his pioneering efforts and record of success as medical director of a rural health clinic in West Virginia. This appointment demonstrated Clinton's commitment to new efforts to fight rural health problems and to reorganize the mismanaged health department.

Clinton and Dr. Young proposed four rural health

clinics, hoping to bring medical services to needy areas. The Clinton administration also made extensive efforts to recruit physicians to medically underserved areas. The federal Department of Health, Education, and Welfare approved a grant for the rural health plan, saying that the plan was a "model proposal" and that "our posture is to be extremely supportive of any state willing to do something innovative. It takes courage on the part of Governor Clinton and Dr. Young to do this."

The plan, however, was opposed by the medical community who did not like the idea of part-time doctors making periodic visits to rural clinics, even though many rural areas in Arkansas found it difficult to attract full-time doctors. Dr. Young's had failed to approach the medical community as a political ally rather than as an adversary, and thus was unable to lay the groundwork needed to win the political support of the physicians and rural areas that would benefit from the new programs. Phyllis Johnston wrote, "Here, as in other areas, Clinton's success was tempered by entrenched political roadblocks to dramatic change and by his staff's failure to enlist, rather than alienate, constituencies vital to the success of new health-policy initiatives."

Throughout his first term, Clinton faced strong special interest groups who controlled Arkansas politics and constituents who were not yet ready to pay for better public services. The Governor's opponents were thus able to use his program increases to their political advantage. The automobile registration issue sent Frank White into the Republican gubernatorial primary. White, a longtime Democrat, had been the director of the Arkansas Industrial Development Commission when Clinton came into office and restructured it. He switched his allegiance to the Republican Party shortly before announcing his candidacy.

In a newspaper circulation war, reporters engaged in hyperbole and sensationalized trivial spending mishaps. First, the state's Economic Development director was reported to have budgeted $450 per month for office plants. Then, the newly created Energy Department shelled out $2,000 for a lakeside conference retreat. The Energy Department also rang up a $37.50 bill for corkscrews for a dinner party.

When an investigative reporter found out that the Special Alternative Wood Energy Resources Project (SAWER) — which was designed to train low-income Arkansans to chop wood and distribute it to the needy — had spent a grand total of $62,000 to produce six woodchoppers and just three cords of wood, Clinton immediately fired the director of the project who was responsible for the waste of taxpayer's dollars. Nevertheless, many held Clinton responsible. Clinton had worked hard to cut wasteful spending from the state budget; however, although Clinton was in no way responsible for any misconduct, his reputation suffered by association.

Some good news did come Clinton's way in early 1980. His wife Hillary gave birth to a baby girl, whom the couple named Chelsea, after Judy Collins' song *Chelsea Morning*. Holding the newborn in his arms, Clinton remarked how privileged he was to be standing there, and remembered that his father had died before he could see him. Clinton later said, "I remember when my daughter was born, maybe the greatest night of my life. I remember thinking a few minutes after she was born...'This is something he never got to feel.'"

Clinton had only one challenger in the 1980 Democratic primary — seventy-seven year-old turkey farmer Monroe

Schwarzlose. Schwarzlose had a long history of running unsuccessfully for office. He campaigned on the car tag issue, and distributed a photograph of his own chopped wood pile, which he noted had not cost him a cent. On primary day, Schwarzlose stunned the political experts and picked up 31 percent of the vote.

Clinton's opponent in the general election, Frank White, also had been given no chance of defeating the incumbent. Then the actions of Cuban communist leader Fidel Casto propelled the little known, newly converted Republican into contention. Castro allowed an estimated 120,00 political prisoners and "other undesirables" to leave Cuba. The so-called Freedom Flotilla sailed to the United States, where President Jimmy Carter made efforts to absorb them. Although it was a federal problem subject only to federal authority, it led to a dramatic crisis for the Clinton administration.

On May 7, 1980, the Carter administration notified Clinton that Fort Chaffee, in northwest Arkansas, was to be a stopover point for almost twenty thousand Cuban refugees, who had sought asylum in the United State along with one hundred thousand others. Rumor had it that the Freedom Flotilla contained Cuba's criminals and mentally ill.

Clinton publicly supported Carter's decision. "I know that everyone in this state sympathizes and identifies with them in their desire for freedom," he said. "I will do all I can to fulfill whatever responsibilities the President imposes upon Arkansas to facilitate the refugees' resettlement in this country." Clinton's statement explicitly acknowledged the intrusion of federal authority into Arkansas. Furthermore, President Carter did not commit funds, staff, or federal troops to assist the refugee resettlement, and

Clinton was forced to make do with Arkansas' meager resources.

At first, Fort Chaffee remained peaceful: the refugee camp provided $22 million in jobs and business to Sebastian County. By late May, the camp's population had grown tremendously and tensions began to mount both inside and outside its walls. The county sheriff watched as residents rushed to gun shops to protect themselves.

On May 26, 1980, one day before the primary election, up to three hundred Cubans turned over barricades and escaped through an unguarded gate, dispersing throughout the county. The federal authorities at Fort Chaffee who were responsible had taken no steps to prevent the Cubans from leaving the military base, and the Governor was furious.

Clinton reacted quickly and forcefully. At dawn on election day, he ordered the activation of 65 National Guard troops to protect the citizens living near Fort Chaffee. He travelled directly to Fort Chaffee to review the situation. He called on the Federal Emergency Management Agency to "beef up security at the base" in order to protect the citizens in the area.

General Drummond, the commanding officer of the base, told Clinton that his federal troops had no authority under federal law to restrain the Cubans. This position was a violation of the understanding that Clinton had reached with the White House, as Carter's staff had assured Clinton that appropriate security measures were being taken and that the Pentagon had been ordered to keep the Cubans inside within Fort Chaffee and maintain law and order.

On Tuesday, May 28th, President Carter discussed the crisis with Governor Clinton by telephone. "There's no control over the Cubans," Clinton told him. "The military

says they have no authority to restrain them on the fort."
Carter said that the other possible location was in Pennsylvania but refused to relocate the Cubans on the grounds
that the weather there was poor.

On Wednesday, the Pentagon called Clinton to notify
him that 150 additional federal troops would be sent to Fort
Chaffee. In the interim, Clinton took the precautionary
measure of adding 20 more National Guardsmen to the
security force. Clinton also ordered the director of the state
police to maintain a security force around the clock at the
fort and to cooperate fully with the local sheriff. Within
days, state troopers and local police recaptured the Cubans
with no help at all from federal officers.

On the night of June 1st, Fort Chaffee exploded as the
Cubans rioted. The press called it "a war zone." The
fighting started on the base, but soon the uprising burst out
beyond the fort. About 1,000 angry refugees charged the
gate, but federal troops did nothing to stop them. About
two hundred Cubans ran down Highway 22 in the direction
of Barling, a small town near Fort Smith. Clinton immediately called out the National Guard and the state police to
stop the riot.

The community of Barling was in a panic. The Cubans
were stopped with force by 33 state troopers who stood
between them and an angry crowd of nearly 500 citizens of
Barling on the city line only 100 yards away. Finally,
officers with nightsticks and guns subdued the two hundred
attackers. 62 people suffered injuries, including five Cubans, who were shot.

Relations between the federal government and the state
of Arkansas reached a new low. The Governor demanded
that federal authorities give the U.S. Army orders to keep
the Cubans on the base. Upon leaving the riot scene, he

called the White House and told officials there, "Listen, you can do two things. You can come down here and fix this tonight, right now, or I'm going to call out the entire National Guard and shut the place down. And I'm not going to let anybody in or out without my approval."

That night, Carter aide Eugene Eidenburg flew on an Air Force plane to Arkansas to meet Clinton. Clinton drove him in the middle of the night to Barling where they saw local residents sitting, armed with guns and rifles, on their front yards. After their tour, Clinton and Eidenburg held a 4:30 AM press conference to explain the actions they were taking.

On June 2, the White House finally complied with Clinton's demand and issued written orders giving federal troops the authority to keep the Cubans from leaving the base. The media was ecstatic. On June 12, 1980, the *Hot Springs News* praised Clinton for his role in managing the crisis: "All Arkansans should be grateful to Governor Clinton for his tenacity in finally forcing Jimmy Carter to stop tending his roses and start tending to the safety of the people that his benevolent open-arms policy has engendered."

The White House acquiesced, but only briefly. In August, President Carter ordered the remaining 10,000 refugees to be sent to Fort Chaffee. After consulting with area residents, Governor Clinton turned down the President's "request," but the White House insisted and overruled the Governor. Again, Clinton succeeded in negotiating a new security plan between state and federal officials and the refugees flowed in despite a public outcry and Clinton's firm opposition.

The Sebastian County Sheriff, the county judge and prosecuting attorney defended Clinton's actions. Prosecuting Attorney Ron Fields commented, "Everyone else was passing the buck and saying they weren't responsible, but Governor Clinton took the responsibility and the risks that went along with it and showed what I considered to be a lot of leadership." Clinton had proved that he was an excellent crisis manager.

Still, some Arkansans blamed Clinton for allowing the refugees into the state and argued that he had mismanaged the crisis, even though he had absolutely no jurisdiction over federal matters. Clinton understood their anger. "I'm the one who bears ultimate responsibility for the security of the citizens in that area," he told the *Arkansas Democrat*. "It was incumbent upon me to act, even considering the possibility that I might be held responsible, because it was the right thing to do."

Publicity about the riots nonetheless hurt Clinton's chances for reelection. Frank White had a slogan that would win him the Governor's Mansion: "Cubans and Car Tags." White scored Clinton for his automobile tax increases — especially on the fixed-income elderly for whom the license fee increase was especially burdensome. He criticized the young governor for not standing up to President Carter during the Cuban refugee crisis. Furthermore, he attacked Clinton for not recruiting enough companies or stimulating sufficient job growth. Arkansas Power & Light and Southwestern Bell, influential industries which had disliked Clinton's pro-consumer crusades against the utility companies, soon endorsed White.

On election night, 1980, the 34-year-old Bill Clinton conceded to Frank White. This was Clinton's second electoral defeat and it hurt deeply. Clinton lost by nearly 35,000 votes of the 840,000 cast. No Arkansas governor since 1954 had been defeated for a second term. He had entered office in 1979 with such high aspirations and with such broad support, and as *Arkansas Democrat* editor John Robert Starr noted, "No one, least of all Clinton himself, imagined that two years later he would be the nation's youngest ex-governor."

The morning after the election, Bill, Hillary, and Chelsea Clinton appeared on the steps of the state capitol. "Hillary and I have shed a few tears for our loss of last evening," he said, "but we accept the will of our people with humility and with gratitude for having been given a chance to serve our state. . . . I grew up in an ordinary working family in this state, was able to go through the public schools and become attorney general and governor and serve people in the way that I had always wanted to since I was a boy."

Hearing her son express his gratitude to the people of Arkansas was a moving moment for Clinton's mother Virginia. "It's easy to be a nice person when you're winning," she said. "The way Bill accepted defeat was the proudest I've ever been of him. I have just never been so proud in all my life, as I was when he walked out on that balcony at the governor's mansion, faced a sea of people standing everywhere there was a place in the yard, and thanked them over and over and over again for giving him the opportunity to serve his state. He was magnificent in defeat."

David Matthews assessed the reasons for Clinton's electoral loss:

In 1980, the stage was set for an upstart like Frank White to knock the props out from under the Boy Wonder. I am convinced that Bill Clinton's defeat in 1980 came about as the result of the five C's: Cubans,

Car tags, Coattails, Carter, and Clinton. None of the five C's would have been enough by itself to defeat him, but the combination edged him out. Under pressure from the Carter Administration, Governor Clinton had agreed to allow Fort Chaffe at Fort Smith, Arkansas, to be a temporary home for the Cuban refugees. Frank White was able to capitalize on the riots at Fort Chaffee in the summer of 1980 with some very provocative television ads. In a effort to improve our highways, Governor Clinton had sought and received a significant increase in the car registration fees in our state. Once again, Frank White was able to use some creative advertising to incite the people over the increase in their car tag fees. Of course, no one can forget that 1980 was the year of the Ronald Reagan juggernaut, and it is impossible to discount the impact of the Ronald Reagan coattail effect in our governor's race. By the same token, many people were frustrated with President Carter and his "malaise". The fact that Bill Clinton was one of Jimmy Carter's strong supporters and defenders did not help him in the governor's race. Finally, some folks believed Bill Clinton had violated the old adage, "your neighbor should be successful, but not too successful."

Bill Clinton recalled that his loss to Frank White was the most painful experience he had ever gone through. As David Osborne notes in his book *Laboratories of Democracy*, Clinton learned that "a reformer must find a way to do what his constituents want, not what he thinks they need." Clinton undoubtedly had made some errors in political judgement during his first term, but he would learn from all of them. These lessons would inform his judgement and influence his strategy and his decision-making skills in future years.

His success did not go unnoticed by the press and the voters. Certain factors in his defeat were beyond his control. He had overcome dozens of special interests in order to help set one of the poorest states in the nation on the right track in education, energy, health and international trade. Despite the volatile mood of the electorate, he had placed a high priority on advocating the best long-term interests of the people of Arkansas.

The standard of education reform set by Governor Clinton during his first term would later establish a model for the nation. He cared about the future of Arkansas and set new goals in every field of progress which had been neglected in one of America's poorest states. If the benchmark for success was providing leadership in meeting public needs for basic services, then Clinton was successful. He was also successful by the standards of President Franklin Delano Roosevelt, who had said, "The test of our progress is not whether we add more to the abundance of those who have too much — it is whether we provide enough for those who have too little." Had it not been for the White House's insistence on moving the Cuban refugees to Arkansas, the OPEC-induced high inflation and the related rise in interest rates after the Federal Reserve Board tightened monetary policy under Chairman Paul Volcker, Clinton might have won.

Clinton's highly developed resilience and determination to make a difference were the raw materials which would fuel his political comeback. Other political leaders are not as persistent in the face of defeat and never become national political leaders as a result. Winston Churchill, who had spent years in the political wilderness before making a comeback to lead the British people against the Nazis in World War II, once remarked: "Politics is almost as exciting as war, and quite as dangerous. In war, you can only be killed once, but in politics many times." Of Clinton, Sarah Ehrman recalled, "I was among hundreds of friends to call to urge him not to quit and I'm glad to say that he did not."

In John Kennedy's Pulitzer-prize winning book, *Profiles in Courage*, published in 1956, the future president examined why the statesmen that he had chronicled took political risks and rejected political expediency in their careers:

> . . . Because each one's need to maintain his own respect for himself was more important to him than his popularity with others — because his desire to win or maintain a reputation for integrity and courage was stronger than his desire to maintain his office — because his conscience, his personal standard of ethics, his integrity or morality, call it what you will — was stronger than the pressures of public disapproval — because his faith that *his* course was the best one, and would ultimately be vindicated, outweighed his fear of public reprisal. Others demonstrated courage through their acceptance of compromise, through their advocacy of concilliation, through their willingness to replace conflict with cooperation.

In the end, Clinton was eloquent and philosophical about his setback. "I have learned," he told his constituents, "that in the long and brilliant history of this country, the political leaders who really make a difference are those who care enough about their people to build for the future, even when the times are hard and when the right course may not be popular."

Chapter Ten

The Comeback Kid

As the youngest ex-governor in the history of the United States, Clinton had a lot of time on his hands. Many expected that he would attempt a political comeback, but no one knew exactly when or what he would be doing in the meantime.

In 1980, Bill and Hillary Clinton went on a religious pilgrimage to Israel with a group organized by the Reverend Worley Oscar Vaught, the pastor of the Immanuel Baptist Church in Little Rock. Their tour included many traditional stops for new visitors to Israel, including the Old City of Jerusalem, the Western Wall, Masada and the Galilee. The trip reinforced Clinton's support for the people of Israel. "Bill and Hillary understood the profound effect that Israel has on American Jews and around the world," said Sarah Ehrman, their friend from the McGovern campaign, "and share a feeling for the security and stability of the State of Israel."

Reverend Vaught greatly influenced Clinton's attitudes toward Israel. "I have believed in supporting Israel as long as I have known anything about the issue," Clinton later said. "It may have something to do with my religious upbringing. For the last several years until he died, I was very much under the influence of my pastor. . . . He was a close friend of Israel and began visiting even before the State of Israel was created. And when he was on his deathbed he said to me that he hoped someday I would have a chance to run for President, but that if I ever let Israel down, God would never forgive me. . . . I will never let Israel down."

After his return from Israel, Clinton briefly considered a run for the chairmanship of the Democratic National Committee, but decided instead to join the Little Rock law firm of Wright Lindsey & Jennings, as a member counsel specializing in commercial litigation. He made it clear that he was just biding his time, waiting for the right moment to reenter politics. Clinton remained with the firm from 1981 to 1983.

Although he was an effective campaigner, Frank White was not much of a governor, by most accounts. He signed into law a bill mandating the instruction of "Creation Science" in Arkansas schools, and later admitted that he had not even read the bill before he signed it. The law was later declared unconstitutional. He offended many Arkansans when he let utility costs increase. State Auditor Julia Hughes Jones quipped that when White said he wanted to approach state government as he would a private company, "he must be thinking about Braniff Airlines" (which went bankrupt in 1982). Soon, a popular bumper sticker made its way across the state: "Don't Blame Me — I Voted for Clinton."

Still, White was a formidable politician. The *Daily Citizen* reported, "We've become fascinated by watching Governor Frank White's acumen as a politician. While he still doesn't have any hint that he understands the governor's job or has the faintest idea how to run state government, he is turning his flair for salesmanship into political hay . . . Mr. White is about as fast on his feet as any politician in memory, and although he doesn't impress us even lightly as an administrator of state government, he isn't going to be anyone's pushover in the 1982 election."

Clinton realized that he had an opportunity to reclaim the governorship. He knew that politics was a tough business and that he would have a tough battle ahead. Still, he could joke about it. "If your opponent picks up a hammer," he told one crowd, "you need to pick up a meat-axe and cut off his arm." He also knew that political hardball was not enough. "You have to really have priorities and make them clear to people," he told *U.S. News & World Report*. "If you do a zillion things, even if you do them well, people may perceive that you haven't done anything."

Years later, at a Yale alumni dinner in 1987, Clinton recalled his decision in 1981 to run again for Governor: "When I decided I didn't want to give up and I wanted to go on in politics, I realized I had to be in better communication with the voters. I began to drive around the state and talk to people." For the last six months of 1981, he traversed the state, apologizing to those who opposed him for not listening enough to their problems and complaints. He spent hours with the citizens of Arkansas. Sometimes Hillary would join him; other times, Betsey Wright, his campaign manager, or Bruce Lindsey, his law partner, would accompany him in his effort to win back the grass-roots support of the people who had voted him out.

At the Yale dinner, Clinton related the story which made him decide to get back in the game. "One day I was going to see my mother, who lives about fifty miles from Little Rock, the state capital. I stopped midway at an old service station, which is kind of a political watering hole. I walked in and smiled. "You're Bill Clinton, aren't you?'

"I said, 'Yes, sir.'

"'Well, I cost you eleven votes, son. And I loved every minute of it?'

"'You did?'

"'I did. It was me and my two boys and their wives and six of my buddies. We just leveled you.'

"'Why did you do it?'

"'I had to--you raised my car license'

"'Let me ask you something. Look out there across this road. Remember when that road right there was in the front page of the biggest newspaper in this state, because cars were buried in it and I had to send tractors down here to get cars out?' "'I don't care, Bill. I still don't want to pay it.'

"'Let me ask you something else. Would you ever consider voting for me again?'

"He looked down at his shoes, and he looked back at me, and he said, 'You know, I would.

We're even now.'

"So I went out, put a dime in the pay phone, and said to Hillary, 'We're gonna run.'"

In February, 1982, Clinton took to the airwaves with a paid television advertisement announcing his candidacy for Governor. He admitted that he had made some mistakes, and promised that he had learned from them. He had a new slogan which conveyed his new attitudes about governing: you can't lead without listening.

John Brummett of the *Arkansas Gazette* noted that "broadcasting a campaign advertisement before actually announcing as a candidate was curious, of course, but it might turn out to be a smart maneuver. If nothing else, the press was intrigued." Brummett was right: it was a smart move because the press replayed the ad many times over on the evening news — at no cost to Clinton's campaign.

Clinton was quick to admit the mistakes of his previous administration. "I was too inflexible," he said. "This is a very personal state that requires a high level of accessibility. I'm ready to correct past mistakes." He was so apologetic that one political cartoonist sketched him as a repentant monk. David Matthews, Clinton's former law student, noted that the hard lessons Clinton learned have served him well over the past decade.

Many people believed, at the time, that Bill Clinton's political career was over. Obviously, that was not true. In fact, the defeat in 1980 was probably the most significant event in Bill Clinton's political life. He learned some great lessons through that defeat. A leader must find consensus. A leader must bring competing factions together to achieve a common goal. A leader must lead by example. And finally, the greatest lesson was that people can be led and persuaded to a desired result, but they cannot be pushed or driven to it. It is that lesson which has been at the foundation of Bill Clinton's phenomenal success in leading Arkansas during the last ten years. Others, unfamiliar with Arkansas politics, have criticized Bill for being "all things to all people." The fact is he has, through the course of his career, fought long and protracted battles with each of the major special interests in our state. In the final analysis, he has always won through sheer perseverance and a commitment to what is right and by convincing his opponents that his course is the right course. The fact that he has battled those groups who now enthusiastically support him is a tribute to his leadership skills.

Clinton committed himself during the Democratic primary campaign to work on three issues: increasing education funds, expanding job opportunities, and holding down utility rates. Clinton won the primary with 41.7 percent, and in the runoff against Joe Purcell, he captured 54 percent of the vote.

The general election campaign against the Republican incumbent, Frank White, was one of the ugliest in recent memory. Clinton's friend Diane Blair wrote, "White's advertisements portrayed him as a tough-minded, no-nonsense, execution-eager, good old boy in contrast to the bleeding-heart, East Coast, Ivy Leaguer, ACLU-liberal Clinton, who specialized in commuting killers' sentences. Clinton's advertisements portrayed White as an untrustworthy interest-dominated plutocrat who might run with the good-old boy hounds by day but slept with the utility foxes at night, while Clinton was just a caring and concerned down-home Baptist family man who wanted nothing more than another chance to fight the fat cats in behalf of the little guys."

Clinton and White battled over education and utility rates. Clinton said that better schools and educational facilities would attract more industries to Arkansas and would lead to job growth. He attacked White for firing three former officials of the state's Energy Department who had helped Clinton fight higher utility rates in 1980.

The Democratic candidate was not the only person who

152

changed. After much soul-searching, Hillary Rodham changed her name to Hillary Clinton. The *Arkansas Gazette* noted, "Mrs. Clinton is almost certainly the best speaker among politicians' wives, probably the only one who can fully engage an audience on her own merits, rather than just as somebody's wife. . . . The name change indicates that she's working at softening her image a bit. . . . And succeeding, apparently. She has become a good hand-shaking campaigner in the traditional Arkansas style."

Clinton promised voters that he would have a better staff running the Governor's office and criticized White for his ineptitude and for raising utility rates. He attacked the incumbent for increasing the price of medicine for Medicaid recipients while at the same time giving away $12 million in corporate tax breaks.

Near the end of the election, Clinton had an encounter that signaled he had a chance to win. He recalled:

"I was in the northern part of the state. I went into a little country store. Another guy was standing there, . . . and he said, 'Aren't you Bill Clinton?'

"I said, 'Yes, sir.'

"'Well, son, I voted against you last time. But I'm gonna vote for you this time.'

"'That's wonderful. Why did you vote against me last time?'

"'I had to. You raised my car license.'

"'Well, why are you gonna vote for me this time?'

'Because you raised my car license.'

"'Look, mister, it's close to the end of the election. I'm desperate for every vote I can get. The last thing in the world I want to do is make you mad. But, if you'll forgive me, it don't make a lick of sense for you to vote for me this time for the same reason you voted against me last time.'

"'Oh, Bill, it makes all the sense in the world. You may be a lot of things, but you ain't dumb. You're the least likely one to ever raise that car license again, and I'm for you!'"

The *Arkansas Gazette* endorsed Clinton, praising his "ability to bring the ideas and leadership the state so desperately needs." As for Frank White, the paper noted, "Mr. White's shortcoming was that he had nothing much in mind to do as governor. His vision was limited to a few clichés."

Despite a constant barrage of attacks, Clinton defeated his opponent with 54.7 percent of the vote. He was the first Arkansas governor to be defeated for reelection and then later return to the statehouse.

The press cited the reasons for Clinton's victory. *Arkansas Gazette* writer Ernest Dumas wrote, "His final televised talk with the voters Saturday night before the election, a rarity nowadays, may have been pivotal in his victory. As a communicator, he rivals President Reagan." Dumas also praised Clinton for his effective organization skills, his choice of Betsey Wright as his campaign manager, and his revival of the previously dormant Democratic party organization.

In late November, Clinton thanked his supporters in the Arkansas Education Association for their hard work. "I think for the rest of my life," he said, "I will look back on this election with a mixture of disbelief that it happened and with a profound sense of humility and gratitude for people like you who worked their hearts out and went the extra mile to do something that no rational person thought could be done."

Clinton's inauguration speech in January 1983 focused

on education and other critical issues facing the state. He proposed creating "enterprise zones," to foster economic growth in depressed areas, an Arkansas Science and Technology Development Authority to encourage advanced worker skills and industrial growth, and tougher penalties for drunk driving. He noted, "We must realize that we cannot go forward if half of us are always falling behind."

A recent Arkansas Supreme Court decision was interpreted as a mandate to increase education funding statewide. Eleven school districts in Arkansas had filed a lawsuit against the state. They claimed that the distribution of education funds was unequal and therefore unconstitutional. The Arkansas Supreme Court agreed. The majority opinion stated that the disparity in property tax revenues among different parts of the state was not compensated enough by the state's partial equalization formula. In short, funding was so uneven as to be unfair.

Governor Clinton appointed his wife Hillary to chair the state's new Arkansas Education Standards Committee, which was charged with setting statewide standards for education quality. Mrs. Clinton had worked since 1973 with Marian Wright Edelman at the Children's Defense Fund, quickly rising in the organization to chairperson. As head of the education commission in Arkansas, she travelled all over the state, holding hearings and meeting with parent and teacher associations. In the end, her commission submitted a proposal for drastic changes in the state's education system. John Brummett told *Working Woman* magazine that "she did a magnificent job. . . . I'm not one of her biggest fans, but I give credit where credit is due. She worked hard and competently and built political consensus for reducing class size, increasing accountability — it was masterful."

Bill Clinton had always believed in education as the springboard to success in life. So he set to work giving the children of his state a better educational system. To achieve his education goals, Clinton called the first of many special legislative sessions. Under normal conditions, the Arkansas legislature meets only 60 days every two years, but the Governor can call it into a special session at any time. Clinton used the first special session to raise taxes to improve education funding.

He asked the legislature for a tax increase to pay for the new funds. The legislature went along with his request, provided that the tax increase be coupled with Arkansas' first teacher testing requirement. The new law required teachers to pass a basic skills test during the 1984-85 school year. Those who failed would have to take remedial courses and a second test; if they didn't pass by 1987, they would lose their credentials. Teachers were additionally required to take an exam in their specialty area, or complete six credit-hours of college work in their field.

The Arkansas Education Association broke with Clinton on this issue and opposed the skills test. Clinton stood firm, even though he recognized the political risks involved. Despite efforts to subvert the law, demonstrations, and boycott threats, well over 90 percent of Arkansas teachers took the test in 1985. The Governor told the *Arkansas Gazette* that improving the education system was "more important to me than anything I have ever done in politics."

Hillary Clinton was also instrumental in the establishment of a preschool program in Arkansas which encourages parents to teach their own children. Aimed at 4 and 5 year olds, the program is called the Home Instruction

Program for Preschool Youngsters, or HIPPY. Hillary
Clinton worked to bring the program to the attention of
educators in Arkansas, culminating in an ground-breaking
state-wide conference on preschool programs.

Developed in Israel by the National Council of Jewish
Women, HIPPY helps young mothers improve their
parenting skills and gives them valuable skills which they
can use to foster their children's educational development.
Arkansas now has the largest HIPPY program in the United
States, with over 2,400 mothers in the program, and the
Clintons speak about it frequently. "The HIPPY program
builds in its own follow-up by changing the parent into the
child's first teacher, which is what every parent should
be," Governor Clinton told author David Osborne.

The results have been spectacular. Initial testing in one
school district showed a 33 month average gain by children
in 16 months of participation. Indications show much
higher than expected scores on the Metropolitan Achievement Test for HIPPY children in kindergarten.

Another successful initiative in this area was creating a
special education committee headed by Ann Henry, the
Clintons' friend from Fayetteville, and a college teacher.
Henry noted that the Governor made sure the committee
was able to pursue its goals without undue political inter-
ference.

Bill Clinton asked me to chair a state committee on
certification, evaluation, and teacher education issues.
The committee was mandated by a bill that had passed
in the legislature in October 1983, the special session
called to reform education in Arkansas. The committee
included classroom teachers, principals, superintendents,
and college teacher education personnel. The deadline

for getting our work done was December 1984 and we were to have a report to the State Board of Education about recommended changes for implementation.

I met with Bill and Hillary at the mansion in the breakfast room to discuss and organize the process. They wanted to make sure that there was an outreach effort to get public input on these issues.

All day working sessions were held and public hearings were held in the four corners of the state: Jonesboro, Monticello, Hope, and Fort Smith. We heard comments and reactions to our draft reports, and attempted to correct misinformation. Occasionally I would get a phone call from Bill or Hillary to ask if certain viewpoints had been heard or represented.

The committee kept state legislators, the Governor's staff, and other interested parties informed about the progress toward our goal. But there was no pressure to adopt a particular viewpoint; essentially all views were held and we came to a consensus as a committee about what we wanted to recommend to the State Board of Education.

Governor Clinton had made education reform a top priority in Arkansas because he knew that throughout modern history, a community or state that neglects the education of its youth undermines its own economic future and democratic system. In a speech given by Benjamin Disraeli in the House of Commons on June 15, 1874, he said: "Upon the education of the people of this country the fate of this country depends." Franklin D. Roosevelt, in a speech in Boston, Massachusetts on October 31, 1932, said that "Knowledge—that is, education in its true sense--is our best protection against unreasoning predudice. . . . "

EDUCATIONAL EFFORT IN ARKANSAS AND THE NATION, 1900-1985

Year	1900	1920	1940	1960	1980	1985
Length of school term (days per year)						
Arkansas	69	124	59	173	175	180
United States	132	162	175	178	178	180
Ark. as % of U.S.	52.3	77.0	91.0	97.2	98.3	100
Per pupil expenditures per Avg. daily attendance (ADA)						
Arkansas	$6	$20	$29	$207	$1,193	$2,542
United States	$17	$54	$94	$472	$2,445	$3,677
Ark. as % of U.S.	35.2	37.0	30.9	43.9	48.8	69.1
Per capita income						
Arkansas			$332	$1,341	$7,099	$10,100
United States			$693	$2,223	$9,494	$13,451
Ark. as % of U.S.			47.9%	60.3%	74.7%	75.7%
Per pupil expenditures per ADA as a percent of per capita income						
Arkansas			8.7%	15.4%	16.8%	24.9%
United States			13.5%	21.2%	25.7%	27.3%
Ark. as % of U.S.			64.4%	72.6%	64.5%	91.2%
Average teacher pay as percent of per capita income						
Arkansas			176%	246%	178%	192%
United States			208%	244%	194%	188%
Ark. as % of U.S.			84.6%	100.8%	91.8%	102%

Source: *Arkansas Politics and Government* by Diane D. Blair

Bill as
toddler
in his
home in
Hope,
Arkansas

Bill's
Grandfather,
Eldridge
Cassidy
watches over
young Bill
as he
recovers
from a
broken leg.

Young Bill Clinton poses on a pony.

Billy Blythe, the father Bill Clinton never knew.
Blythe died in a car accident before young Bill was born.

Bill's Grandfather
(seen to left
in photo)
in his country store:
Hope, Arkansas.
The equal-handed
way in which he
treated all his
customers made
a lasting impression
on young Bill
(photo to right).

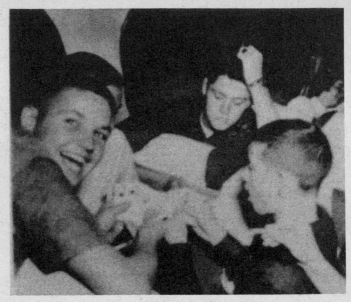

A teenage Bill spends time with classmates.

Edith Irons, Clinton's
high school counselor,
who participated
as an Arkansas delegate
for Clinton in the
1992 Democratic
National Convention.

THE AMERICAN LEGION
BOYS NATION

1963: Arkansas' most promising delegate to
Boys' Nation pauses for a photograph with a friend.

A significant moment in Bill's life. He shakes hands with
President John F. Kennedy in the White House Rose Garden . . . .
Tenor saxaphonist and high-school all-star, Bill Clinton plays
in his school orchestra.

June, 1964: a proud Hot Springs high school graduate.

1974: Clinton's first campaign was a home-made grass-roots effort.

Young politician,
Clinton reviews
a campaign speech.

Clinton on the congressional campaign trail.
He speaks with a volunteer working for the gubernatorial candidate
(now Senator) David Pryor.

Bill Clinton shakes hands with author, Robert Levin on May 21, 1992.
. . . Clinton's mother, Virginia, pauses for a moment with Editor Shawn
Landres, amid the excitement of the Democratic National Convention
in New York City.

October 3, 1991: Following his announcement that he will run for president, Bill Clinton hugs his daughter Chelsea. His wife, Hiliary applauds . . . .

Bill Clinton campaigns in Louisiana in 1992.

Clinton also hired his tenth grade world history teacher, Paul Root, as a special assistant in the Governor's Office. It was a "teacher's dream" for Root. He reflected on Clinton's talent for understanding different sides of issues and about the governor's compassion for people's needs.

When I became his assistant, at age 50, in the Arkansas Governor's office in 1983, our roles were reversed. He was now the teacher and I was the willing student.

I was amazed at the reality of the relationships between the areas of his study at Georgetown University and as a Rhodes Scholar in England and the needs of Arkansas. Teachers in Arkansas were traditionally either the lowest paid or next to the lowest paid in the United States. Farmers were filing bankruptcy in alarming numbers. Unemployment in Arkansas was higher than the national average. (In some of the Delta farm counties, it was holding at about 15 percent.) The federal government was cutting aid to the states.

Now Governor Bill Clinton was speaking five or six times daily, all over Arkansas, to varied mixtures of people on the need to understand the changing nature of our economic system. In one day, I heard him speak to a farm group, a united steel workers union, 5,000 Baptist young people, a group of school superintendents and a group of retired persons. His message changed little from group to group. He was helping people to see the changing nature of the workplace as we approached the reality of a growing world economy.

This was an amazing lesson for me. I had been telling my students for years, "You need to understand these concepts" as I taught world history. I always dreaded the question, "Why?" and was never very satisfied with my answers. But here was my proof. My former student was demonstrating to me (and others) that an understanding of history and economics could enlighten people with interests as varied as the groups mentioned above as to their basic problems and a possible answer to those problems. The connection between education and jobs and the role of government in that process was the message.

Suddenly, I saw my former student as a great teacher. His classroom was the state and he was covering it tirelessly and effectively. Once people understood the problem another part of his job became obvious. He had to get people to commit themselves to solve the problems they had come to understand. Night after night, in town meetings all over Arkansas, with some counties showing unemployment above fifteen percent, he was asking people if they would lower their own standard of living by raising their taxes in order to ensure that the young people of Arkansas could have an education that would allow them to compete in a world economy. He was getting 80 percent positive answers.

I was raised on a farm, so I was accustomed to rising early and working late during the planting season. It had been several years, however, since I had planted anything except an occasional rose bush. Governor Bill Clinton and his chief of staff, Betsey Wright, reintroduced me to the 14 hour day. While the legislature was in session, we started the day at 7:15 am with a staff meeting. My job was to inform the Governor of bills that would possibly come to a vote in the education committee that day, either in the House or the Senate. I would talk about each bill in terms of what it would do to or for classroom teachers, mostly in terms of attitude. Don Ernst, assistant for education, would add a few words about small schools and expected reactions from them.

The Governor would then talk about the implications of each bill in terms of finance. I thought he always understood what I was saying better than I did and he always ended by teaching me a lesson in school finance. Minutes later, I would listen in amazement while others covered the issues that would come up in other committees — local and state government, revenue and taxation, insurance and commerce, public health, welfare and labor, aging and legislative affairs, energy, joint retirement and social security, public transportation, agriculture, and others.

The Governor would know about the major issues in each area, how they would affect people over the state and who was for and against most every bill. We were looking at about 150 bills per day that could be passed by the House and/or Senate. I sat and wondered day after day how anyone less educated and endowed with less ability could be governor.

I understand that information does not always translate to wisdom or the capacity for sound judgement. In Governor Clinton, however, the deep understanding, the insight, the love for and knowledge of the people of Arkansas and the deep and abiding belief in democracy combined to produce decisions aimed at an improved quality of life for the majority of Arkansas' people.

I traveled with the Governor to a breakfast meeting in western Arkansas to meet with a group of local deer hunters. The Game and Fish Commission had ruled that the deer herd was somewhat depleted in their area so they would not be able to run their dogs in the December season. In Arkansas, the Game and Fish Commission is not directly answerable to the Governor even though he does appoint them. These hunters were mad and the Governor was there so they just forgot about the Game and Fish Commission and yelled at him.

When we returned to the car to leave, I suggested that these men were completely out of order and they didn't try to understand his role in the ruling. His answer surprised me. He said, "We have to understand that these men are never going to Little Rock to a Game and Fish Commission hearing and stand up and speak their objections before an auditorium full of people. Their only recourse was to yell at me for appointing commissioners they did not appreciate. I come out here every two years and ask for their vote. The political issue that concerns them now is 'Can we run our dogs in the December deer season?' As far as they are concerned, I have let them down. They have a right to be concerned." By the time he finished his explanation, I had a different attitude toward the hunters.

I have had several such conversations with Governor Clinton. I have been pleased at his compassion and unflagging belief in democracy as worked through difficult situations. He is as tough as anyone I have known and as concerned about others as anyone I have known.

Clinton's leadership style changed significantly between his first and second terms. Perhaps because he spent much of his childhood making peace between warring parents, he has always preferred consensus to conflict. Clinton began to work with the opposition to get his proposals passed. He served as his own lobbyist, calling legislators at all hours of the night and wandering the halls of the legislature armed with a notepad and a cup of coffee.

At the outset of his second term, perhaps due to criticism that he had sought a national profile at Arkansas'
expense, Clinton "went native," hiring mostly Arkansans
for his staff. But in 1984, Clinton told one audience, "The
old notion that Arkansas was the only state that could
produce all it needed to survive was probably never true,
but it was never more untrue than it is today."

The Governor took advantage of the large network of
friends he had built up over the years, frequently calling
upon their expertise. Jim Crawford, a fellow Rhodes
Scholar, regularly consulted with him.

In 1983 my wife, Alicia, and I traveled to England to
combine a two week vacation with attendance at the
80th anniversary of the founding of the Rhodes Trust.
Bill and Hillary, Alicia and I, and several other friends
had a rousing dinner together on the first night of the
celebration, and then shared a picnic at the Perch Tavern on the last day. By then I had spent five years at a
public company, Mark Controls, in Chicago. As I
remember, I was the only one of our friends at that
gathering who had a career in business — and manufacturing at that.

Bill by then was Governor of Arkansas, . . . and the
economic health of his home state was very much on his
mind. I found myself bombarded by endless questions
about business, how plant and office site decisions are
made, and what advice I might have on luring companies and jobs to Arkansas. I remember being struck by
Bill's same gregarious openness that he had displayed
when we were together in Hot Springs, but overlaying
that was a new seriousness. He gave the impression that

every contact with a friend was an opportunity to learn something that might help him in his chosen political career. We talked at length about my experiences at Mark Controls, and I left with the feeling both that I had been with a friend whose friendship had not diminished in a decade, and that I had come into contact with a man on a mission, who had picked up every idea I had about business, and who had tried out on me all of his ideas about attracting business to Arkansas. That feeling was altogether pleasant, as if in some small way I might have contributed to formulation of an idea or two that really might improve the Arkansas economy.

During Clinton's second term, an event occurred which deeply affected the governor and his family. In May, 1984, Clinton received a telephone call from Colonel Tommy Goodwin, director of the Arkansas State Police. Goodwin told him that Clinton's brother, Roger, was under investigation for cocaine distribution. Clinton was stunned. Roger had been abusing drugs since he was 15, and took as much as four grams a day. Clinton recalled to the *Arkansas Gazette*, "If he hadn't been in incredible physical shape, he would have died."

"What do you want us to do?" Goodwin asked.

"Do what you'd normally do," Clinton replied with a heavy heart.

The next weeks were some of the most difficult Clinton had ever endured: he had a shattering secret which he could not share with anyone in his family except his wife. Together, they studied all the literature on drug addiction they could find.

Roger was arrested in Hot Springs three months later. After his brother was taken into custody, Governor Clinton said, "This is a time of great pain and sadness for me and my family. My brother has apparently become involved with drugs, a curse which has reached epidemic proportions and has plagued the lives of millions of families in our nation, including many in our own state. I ask for the prayers of our people at this difficult time for my brother, for my family, and for me. I love my brother very much and will be of comfort to him, but I want his case to be handled exactly as any other similar case would be."

At first, Roger denied that he was an addict. "You don't understand," Clinton told him. "If you're not an addict, I want you to go to prison for ten years. You've been putting cocaine into the bodies of others for money. You're my brother, and I love you, but I want you to go away for a long, long time."

In November, Roger changed his plea from innocent to guilty on two drug related charges. He received a suspended three-year sentence on the first charge, but was sent to prison for two years on the second.

After Roger's sentencing, Governor Clinton told the press, "I accept the judgement of the court with respect. Now all of us in my brother's family must do everything we can to help him free himself of his drug dependency. I hope the publicity this case received will discourage other young people from involvement with drugs and will increase public awareness of the staggering dimensions of the drug problem in our state and nation. I am more deeply committed than ever before to do all that I can do to fight against illegal drugs and to prevent other families from experiencing the personal tragedy and pain drug abuse has brought to us."

At first, Roger felt betrayed by his brother, according to the *New York Times Magazine*, but he soon realized that

Bill had saved his life. Bill, too, came to the realization that he had ignored the needs of the people he cared about as his own ambitions had gotten out of control. "I finally realized how my compulsive and obsessive ambition got in the way," he said. "I think that dealing with [Roger's drug problem] helped me to achieve some better balance."

Roger recalled, "He was my best friend, . . . my brother . . . my father . . . my protector." He once told a radio talk show host, "It's always wonderful and never difficult to be the brother of Bill Clinton because he's a wonderful person. It's just his position that's sometimes awfully tough to handle."

Since his release, Roger has made numerous presentations about the dangers of drug abuse to children across Arkansas. The presentations are not a condition of parole or probation — Roger does them because he cares deeply about helping young people avoid what he went through. Almost two years later, speaking to a Children's Defense Fund dinner, Bill Clinton commented, "Now 100,000 kids in my state know what can happen to them." Today, Roger is a production assistant on the television series *Designing Women*, in Los Angeles, and is a singer and songwriter.

Despite the publicity over his brother's addiction, Clinton remained a popular figure in Arkansas due to his successes as Governor. He entered his 1984 reelection campaign with confidence, making economic growth as well as education improvement the centerpieces of his campaign. After winning the Democratic primary, Clinton faced his Republican opponent, a contractor named Woody Freeman. At one point, former Secretary of State Henry Kissinger made a campaign appearance for Freeman. The foreign affairs expert had little of substance to offer Freeman other than his distinguished reputation. Clinton got a lot of mileage out of the appearance when he addressed the 1984 State Democratic Convention. "I hope Mr. Kissinger tells us everything he knows about what Arkansas needs," he told the crowd, "and I hope my opponent tells Mr. Kissinger everything he knows about what Arkansas needs in a utility contractor."

Humor aside, critics attacked Clinton for not paying enough attention to Arkansas' economic growth. Woody Freeman had pledged not to raise taxes and promised — as Frank White had — to run the state like a business. Clinton responded by releasing his 1985 legislative package: an economic growth plan which included job training and new funds for industrial development. Clinton also said that he intended to launch a nationwide campaign to attract tourism and new business to Arkansas.

One of the challenges of running as a Democrat in 1984, however, was that nationally, the party had nominated Walter Mondale, an old-time Northern liberal, to face off against the extraordinarily popular President Ronald Reagan. Many Arkansas Democrats either endorsed Reagan outright or distanced themselves from the Democratic nominee. Clinton announced that while he was a Democrat, "by both heritage and conviction," he would not hesitate to criticize his party if he felt it necessary.

Clinton also made efforts not to run with the advantages of incumbency -- especially considering how those advantages affected him in 1980. He said, "I'm going to run as if I were starting out as an unknown and if I were behind. I enjoy this and I'm ready." He ended up winning easily, with 63 percent of the vote.

Clinton seemed more confident when he took office in January. In his third inaugural address, he promised that his efforts at job growth would be as enthusiastic as his efforts at education improvement. His plan, which promised to make up to $400 million available for investment in Arkansas, had two major parts: the Arkansas Development Finance Authority, which would issue tax-exempt bonds to finance new projects; and incentives for Arkansas' three pension funds to invest at least five percent of their assets within the state. The bill was passed almost unanimously by the legislature. Furthermore, the Governor secured passage of laws requiring trials to be held within nine months of indictment and legislation protecting crime victims' rights.

The 1985 session also produced Arkansas's first law limiting abortion to those after the first trimester without mentioning earlier terminations of pregnancy. The act, sponsored by State Senator Luther Hardin, Clinton's former law student, prohibited abortions after the 25th week of pregnancy and prohibited the abortion of fetuses which could survive outside the womb. Clinton signed the law, saying that it was in accordance with the mood of the Supreme Court. The bill made no mention of abortions prior to the 25th week and abortions remained legal within those parameters.

Clinton maintained and continues to maintain that he is committed to a woman's right to choose. He opposed a 1988 initiative which severely curtails abortion rights, but the voters approved it over his objections. His close friend, the Reverend Worley Oscar Vaught of the Immanuel Baptist Church, helped him resolve his initially conflicting feelings about abortion. He told the Governor that his understanding of the Hebrew Bible was that it did not specifically prohibit abortion in all circumstances, Clinton told the *Washington Post.* "He read the meaning of life and birth and personhood in words which literally meant 'to breathe life into' so he thought the most literal meaning of life in the Bible would be to conclude that it began at birth," Clinton recalled. "It didn't mean that it was right all the time or that it wasn't immoral, but he didn't think that you could say it was murder."

By the mid-1980s, Bill Clinton was becoming a national figure. In May 1985, he told the *Atlanta Constitution,* "It would be fun to run [for President], even if you lost. It would be a challenge to go out and meet the people and try to communicate your ideas and bring the different parts of the country together." That summer, Clinton was elected chairman of the Southern Growth Policies Board and Vice-Chairman of the National Governors Association. At the end of the year, he led an international trade delegation from Arkansas to Japan, where he received a warm reception. His corporate hosts expressed their pleasure at doing business with Arkansas and manufacturing products there.

In June 1986, Clinton served as the co-chairman of the National Governors Association (NGA) task force on welfare reform. The panel called for programs which would return welfare recipients to the work force, encourage strong, responsible families, and provide better medical attention to young children. At the press conference announcing the package, Clinton said that a welfare program should be a jobs program. Applying similar principles in Arkansas, the Governor set up a program which, by 1991, was helping over 200 people per month move from welfare lines to the work force.

Clinton was elected chairman of the NGA that August. In his address to the group, he reminded his fellow governors of their "responsibility to make Americans more competitive from the ground up and to reverse the tide of lost human potential in those who have fallen through the cracks."

During the 1986 campaign for governor, Clinton was the only candidate to focus on education as a top issue. The other candidates, almost completely ignoring it, centered their attention on economic growth. Clinton took 60.5 percent of the primary vote, despite a comeback attempt by 76-year-old Orval Faubus. Some 64 percent of Arkansas voters returned Clinton to his fourth term as governor that November. The election was significant for another reason — this would be the first time in more than 100 years that the gubernatorial term would be four years, not simply two. In 1984, the voters had approved a constitutional amendment lengthening the term of office from two to four, and Clinton was the first to benefit from this extension.

Clinton's inauguration festivities were accompanied by bad news from the budget office: Arkansas faced a budget shortfall which required immediate attention. Despite being first in Southern states in manufacturing job growth through 1986, the state needed an immediate revenue boost. Many observers were unsure whether the state would need to raise taxes again, and some were critical of moves in that direction. The legislature took weeks to make progress.

Clinton attempted to raise revenue by rewriting Arkansas' tax code to resemble more closely the federal income tax code. His plan made it as far as the Arkansas State Senate, but stalled when it reached the House. It would have generated $35 million in new revenue. The House passed a watered-down version which only generated $20 million. A compromise proposal — providing $26 million — failed at first, but passed a few days later, after Clinton personally lobbied state legislators who cast the deciding votes on the bill.

<u>Budgeting In Arkansas 1978-1990</u>

All money figures are in current (not adjusted for inflation). Years for which Clinton did not prepare the original state budget are marked by asterisks

Fiscal Year	Total Rev. (millions)	State Tax Rev. (millions)	% Change Ark.	% Change U.S.	Total Spending (millions)	% Change Ark.	% Change U.S.
1978*	1,840	926	17.3	10.1	1,685	10.7	6.6
1979*	1,968	995	7.0	9.8	1,897	12.6	10.2
1980	2,295	1,161	16.6	12.1	2,148	13.2	14.8
1981	2,529	1,265	10.2	12.2	2,356	9.7	13.1
1982*	2,506	1,338	-1.0	6.5	2,362	0.3	6.4
1983*	2,739	1,541	9.3	8.1	2,488	5.3	7.6
1984	2,967	1,745	8.3	11.0	2,636	5.9	5.2
1985	3,342	1,827	12.6	10.5	3,018	14.5	11.2
1986	3,623	1,889	8.4	9.6	3,355	11.2	8.5
1987	3,888	1,889	7.3	7.4	3,473	3.5	7.4
1988	3,959	2,022	1.8	4.7	3,570	2.8	6.4
1989	4,299	2,172	8.6	8.3	3,840	7.6	8.3
1990	4,511	2,261	4.9	6.6	4,223	10.0	8.9

The state still faced a massive budget shortfall, so Clinton proposed a quarter-cent increase in the sales tax. The measure failed, and the session came to a close. A June special legislative session finally managed to produce another $21 million in additional revenue, including $7 million in new tax dollars. The sales tax in Arkansas can be raised by the legislature by a simple majority vote. It is practically impossible to raise the business and income taxes, which require a three-fourths vote of the state legislature in order to approve. As a result, the Arkansas tax structure is fairly regressive, since sales taxes and user fees, which are imposed equally on people of all income levels, are a greater burden on the poor.

Arkansas' Tax Rankings 1984-1990

State Policy Research, Inc.

(Rankings among the 50 states)

Individual Taxes	1984		1990		National
Per Capita	Rank	$ amt.	Rank	dollar amt.	Average
Property taxes	—	$162	—	$201	$538
Sales taxes	—	202	—	543	636
Income taxes	—	204	—	298	456
Total	49	771	49	1,113	1,772

Clinton attempted to reform the tax code to make it less regressive, but the legislature blocked his efforts. When it came time to raise funds to bring the Arkansas school system into the twentieth century, the sales tax was the most politically palatable source of funds. Clinton would have preferred that the Federal government share a greater portion of the state and local government's burden of paying for school budgets. Federal revenue sharing with states and municipalities declined during the 1980s, so governors and mayors had no choice but to raise taxes to meet the local needs.

Clinton has been a fiscal conservative and has delivered eleven balanced budgets as required by law. Despite some increases in taxes in order to finance desperately needed improvements in education and other services, Arkansas remains a very low-tax state, well *below* the national average for state taxes. On a per capita basis, the ranking of Arkansas state taxes among the 50 states (plus the District of Columbia) has ranged between number 46 and number 38. In other words, over 75% of the other states in the United States have had consistently higher tax rates than that of Arkansas. Today, Arkansas has the second lowest per-capita tax burden in the nation.

As Clinton's popularity as governor increased, rumors began circulating that Clinton might be a presidential candidate in 1988. Don and Susan Bucknell-Pogue, his old friends from New Haven, recalled his decision not to run that year. Susan ran into Hillary Rodham in Washington, DC.

After our student days together we maintained contact through Christmas cards, notes on fund raising letters, and the odd phone call. I used to meet up with Hillary at Children's Defense Fund Conferences in Washington. As Chair of the Board, these conferences were extremely busy times for Hillary. But she always made the time to snatch a lunch with me and renew our friendship. I remember these lunches with pleasure. The conversations were a delightfully intense mixture of children's social policy issues, a catch-up on our careers, and very personal exchanges on how many children we hoped to have and the tensions of balancing family and work and especially politics.

Was Bill going to run for President?"

I asked on one occasion.

"Not this year," she said. "We both decided it would take too great a toll on our daughter, Chelsea." At one of these lunches, I heard Hillary speak. I was impressed by how "grown up" she looked and how accomplished a speaker she was. I was struck by the strength of her passion for changing children's lives for the better; and by how much she had matured and developed from our early student days.

One year Bill was a keynote speaker. I remember being embarrassed going up to speak to him afterwards, worried that he wouldn't remember what I looked like. After all, it was quite a few years since we had actually seen each other face to face. I need not have worried. In his typically warm way, I was enclosed in a bear hug in an instant. Bill hadn't changed a bit. His commitment to friends, his warmth, and his ability to include everyone were still there. He invited me to join a select group of friends and political allies for an evening get together. As I listened to the political conversation in the room and watched Bill in action, I realized that although the essential Bill hadn't changed, he had become an enormously accomplished, and experienced politician with an insatiable energy for people, relationships, and promoting political change. I remember thinking that maybe he wouldn't run for President this time; but it would be soon.

In January, 1988, Governor Clinton called a special session to consider his proposals for a tough new ethics law for public officials and a new disclosure requirement for lobbyists. The legislature refused to pass them, so Clinton took his case to the people with a petition drive. The ethics package was on the ballot alongside the so-called Fair Tax Amendment, another Clinton proposal which would have allowed the legislature more flexibility in setting tax rates. Groups opposed to the ethics package took advantage of the presence of the tax plan, and formed a coalition called the Committee Against Higher Taxes. They launched a massive television advertising campaign against both initiatives.

The Committee charged that the tax plan would enable Clinton to raise $200 million in taxes for his 1989 legislative proposals, and told voters, "There's nothing fair or ethical about higher taxes." Clinton retorted, "It's a sneaky way by the favored few who have had their way in the legislature for years . . . to try to beat the Ethics and Fair Tax amendments, but worst of all to try to cast aspersions on this educational program." Clinton charged that many of the lobbyists behind the "fear and smear" campaign actually were working for corporations sympathetic to his education agenda. Despite the massive advertising campaign against the ethics plan, 60 percent of the voters approved the measure in November 1988. The Fair Tax amendment, however, did not pass.

Clinton had the opportunity to increase his national stature when he nominated Massachusetts Governor Michael Dukakis for President at the 1988 Democratic National Convention in Atlanta, Georgia. Political observers familiar with Clinton have noted that Clinton does not normally speak from a prepared text, preferring instead to make brief

notes and speak extemporaneously. At the last minute,
Dukakis's political advisors insisted that Clinton use the
written text they had prepared for him. Unfamiliar with the
text and unused to reading Teleprompters, Clinton did the
best he could. His 33 minute speech never seemed to end,
and the only applause he got was after he said, "In conclusion . . . ." Clinton later told John Brummett that he was
torn between his desire to wrap up the speech — and risk
Dukakis's anger — and his self-perceived obligation to
complete his duty.

A few days later, Clinton regained some public appeal
by playing his saxophone on the *Tonight Show* and by
making fun of himself on the show. His rendition of
Summertime with Doc Severinsen's band was a resounding
success. Clinton's state reputation was never in doubt —
Arkansans have traditionally rallied around their own when
under fire from the national establishment.

Clinton continued to search for new ideas to bring
economic development to Arkansas. He ran into fellow
Rhodes Scholar and economic idea man Jim Crawford
again in 1988.

Bill was in Chicago for the opening of a photography
exhibit on Arkansas Black History that was being displayed at the South Shore Bank. Bill sent me an invita-
tion, and I decided to attend. Since 1984, I had been in
my third career: a venture capitalist, investing other
people's money in growing, private companies.

I attended the opening, along with about 150 other
people. As Governor of Arkansas, Bill spent the evening
in a swirl of greetings, well-wishers, and press. Not
wanting to monopolize Bill's time, I said a brief hello
and then occupied myself looking at the photo exhibit

and testing the hors d'oeuvres. To my surprise, later in the evening, after the press had left, Bill made a point of seeking me out: again, the same Bill Clinton, just saying hello to a long lost friend, asking about Alicia, and making small talk; and, as at Oxford, again the Governor of Arkansas on a mission. He had learned from Bob Reich's regular *American Oxonian* reports that I was in the venture capital business. We talked for twenty minutes about the infrastructure required for information technology companies to prosper, and he asked my advice on how to encourage that infrastructure in Arkansas. It was a casual conversation, but I could tell that Bill was filtering my ideas, adding them to others, and deciding whether there was some way I could help him solve the challenges he faced in Arkansas.

At the end of our conversation, Bill asked if he could have one of his aides call me for additional suggestions. I agreed, and as promised, about two weeks later, I received a call from a member of Bill's staff who was responsible for entrepreneurial initiatives in the state. We talked at length, and perhaps he picked up a good suggestion. I hope so.

Bill has left me with the impression of a serious professional who would never pass up the opportunity to ask another question, and learn a little more that might help him improve the economy of his home state.

In the fall Clinton received recognition for his avid support of child care. The National Women's Political Caucus included Clinton in its 1988 annual list of "Good Guys." Irene Natividad, the group's executive director, told the *Arkansas Gazette* that Clinton had been chosen "primarily for his national and statewide advocacy on behalf of child care. He has been an eloquent speaker — the Democratic convention notwithstanding . . . on the paucity of child care in this country."

That December, Clinton set out his latest family policy, designed to support the survival of two-parent families and the growing number of single parents. Clinton proposed providing cash assistance and medicaid to two parent families, providing that at least one parent remain in the home for six months out of the year and that the parents enroll in an education, training, and work program. For single parents, Clinton called for child care and medical coverage, so that the parent could work during the day. Finally, the Governor argued that absentee parents delinquent in their child support payments should have their debts automatically deducted from their paychecks.

In 1988, Clinton succeeded in tightening enforcement of child support laws and in reforming the juvenile justice system. He signed into law a bill mandating military-style "boot camps" — instead of jail — for first-time offenders. At these camps, offenders were subjected to a strict disciplinary regimen and were given rehabilitation and training in order to get a second chance. Statistics have shown that very few boot camp graduates end up in prison a second time.

Clinton also worked hard getting his education reform package through the legislature. He established an Office of Accountability within the state Department of Education, to issue report cards on educational quality. He implemented a public school choice plan. He gave the Department of Education power to step in and take over school districts suffering from low test scores, and required college faculty to submit to annual performance evaluations.

In September, 1989, Clinton travelled to Charlottesville, Virginia, to take a leadership role in President George Bush's national education summit. Clinton was very influential in the formulation of the six national education goals which emerged from the conference.

Hillary Clinton, herself a vocal advocate for children, took the opportunity the summit provided to express her views on other urgent childhood issues. During one luncheon at the education summit, Hillary sat next to the President and spoke with him about children's health care issues. She said, "You know, Mr. President, depending upon what statistic you look at, we're at 17th or 19th in the whole world in infant mortality."

Bush replied, "Well, Hillary, whatever are you talking about? Our health care system is the envy of the world."

"Well, not if you want to keep your child alive to the year of his first birthday," she replied. She explained that she did not believe that the United States had done enough for children's health. Since she did not think the President knew enough about the issue, she offered to have her husband bring the statistics to the next day's working session.

President Bush probably was not enthusiastic about reading statistics provided by a Democrat. He said, "Well, I'll get my own statistics."

Hillary replied, "Well, fine. I wish you would."

The next day the President handed a note to Governor Clinton. It read, "Tell Hillary she was right."

In 1990, Bill Clinton was called upon to enforce the state's death penalty law, which preceded his term of office. As of 1989, there were 31 inmates on death row in Arkansas. Bill Clinton sought Reverend Vaught's counsel when he was wrestling with this difficult issue. Clinton told the *Washington Post*, "He made his arguments about why the ten commandments did not prohibit capital punishment. In the ancient Hebrew and Greek, he said it's 'Thou shall not murder'. He said you can make your own judgement about whether you think it's right or wrong, but he said you must never worry."

No one except Bill and Hillary Clinton knew whether or not the Governor would seek an unprecedented fifth term in office. Political advisors warned the Governor that another term might harm his long-term national ambitions, but in early March 1990, he declared that he would seek a fifth term. "Even though the fire of an election no longer burns in me, he said, "I decided that I just didn't want to stop doing the job."

Clinton defeated Winthrop Rockefeller Foundation Chairman Tom McRae handily in the primary race, especially after Hillary Clinton appeared at a press conference McRae was giving while the Governor was away in Washington, DC. She accused McRae of hypocrisy for attacking Clinton. She displayed reports McRae had authored which praised the Governor. Mrs. Clinton told McRae, "I went through all your reports because I've really been disappointed in you as a candidate and I've really been disappointed in you as a person, Tom. . . . For goodness sake, let Arkansas stand up and be proud. We've made more progress than any other state except South Carolina and we're right up there with them."

During the 1990 campaign the issue of marijuana use was raised in the press. When asked if he had ever used drugs, Clinton replied, " . . . Not as an adult in Arkansas." Two years later, Clinton acknowledged having tried marijuana, but added, "I didn't like it and I didn't inhale." Many Americans wondered how he could know that he juana in England, but added, "I didn't like it and I didn't inhale." Atypical of his generation, Clinton has never used drugs. Over 50 percent of high school students since 1975 reportedly have smoked marijuana. This "soft" drug seems harmless in comparison to the health risks of alcohol and tobacco which have been used and abused by over 90 and 75 percent of students, respectively, since 1975. Clinton later addressed the marijuana issue head-on and said that his answer to the question, although honest, seemed evasive, and recognized that he should have admitted to experimenting with marijuana the first time he was asked.

Clinton was trapped by the double standard too often applied by the mass media: even though a majority of young Americans have smoked marijuana since the late 1960's, candidates for political office from that generation are still held to a higher standard than their peers. Furthermore, as John Brummett wrote in 1990, Clinton's severe allergies explained his extreme unease with any drug use. "A couple of beers puts him to sleep," he wrote. "A glass of wine with dinner activates his allergies and makes his face puffy." Brummett further noted that Clinton clearly had not tried marijuana in two decades, and that he had served competently as governor; thus, he argued, it made no sense to force the matter further. On a more relevant issue, Bill Clinton has led the war on drugs in Arkansas.

In the general campaign, Clinton faced ex-Democrat Sheffield Nelson. During his debates with Clinton, the GOP nominee charged that SAT scores were falling. Clinton replied that Arkansas's national reputation was in fact improving, and that school graduation and college matriculation rates were up sharply. He criticized Nelson for reversing his stand on a tax increase for education. Nelson countered desperately that in four more years, Clinton cial to Clinton's 1982 victory had long since dissolved. Clinton campaigned with the support of neither teacher nor labor groups. During the primary, the AFL-CIO declined to endorse Clinton or his opponent. Clinton attacked the labor confederation for supporting him only when it was convenient. "You'll get the reputation," he warned, "of saying, 'If you side with us and we lose, we'll blame you.'" As for the AFL-CIO's concerns about labor policies, Clinton was just as blunt. "My job is to save jobs,' he said. "I don't ask you to agree with me. Just put yourself in my position."

Clinton prevailed on election day with 57 percent of the vote — his narrowest margin of victory. Nelson conceded, saying, "The people said they wanted Bill Clinton for four more years, and I don't think it would have made any difference who was against him. He was just that strong."

January, 1991, opened with a string of new proposals from the newly reinaugurated governor. He endorsed bills which would require drivers under eighteen to show proof of school attendance, as well as one which would raise the compulsory school attendance age limit from sixteen to seventeen. He proposed a full-blown apprenticeship program for high school graduates not going on to college and supported expanding the adult literacy program. For those with college plans, Clinton sought passage of a college scholarship plan for students with at least a B average.

In health matters, he secured passage of a law requiring the social security numbers of both parents on children's birth certificates, and allowing the use of those numbers to enforce child support orders. He submitted plans to expand recruitment efforts — including scholarship opportunities — for medical students who pledge to set up practices in rural areas.

On the environment, Clinton wanted to implement

tougher recycling requirements. He called for a moratorium on new landfills, and advocated an income tax credit for waste reduction and recycling. Clinton also sought to include environmental education as a mandated part of the school curriculum.

The Governor also endorsed a plan to tighten public disclosure requirements for state officials who seek reimbursements for expenses.

Bill Clinton's leadership skills sparked admiration from his colleagues. *Newsweek* magazine reported the results of a June 1991 poll of America's fifty governors asked whom they considered to be the nation's most effective state executive. 39 percent of them — Democrats and Republicans alike — chose Bill Clinton of Arkansas.

Part Two

Who Will Tell the People?

The destiny of mankind is not decided by material computation. When great causes are on the move in the world . . . we learn that we are spirits, not animals, and that something is going on in space and time, and beyond space and time, which, whether we like it or not, spells duty.

WINSTON CHURCHILL

Rochester New York, June 16, 1941

A Circle of Friends

The morning of October 3, 1991, dawned bright and clear. At noon that day, on the steps of the Old Capitol Building in Little Rock, Bill Clinton made an historic announcement to the waiting crowd: that he had decided to seek the Democratic nomination for President of the United States. He set out on an eight month journey across the nation for the primary season.

Despite his hectic schedule, Clinton always found time to return to Arkansas and to his hometown friends. Ever since his school days, he has kept up with his friends' lives, and with the lives of their children. He does not come home to unload his frustrations on them, nor to expound his political views to sympathetic listeners. He seeks simply to stay in touch with his roots, with the people he truly cares about.

These qualities can best be described by the people who

knew him then and now, so it is perhaps best that their words make up this chapter.

Glenda Johnson Cooper, one of Clinton's high school friends, returned to Little Rock in 1987 after a number of years away.

We all got together at Carolyn's house the week before he announced for President, and he questioned us about values affecting our lives. We discussed the outrageous cost of health care, lack of decent job opportunities, our worries about sending our kid's to college, and our fears about racial divisions becoming stronger than ever in our country. He listened and asked the right questions. Bill really wanted our honest opinions about the problems facing ordinary Americans. Dixie Harvey and I are single parents struggling to raise our kids alone and he has always shown sympathy for that. Bill has always been on the right side of women's issues — very sensitive to our needs and problems. He was, however, worried about getting his message across in the age of eight-second sound bites and how to overcome that.

Later, at our last Christmas party, he was exhausted from campaigning for the New Hampshire primary, but anxious to tell us what he had learned and related many stories he'd heard of the campaign trail. He was tormented by the overwhelming problems, needs, and fears Americans are facing in this election year. But, he wanted us to know that all this had deepened his commitment. He is not a quitter — he just worked harder against overwhelming odds in the months to come.

In March, we had lunch again and we were so upset about all the negative publicity he had received. Really, we were angry that this good man of strong character and integrity who adores his wife and child could be so maligned. He had to reassure us that it was just part of the process and we all had to be strong. He believes in the power of redemption and said, "I hope that day I die, I'm a better person than the day before."

Ann Henry, their friend from Fayetteville, became a member of the *Arkansas Travelers*, groups of Arkansas who visited key primary states, knocking on doors and holding town meetings on behalf of their favorite son candidate.

The greatest chicken and egg question for many of us is whether Bill Clinton turns all his friends into campaign workers or whether all campaign workers turn into friends. We have never agreed on the answer. All of us campaign workers and friends have been sounding boards for him on issues and opportunities to help people. During the campaign this spring in Little Rock, I was not surprised to meet law school classmates coming in from around the country to consult and discuss the campaign issues. Over the years at every inaugural we have met college classmates and other friends. Carolyn Staley and Betsey Wright have become my friends because of our mutual friendship with Bill and our work together. Carolyn and Morriss and I worked the polls in freezing weather in New Hampshire and had a good time being interviewed by foreign correspondents from all over the world. We probably thought that singing *The Arkansas Traveler* for the BBC was the most fun.

David Leopoulos, Clinton's old friend from grade school, went up to New Hampshire when things got rough.

When I drove to New Hampshire to campaign for my friend I wanted to educate everybody I could about this man. I would ask each person if they thought Bill was a rich, spoiled kid that had just assumed his place in politics through his family connections like others we all know are around today. Most people that I talked with said they thought that Bill was rich, arrogant and not very intelligent. Once I told them that Bill, after being in politics for 20 years, is not rich, they could not believe it. When they found out that he is a true intellectual and worked his way through college people were amazed. The clincher came when they found out that he has been a real friend to me for 37 years — me, a little middle-class guy. The citizens of New Hampshire could tell that Bill indeed had character and was a real person. I am sure many of the voters that met me and the other Arkansas Travelers did vote for Bill. They knew we were honest and telling them the truth. If you get to know many of the close friends of an individual, you get to know that individual.

Bill Clinton is a very rare combination of qualities. He is extremely intelligent. He can absorb great amounts of knowledge and use it wisely. His decision making is based on facts from the source of the problem, not stabs in the dark. His energy allows him to work long hours. Bill's middle-class personal life experiences have focused his heart towards the right priorities. Personal wealth is not the driving force in his life. The ability to get people to communicate with each other in order to make decisions and progress is acute. He demands fairness and what is right. He listens. He cares.

When the campaign reached Connecticut, Yale friends

Susan Bucknell Pogue and her husband Don were ready to help.

Certainly, it was exciting when the time came and we got a call from Hillary saying that they would appreciate any help Don and I could give Bill in his Presidential campaign in Connecticut. Of course we were on board. We had no doubts about Bill's candidacy. When Bill came to Connecticut before the primary we went to hear him speak. We hadn't thought about the possibility of getting together. We assumed his schedule would be too tight. But we lined up close to the entry way to the platform as we at least wanted Bill to see us in the crowd and know we were there. As he came in he did see us: and despite secret service personnel and an anxiously awaiting audience, he stopped and embraced us both warmly, showing obvious pleasure that we were there. Indeed, much to our embarrassment, he ended his speech by thanking everyone for such a warm welcome and saying specifically how good it was to be greeted by old friends in Connecticut, including his good friends Don and Sue Buchnell- Pogue.

So Bill hadn't changed. But when we heard his speech, we changed. As he drove home the themes of change in America, of competitive economic development based on investments in human capital; of healing racial rifts, of family and community, of social policy that empowered rather than paternalism, we realized the strength of his vision and mission; that he truly was a candidate who could bring about the kinds of change in government that we had been committed to as students. Here was a candidate that really was worth working for. Our own excitement was matched by those in the crowd around up. A long time union leader of some standing in Connecticut looked somewhat incredulous as he turned to us and said that we might have another Kennedy here. An African- American woman, who earlier had told us that she had personally spent hours ironing the folds in the banner that hung behind the platform, said it was worth it and she wasn't disappointed. She couldn't wait for the morning because Bill was meeting with her church group in the North End of Hartford and she intended to get up her grand children at 7 AM to meet him. Certainly, he reached the young people, including one of our daughters, who at 14 was measurably impressed.

As Bill ended his speech, he sought us out, urging us to join him for supper. As he earnestly responded to the questions of those anxious to talk to him, we dodged secret service personnel and his campaign staff to secure time and place. Later that evening, in the Presidential Suite, Don and I, our daughter Tamara, along with another old friend of Bill's and two or three close Connecticut political allies, joined Bill for an intimate supper. The depth of Bill's grasp of a wide range of policy issues was impressive as the conversation moved from health care reform, economic development, school reform, poverty, social service reform, and international affairs. Bill was well informed and thoughtful and clearly developed his views from listening carefully to people and learning from their experience. Most compelling to me was what he had learned from talking to teachers and young people in inner city schools about what was really needed behind the popular rhetoric of school reform. The conversation was interspersed by his campaign manager's insistence that Bill make some required calls to Connecticut dignitaries. We then returned to our discussion. We asked how his daughter Chelsea was coping with the campaign. He laughed and said that she made sure she kept close to her father. One night, he told us, he got home at 2 AM to find a note on the kitchen table asking for some algebra homework to be checked before morning. "What did you do?" we asked. "Did it, of course," he replied, "but it took me a couple of hours."

Clinton's devotion to his daughter Chelsea extends far beyond faxed algebra homework. "The morning is our time," Clinton says. He has driven her to school every day since she was in kindergarten, except when he was out of town. An aspiring ballerina, Chelsea often gives dance recitals which conflict with pressing political business — but the governor is always there to see his daughter perform.

Chelsea Clinton has inherited her parents' intelligence and focus. She is a grade ahead in school, and would like to become a scientist, perhaps designing and building space stations. When she is not dancing, she plays volleyball and softball, and can often be found beating her mother and father at a game of pinochle or hearts. To those who do not know her well, Chelsea seems reserved, even introverted. But as a family friend told *People* magazine, her reticence disappears when she has a deck of cards in her hands and is challenging her parents: "she plays a hard game and likes to kick ass." In that she has followed her mother's age old advice: "When you work, work hard. When you play, play hard, and don't confuse the two."

Susan Bucknell continued:

It was an exciting evening. I thing we can thank Bill for awakening a political interest in our daughter that will shape her life. She organized a leafletting group for Bill the next morning and began expressing some Presidential aspirations herself. As for Don and I, the evening rekindled in us a dream and a vision that we could have a Presidential candidate that could be a leader for the country ad bring about change, yet at the same time was an enormously genuine and caring person. Bill's commitment, political intensity and energy for the campaign were evident. Yet underneath, he was the same Bill — warm, funny, affectionate and unassuming. "Am I too fat?" he asked, as we got up to leave. "I have lost ten pounds."

"You'll have to watch it," we said. Then we embraced warmly and left, holding onto our deep excitement about Bill's campaign and a sense of privilege that we had known Bill and Hillary in our formative student years and as friends.

Having won enough delegates to assure a first-ballot victory at the Democratic National Convention in New York City, Clinton went home to Hope before departing to accept the nomination. McDowell Turner, who had known him since before he was born, was there.

Recently, Bill Clinton came to Hope, Arkansas, his birthplace, for one last visit before the Democratic Convention. My wife and I had heard that he was in town, so we drove to the business section to see if we could get a glimpse of what was happening.

We found Governor Clinton in front of a feed and seed store surrounded by *Time* magazine reporters and photographers and secret service and local policemen.

I was standing across the street at least one half city block away with several other people. The Governor looked in my direction, raised his arm and waved. I thought, "Surely, he is not waving at me." So I didn't acknowledge his greeting. Then as he and his entourage prepared to leave, he walked across the street, came directly toward me, and said, "Mac, I would not leave here until I could speak to you." And he gave me a big bear hug. Here was a man who had traveled from coast to coast, from large city to large city. He had greeted thousands of people. And here was I, citizen John Doe, but he remembered me and called my name without any prompting.

That's why I know when elected President he won't forget the people of the nation.

That Bill Clinton should remain close to his friends despite his hectic campaign schedule came as no surprise to Carolyn Staley and David Leopoulos, who have known for years how dependable he is.

Carolyn Staley recalled:

We shared happy times together like weddings and the birth of our children as we grew older and moved apart. We've also shared the death of parents and attended funerals together. We've even talked about designing and building some condominiums together so that we can grow old together.

I was so surprised and pleased that Bill offered to come to Mississippi when my father died in 1987. (My father's last pastorate was in Greenwood, Miss.) I never expected him to come, but he flew in and the

Mississippi State Police escorted him to the church where he met the family and walked in with us. He even gave a brief eulogy and came back home with us for a meal. He said he just wanted to be with us. Friends are like that. Bill also was the second caller to David Leopoulos when his mother died, only after his father had reached him with the news. Bill tracked David down to a remote town in Italy where he was stationed in the Army. David has never forgotten this gesture of friendship.

Clinton has an intense one-on-one charm which conveys a deep and sincere concern for others. David Leopoulos recalled how Clinton helped him make it through those trying days in the spring of 1969.

In 1968 I graduated from Henderson University in Arkansas and went into the Army. I had orders to go to Vietnam. I, like most of the other Officers in my training school did not want to go. I was given the opportunity to extend my tour of duty. If I extended I could choose any duty station for the next year. I chose to go to Italy. In the spring of 1969 I was working the midnight shift in a communications site in Caltano, Italy. This place was in the middle of nowhere. The phone rang. It was the Red Cross. They asked for me. I took the phone from my good friend Steve Gorman. The Red Cross person said, "Hold on." My dad got on the line. I could not understand what he was saying. He was crying and delirious. He was saying, "Come home, Dave, come home."

My Uncle Harry finally got the phone from my Dad and told me that my mother had been killed and to get home as quick as possible. I was devastated and very worried about my father. They had been married for many years and I was afraid for his life. I could not leave for home until the Red Cross got it approved. I went into my office, turned out the light and put my head on my desk. At that point I did not know what to do or what to think.

The phone rang on my desk. It was Bill. In a low voice he said, "How are you?" Our conversation gave me strength to make it through the painful times I would experience.

On December 27, 1971 Linda and I were married in Pine Bluff, Arkansas. I did not tell Bill about it. He was far away at the time and I did not want to ask him to come so far just to be my best man. When I walked out to the altar of the Church, there was Bill sitting in the back of the congregation.

Bill Clinton's complete intolerance for prejudice and discrimination is reflected not simply in his political attitudes but also in his friendships. Two who have come to know him well are David Mixner and Bill Coleman.

David Mixner kept in touch with Clinton long after the Vietnam moratorium movement came to an end.

There was a group who bonded in the Kennedy and McCarthy days that kept in touch. We would visit, have reunions and support each other both in good and difficult times. People such as Eli Segal, Harold Ickes, Sam Brown, Anne Wexler, Susan Thomasas, Don and Judy Green, etc. stayed in touch and formed an informal network based on a mutual commitment to change the world and to be the future leaders.

All though this time period none of them, including Bill and Hillary Clinton, knew that I was a closeted homosexual. I had lived in total fear of being discovered and not being allowed to participate in changing the country or politics. The terror and pressure of living this closeted life is indescribable. In 1977, Anita Bryant began her campaign against homosexuals. Her efforts made it impossible for me to continue living in the closet; I realized that my own civil rights were in jeopardy. I decided to fight back and come out of the closet. I sent a letter to all of my friends informing them that for 15 years I had lived a dual life as a gay man. Never have I known such fear as when I sent out that letter. I had no idea what to expect from my friends and political allies.

I received a variety of reactions to that letter. Many friends were supportive, loving, and caring. Many friends were disappointing and the nature of our friendships changed. Among those who were the most caring, compassionate and loving were Bill and Hillary Clinton. They were supportive and concerned about how I was doing. They treated me no differently. I was their close friend — end of discussion.

In the early 1980's, Bill and Hillary were making trips to California to generate business in Arkansas. They also were using the opportunity to met people in the film industry and government to assist them with that goal. They called Peter Scott (my friend and partner) and myself, to ask us to host a major event for them at Peter's home. This was a time when many California politicians would not even attend a gay/lesbian event let alone ask us to host one in our home. It stunned us that a Governor of Arkansas would publicly come into the home of openly gay people and embrace us as friends and allies. For him, it was a courageous action. For us, it was something that we would never forget. To me, it was an act of unbelievable friendship and courage. He wanted to be sure that a photographer was present so that people could have their picture taken with him and Hillary.

Bill Coleman, who had watched as Clinton single-handedly integrated the "black table" at Yale Law School, long ago noticed that Clinton was one of only a handful of white alumni who maintained their friendships with black classmates.

Although Bill behaved just like another student trying to survive the rigors of law school, even then, most of his classmates felt he possessed a unique blend of qualities that would some day thrust him into a position of national leadership. After we graduated and went our separate ways, despite becoming America's youngest governor, it was Bill who initiated and maintained contact with his classmates, including his African-American classmates. Eric Clay, a senior partner at Detroit's Lewis, White & Clay, one of the nation's leading minority firms, has maintained a close relationship with Bill throughout the years, and is currently active in Bill's campaign in Michigan. When Bill was last re-elected governor of Arkansas, I flew to Little Rock to celebrate his inaugural. Despite the intense demand on his schedule at such a politically demanding time, Bill and Hillary nonetheless found time to be gracious hosts, and assured that my visit to Arkansas was memorable.

A few years ago, Lani Guinier, currently a member of the University of Pennsylvania law faculty, and formerly a law clerk for the Honorable Damon Keith and a senior litigation counsel for the NAACP Legal Defense Fund, was married in Massachusetts. The wedding provided an opportunity for a reunion of the African-American members of Yale Law School's class of 1973. Approximately half of the African-Americans in my class were able to attend. The only non African-American member of our class to attend: Bill Clinton.

When Clinton returned home to run for office, he kept up with his old friends even as he made knew ones. Not only has he stayed in touch with all of them, but he has shown interest in their children's lives as well.

Mary Nell Turner, McDowell's wife, saw Clinton speak to a group of aspiring reporters.

Although I've known Governor Bill Clinton's family — mother, grandparents, cousins — for many years (I'm almost 73), I heard him for the first time at an Arkansas High School Press Association meeting where I had taken my journalism students. We were really impressed with this curly headed handsome young speaker.

Then when he became our governor, I was the official photographer for Arkansas Girls State. I have photographed him many times at the inauguration program, at the capitol, etc. The girls loved having him and always gave him a standing ovation. When they had the opportunity, they swarmed around him asking for autographs and answers to questions.

On one occasion he came down the aisle between the

cheering girls, and I waited with camera poised. To my complete surprise and the girls' delight, he picked me up, swung me around, laughing all the time. We all enjoyed the moment.

Every so often, Ann Henry of Fayetteville gets a call from one of her children who has run into her old friend, Governor Clinton.

Over the years Bill has remained in touch not only with his high school friends but with all of us who were his earliest supporters. He has corresponded, visited our home, mentored our children, and kept up with us. Paul, our oldest, went to medical school in Memphis, Tennessee, but occasionally got to got to Little Rock with friends. As he tells it, "We were at a restaurant when Clinton walked in. Bill recognized me and came over to visit. I didn't think he would know me because it had been a year since I saw him last. He was asking me about finishing medical school and what I was going to do after that. We talked about health care issues and really had a nice visit."

Two years ago, Katherine was a freshman in medical school and Bill had been invited to speak to the class. She called me on the phone: "Mom, Bill Clinton saw me and walked up the aisle in the classroom and gave me a hug in front of the whole class. He seemed really glad to see me."

Our children have been around a lot of politicians who never could sort them out as individuals. That is why they appreciate Bill's support of them and their goals and his treatment of their ideas as valuable.

Today, Clinton continues to stay in touch with his

friends, meeting regularly for lunch, playing Trivial Pursuit, and spending every Christmas together. Glenda Johnson Cooper is part of his circle of friends.

In 1987 when I returned to Little Rock after living in the West for 13 years, there were many old friends from Hot Springs who were very supportive and inclusive. I was quickly a member of the "lunch bunch" group which met once a month (Bill Clinton, Carolyn Staley, Joe Newman, Dave Leopoulous, Dixie Harvey). I think we became Bill's touchstone — maybe a reality check. He listened to our life stories, daily trials and tribulations, mid-life crises, troubles with health care, education for our children as well as their accomplishments. He often did most of the talking, unable to contain his enthusiasm for his legislative programs, particularly those involving education, health care, and creating jobs.

Bill has always been ambitious but not only for himself. He was born into poverty in a traditionally poor state. He has been motivated by a transcendent cause: improving the lives of average people through better educational opportunities affordable health care, decent jobs and, of course, hard work as tirelessly as Bill Clinton. He has never been afraid to follow his dreams and in that respect he has been an inspiration to me. Believe in yourself, work hard and care for your fellow man, and you will have lived a magnificent life.

Our annual Christmas parties at Carolyn Staley's house will remain among the best memories of my life. She was a great old home not far from the Governor's Mansion in downtown Little Rock. It's always decorated beautifully and is always full of love, good cheer, games, and singing from cards to high school 60's music. I think Bill, Hillary, and Chelsea enjoyed sneaking away from official functions to join the fun — singing around the piano that Carolyn plays so well and just talking — not being a public figure in a safe, relaxed atmosphere with old friends.

Bill and I are both spirited, competitive Trivial Pursuit players. He loves a challenge. One Christmas I couldn't get out of my house, He kept calling Carolyn to find a way to coax me out because he really wanted to play. The point here is that he is a *real person* — not some phoney government official all wrapped up in self-importance and influential people. I'll never forget one Christmas about four years ago when we had played lots of games, talked and sang until we were hoarse and were quite ready to go home. The tape deck was playing some 60's oldies when Bill grabbed Hillary and they danced and the love and admiration they have for each other was so evident. There were no cameras, no attempt to impress a public not present — just a joy and happiness to be with each other at a special time of the year in the presence of warm and loving old friends.

What I would want people to know is that Bill Clinton is a man of extraordinary intelligence who genuinely loves people and values their concerns. He is a self-made man who honestly cares for the people of this country and understands what we need and the direction this country must take to become competitive again in a global context.

Our country needs leadership, hope, and love. Bill Clinton can give us what we need.

Bill is a voracious reader, devouring books when he travels. Since we first realized that we shared an all

202

time favorite book, *One Hundred Years of Solitude*, by Gabriel Garcia Marquez, we have avidly discussed new reading material during our lunches. Despite the fact that I have more time to read that he does, I've always been hard pressed to keep up with him.

He and I both love Tony Hillerman mystery novels, in part because of the cultural information about Native Americans. I gave him the latest Hillerman novel for Christmas and his eyes lit up. Within two weeks, I received a thank you note from Bill and Hillary saying they both read and enjoyed it.

Bill loves history and political books and suggested in spring 1991 that I read *Why Americans Hate Politics* by E.J. Donne, Jr.. He said this book explained so much about the stagnation in American politics today. He was very excited about this book.

Finally, despite the rigors of the New Hampshire campaign, Bill told me at the Christmas party that he was reading several books about American corporations in order to have a better understanding of the history and culture of the corporate world. He loves to read and learn and believes that when you cease to learn, when you lose your curiosity about life, then your life is diminished.

Even now, Carolyn Staley continues to provide musical accompaniment to her friend.

Today Bill still loves music. He is called upon from time to time to play the saxophone in impromptu settings with bands which are entertaining for some function he may be attending. I am often asked to play the piano for official functions at the Governor's Mansion.

Bill always comes by the piano to say hello and to sing a bit and chat with others who are standing around the piano. And almost always at the end of the evening, when all the guests have gone home, Bill will ask if we can play and sing awhile. We'll sit at the piano bench and play and sing everything from folk songs to hymns. After the dinner at the mansion at the end of his presidential announcement day, he asked me to sing and play *Amazing Grace* and he sang along. It was a perfect ending to an amazing day.

Bill has invited me to sing at all his inaugurations as Governor and he often suggests some song for me to sing. He asked me to be in charge of the music for his most recent inaugural dedication service, and he specifically requested several gospel songs to be sung by a Black ensemble (*Goin' Up Yonder* which was sung at Hubert Humphrey's funeral and which Bill loves and tells me I'm to sing at his funeral), *Then My Living Will Not Be In Vain*, sung by a Black male soloist and which was also sung at Martin Luther King's funeral, and *Holy Ground* sung by a White Pentecostal singer and dear friend. To balance the gospel music I sang *Alleluia* by Mozart as a Call to Worship at the beginning of the service. As the Clintons walked up the aisle to the pulpit at the beginning of the service, the organist played *Jesu, Joy of Man's Desiring* by J.S. Bach, at Bill's request. Later Bill wrote to me that this was the best music at an inaugural yet.

Now we still enjoy parties together with our families in tow, playing Trivial Pursuit or Pictionary or other competitive board games. We always get together at Christmas and other times throughout the year, usually at my house. We sometimes don't wind down until the wee hours, when we have the luxury of a holiday to sleep the next day.

Somehow I knew from the moment we became friends that Bill Clinton was not only to become one of my best friends but that his life was destined for greatness. His deeply caring and loving heart, his sense of justice and fairness for all people, his charisma, intellect, and personal drive indicated to me that he was an extraordinary man. One of the most remarkable attributes of Bill Clinton is that, no matter where he has traveled nor whom he has met, he has remained the same person I have known from the beginning. He is humble and awed by the opportunities which life has given him and believes that he has a responsibility to help make life better for all people. His life has been marked by struggles along the way, both personal and professional; however, all these times have served to strengthen Bill, to refine and mature him, to add wisdom and a renewed vision for service to our country.

Bill Clinton's grade school friend, David Leopoulos, has always appreciated Clinton's selfless compassion which characterizes his closest friendships.

There have been countless times that Bill has touched my life. I will get calls late in the day, sometimes late in the evening, and the voice on the line says, "How are you?" Never, "Guess what I did yesterday," always, "How are you?" The special thing about this great man is that he treats most people he knows the same way he treats me. Whether he knows someone for 37 years or 37 minutes he cares about them and will do what he can to help them. During the Christmas Holidays Bill has a personal thing he likes to do. He delivers presents and food to needy families in Little Rock. Two Christmases ago, Little Rock had a terrible ice storm on Christmas Eve. Bill went out to shop for the presents and food, wrapped the presents with Chelsea, his daughter, and delivered them even though the street were extremely dangerous. It was not a press opportunity. He does these types of things as part of his very private life, not for recognition or to build up his public image. I am sure he will not appreciate me exposing this to the public, but the everyday person needs to understand the real Bill Clinton and not the press's version of my friend.

I have known for a long time Bill would be President. Ronnie, Carolyn, and I used to joke about playing touch football on the White House lawn. We will finally get to next January.

Peer Review

David Walters, Governor of Oklahoma

In the summer of 1988 when I was scrambling to find a speaker for a major political event in eastern Oklahoma during the Presidential campaign. It was a time in which Oklahoma was not one of the states targeted by the Dukakis campaign and therefore surrogate speakers were very difficult to come by. I called Bill Clinton's office, however, and he graciously agreed to speak on a hot August day in a state park to a thousand or so Oklahomans. I flew to Arkansas to pick Bill Clinton up and our first meeting was troublesome in that when he met me he handed me a note which indicated that my youngest daughter had been slightly injured and that I needed to call home. After making some rushed phone calls to check on her condition and finding her okay, I then traveled with Bill back to Oklahoma where he delivered a marvelous speech.

We then parted ways and I went on to see my daughter and he traveled back to Arkansas. During that brief first meeting and our opportunities to talk in the plane and in the automobile I discovered a man who really had public policy all together. He knew how, exactly how, to identify the problem. He could lay out several options for the solution of the problem. He could tell you which one he preferred and exactly how he was going to implement it or had implemented it in the past. We talked about real economic development, health care, education, maternal and infant child care, and on each of these topics he was very well informed and had a strong intuitive sense of what needed to happen.

After I was elected Governor of Oklahoma in 1990, I immediately had a number of communications with Governor Clinton and began meeting him frequently at a variety of National Governor's Association meetings. Bill always went out of his way to be friendly and gracious, as he did with all the governors. And he was always working. Huddling with two or three governors working on a particular problem, working on a national initiative, providing leadership for welfare reform or education improvements. He did this in a way that was not overly aggressive and yet fervent and he always had time to listen and to understand.

By the summer of 1991, when it was apparent that Bill would run for president at our Seattle National Governors' Association meeting, I indicated to him that I wanted to help secure the support of other Democratic governors. Most of the governors were very high on Bill Clinton, but it was early and governors and other elected public officials tend to hang back to see who else is running. So at his request I made points that I thought would be helpful to him as we talked about future Democratic Governors' Association meetings and talked to a number of Democratic governors about the importance of early endorsements.

With all of the personal contact with Bill Clinton, I guess I was still overwhelmed by the depth of his command of the issues when I read his announcement speech, and a series of issue speeches given at Georgetown University. These addresses were the most comprehensive statements of national policy that I had ever read and it gave me renewed hope for our system of government and our ability to deal with very complicated controversial problems.

I lost my son Shaun in December of 1991 and Bill Clinton visited Oklahoma shortly after my son's funeral. I believe during his visit here, I got an opportunity to have one of those rare glimpses into an individual's character that doesn't often happen in public life. In the process of addressing a fund raising luncheon and then later appearing with hundreds of supporters at a major press conference, Bill, as usual, did an excellent job of recognizing everyone and saying hello to everyone and giving some very fine remarks.

He asked to see me in my office after his presentation and we walked there and sat down, just the two of us, to talk. The only topic that he wanted to discuss was my son. He wanted to hear about him and about the tragedy and how we were doing. He asked if it would be okay to call my wife and visit with her, which he did by telephone. We spent some time together in which two grown men were able to share a common tear, embrace and wish each other the best. To say that Bill Clinton cares about people, or to say that he is compassionate about the human condition is really an understatement. I saw a man who was able to isolate himself from a very public schedule in order to spend some time sharing the grief of a friend. It was a genuine and heartfelt and will forever be appreciated.

I went to New Hampshire in one of Bill and Hillary

Clinton's darkest hours. They were under attack and his continuing in the race was actively being questioned. I met Bill at a hotel conference room in New Hampshire on a cold Saturday morning and found a man who was thoughtful and reflective. He talked about what it meant but never for a moment did he express frustration or bitterness or suggest that he had lost faith in the system. We campaigned that day and I realized just how tenacious and how faithful he is to the political process and to the ways that we achieve significant change in America. He was taking a beating, he was being derided and yet he continued to speak from his heart and from his mind about his plans and his hopes. The New Hampshire voters listened.

After the Super Tuesday primaries in which he won Oklahoma by a very large margin, both he and Hillary got on the phone to thank me for our work in our state. They as always were excited and gracious and thankful. When I hosted Hillary Clinton on a trip to Tulsa during the campaigning for the Super Tuesday primary I stood behind her as she gave a great speech, touching on domestic and international policies. I leaned over to her as she was receiving a standing ovation from an appreciative audience, and simply said, "I hope Bill has as strong a command of the issues as you do." And she modestly replied, "I've learned everything from him."

We have a rare opportunity in America to put in the White House a man who cares, a man who has experienced good times and bad, a man who deeply feels for the future of our country and who has a wonderfully gifted mind and an ability to understand the issues and identify the solutions. I've been to the White House during my brief term as governor and I must say it would be a tremendous benefit to the state governments and to the American public to

210

have someone there who is not speaking from prepared remarks and not standing in a marked spot, someone who could listen, who could respond and who could then exercise good judgement in moving our country forward. Bill Clinton is a remarkable man. For all the complaining that we do about the American political system it is amazing that remarkable women and men continue to wind their way through the process to reach the top. Whether or not Bill Clinton wins in November of 1992 he has already taught us all some very important lessons about faithfulness, tenacity and loyalty to one's own ideals and dreams. I hope we have an opportunity to call him Mr. President. It would be a great achievement for the United States if we're able to elevate somebody of Bill Clinton's quality and capacity to the White House.

Famous Friends

Mary Steenbergen

In the movie *Parenthood*, my character and her husband's elderly grandmother have a discussion about life. The grandmother compares life to a rollercoaster, with its twists and turns and high views and plummets and ascents.

My own life has felt like a rollercoaster this year. It's strange to have a friend run for President of the United States. It's hard to have people that you know and love dissected and doubted. It's even hard to hear them cheer by the masses, in a way, because, like the exhilaration of a rollercoaster, the turns come so fast.

I've known the Clinton family since the late seventies. I, too, am a native Arkansan. My family still lives there and so does a large part of my heart.

Arkansans are both proud and defensive about their state. We knew growing up in the sixties that the world had focused upon us as a symbol of racial injustice. It wasn't comfortable sitting on the fence. I know that much of the fuel that Bill runs on today is a desire for fairness that was born of a time when fairness was so miserably absent.

Recently, I stood with Bill and Hillary at a rally in Little Rock. It was a very hot day and as I looked out I was concerned to see how many older people were standing in the baking sun. Then I noticed how many college age people were there and that near half the crowd were African-American. And I realized that I was looking at the most *diverse* gathering of people that I had ever seen in Arkansas. And that the faces gazing back at us had one strong thing in common — they were there to honor a man who tried mightily for the last twelve years to give them something to be proud of. Arkansas has a long way to go but, with Bill Clinton's leadership, the doors to the land of opportunity have opened a bit more for everyone.

At this writing, the rollercoaster hasn't slowed down a bit. I don't know what's around the next bend.

Here's what I do know and I base some of my feelings about what kind of President Bill would make on what kind of friend he is. As your friend he is utterly there for you.

Bill Clinton is one of the most brilliant, most compassionate, most capable people I have ever known.

Bill is a legendary listener. This is not a party trick developed for Campaign '92. He gets lost in people. He always has. I've never been out to dinner with him in Arkansas that someone didn't approach him — a farmer, a teacher, a teenager — with a suggestion or complaint or a story. Bill turns all the way around to them and gives them his full attention and we've got lost him for awhile. When he turns back to us it's "Listen to what he just told me!" or "Did you hear her idea? Listen to this!"

My dad was a freight train conductor. I was terribly proud of him. I have a passionate intolerance for snobbery. Bill Clinton doesn't treat *anyone* as if they're more important than someone else. When he says that this country doesn't have a person to waste, it resonates from the very essence of who he is.

One more thing about Bill Clinton. He's married to one of my favorite women on Earth. Together they produced one of my favorite friends: Chelsea. As a family, they are fun, engaging, and committed. They are a marriage of people who are clearly rooting for each other and who are buoyed, rather than diminished by each other's victories and accomplishments. Only a weak man feels threatened by a woman being everything that she can be. Bill can't keep the grin off his face when Hillary shines.

I don't agree with Bill Clinton on every one of the many issues that face him. I'm against the death penalty, for example. I disagree adamantly with him on the subject. But I find all his positions on such difficult subjects are weighted with the honest soul-searching of a thoughtful man.

Caroline Kennedy, in a recent essay, *My Father's Legacy,* lamented this age in which a man is criticized for wanting to be President. Well, Bill Clinton wants to be President. I think he sees the job as a noble exchange between a politician and a citizen, the giving of a person's experience, ideals, heart, courage, intuition, and capability in exchange for a vote — a vote that represents another's hope and trust. I don't think that Bill has ever had a moment of indifference to the concerns of the American people. This year he has given us, as voters, the dignity of a substantive campaign. He's stood up to the incredible tests of this campaign with dignity and determination. Obviously I'm proud of my friend. I don't know where the rollercoaster will stop — but, for the sake of all of us, I hope it's Washington, DC.

Part Three

The Media, Character and Politics

The men with the muck-rakes are often indispensable to the well-being of society — but only if they know where to stop raking the muck.

President Theodore Roosevelt, 1906

The Media,
Character and Politics

Academics and media professionals believe that the standards by which we judge public figures and presidential candidates have changed dramatically in recent years.

The growing role of primaries and caucuses in the election process has greatly diminished the influence of national political parties and party bosses. The changing system has put the decision-making powers into the hands of different state party organizations. As a result, the media (for better or worse) frequently finds itself working in the leadership vacuum that this newly evolved election system has now created, acting as the unofficial arbiter of the political process. The media is not necessarily well-suited to fill this role due to its fragmentary and competitive nature which results in coverage that is often inconsistent and chaotic.

In the new political process, the media has developed the power both to build up candidates and to destroy them. They also have developed the power to ultimately set the agenda of political campaigns. For example, the media set the stage for the character issue in the 1988 election; and they have done so again in 1992. The issue, of course, is whether the media is acting responsibly in setting the agenda and placing its definition of character high on its list of priorities. The voting public has readily responded to and now actually demands the media's growing focus on the character issue. The two forces in fact have begun to feed on each other, for better or worse, in creating a new tenor to political campaigns.

Today's pressing issues and problems have become too complex and the response time too condensed to put our faith in a candidate's position papers. The American people are consequently left to search out leaders whom they sense are strong, sincere, fair, and compassionate. We want to feel comfortable that our selected leaders will use good judgement. We therefore feel compelled to know and understand our leaders in greater detail than ever before.

Disillusionment with government and politics has contributed to the public's fascination with the media's increased interest in the character issue. The public's growing concern with character may be considered instinctual. Too often, in recent past, voters have reached out to candidates with neatly packaged virtues — characteristics they often fail to have in reality.

There is another reason why the American people have "encouraged" the media to dissect the politicians as never before. Political parties have seldom been more interchangeable. Ideological differences have become blurred. And the nation's social and economic problems are too complicated to submit to clever political slogans. Consequently, most of the candidates now play it safe on the issues, relying on their rhetorical skills to produce the greatest number of sound bites that say as little as possible. The character issue becomes a way to sell candidates and to set them apart from each other.

This phenomenon is having a powerful influence on the 1992 presidential race. Never before has the American media entered a presidential campaign more self-consciously than in this current election season. And never before has the role of character so dominated a presidential campaign.

The issue of the media and character raises a number of important questions. Has the media gone too far in attempting to define what character is and what role it should play in identifying the differences between political candidates? Are the print media and television really responding to the public's growing desire for a greater "need to know" their candidates or are they manufacturing everything, no matter how trivial, in hope of selling more newspapers or achieving higher rating points. Is the media being responsible in defining the role of character in a political campaign? The deluge of coverage and the intensifying competition among the news organizations have led to more reports about the candidates' personal and especially sexual lives, says political science professor Larry Sabato, author of *Feeding Frenzy.*

As the bigger more important issues become increasingly more complicated, the media has begun to focus more and more attention on the trivia. Character no longer becomes a question of how a candidate may handle an international crisis or prioritize a domestic agenda but whether the candidate cheated on a college exam years ago or committed adultery. By elevating character as an important element in the presidential election, has the media lost sight of properly defining character and the role it should play in identifying the best candidate?

The following is a collection of essays from members of the media and academic world who examine the changing role of television and journalism in the political election process. Specifically, the authors address the growing power of the media to control political choices. Most importantly, these essays alert the American voter of the need to actively take the time to learn more about their candidates' political character and capability. They argue, in short, for an informed voting choice — one that enhances the very tradition of American democracy.

We Need To Know

James David Barber

Voters need to know what a potential President is likely to do — or not do — if he wins. Obvious? Yes, but voters are not getting that knowledge from the nation's news stories.

To choose how to vote, we need to know each candidate's Presidential character, based on the real story of his or her life so far. The candidate's stance on issues is also important especially if he brings forth real priorities and tells us which other politicians, in the House and Senate, have joined with him to make the right things happen starting next year. In the excellent biography that you just have read, a citizen can see straight out statements by people who have known Governor Clinton. Those friends not only tell us how they feel about him, but also give us information about what he actually did and how he did it. Americans who remember that our elected authorities are supposed to do "government by consent of the governed"

— us — ought to dig into such evidence and come to the best possible decision for tomorrow's policies.

For that purpose, regular news could be better. Too much news is hard to understand. Many voters have trouble reading, but all of us are flooded with high-tech words, such as "paradigm" which most of us don't really understand. We bump into all sorts of "-ion" abstractions, bureaucratic complexifications, technological obfuscations. So naturally we are tempted to turn away from all that cloudy, complicated news and not even bother to vote at all.

Fortunately a lot of citizens do not give up. Many of us realize that we have the duty to vote, however hard it might be. But figuring out how to vote is hard, we can also be led away from what we really need to know, off into political dreams. Confused citizens can make weird mistakes.

Trouble #1 is to judge a candidate by his ordinary morals. In fact, what we need to know is not just private character, but *Presidential* character. How will this candidate operate as President? That kind of public morality is far more important than a handful of possible one-time blips against virtue in the past, however true or false they are. It would be fine to have a saint be a President, but in real life we need to be looking for fundamental Presidential morality — the morality of leadership, to save the environment and human life and protect freedom here and everywhere. President Kennedy could have done better in his marriage morality, and Prime Minister Winston Churchill should have drunk less whiskey in the morning. But compared to Nixon and Hitler, those two did better with top authority and led exemplary public lives.

Trouble #2 of judging a Presidential candidate is to focus on how he comes across as an actor. How does he

seem? How does he look? How does he make you feel? But
is how he *seems* actually what he is? Consider Warren G.
Harding, elected President of the United States in 1920.
Harding seemed swell. He came across as a tall, handsome, red-faced and white-haired candidate who seemed to
remind us of George Washington. Harding was a super
speaker: loud and clear enough to be heard by the audience
in the last row, and using fancy and funny words as he
waved his arms. He won the election. But later on, for
decades, Harding was rated the worst President ever, because he gave in to crooks in the White House. So the
Harding lesson is clear: don't decide on your choice of
President in the movies. Decide in your head — with
evidence.

Trouble #3 is even simpler: let the other people decide.
Polls and votes in the primaries come forth as showing
which candidate is ahead. Is the one who is ahead the one
who is best? Not necessarily. Polls are opinions, not
decisions; preferences, not reasoning. The numbers jump
up and down as different impressions hit people. To rely
on that as your own decision is to pass your citizen's duty
out of your own head into the mouths of others.

The main thing we need to know is the real story of
each candidate's life, as it relates to one particular line of
work, the Presidency. Those life stories need to be done
now, not just a few years after a President left the White
House. A baseline is whether they are politically energetic
(active or passive) and whether they enjoy politics (positive
or negative).

We need to watch out for candidates whose personalities are dominated by dangerous desires. For example,
some candidates (passive-positive) in the twentieth century, such as Harding and Reagan, have been intensely

hungry for affection in politics. That obsession can make them dangerously dependent on their top advisors close to them in the White House, rather than relating to the rule of law by Congress. But other Presidents (active-negative) have been almost opposite: obsessed to drive forward their own, highly personal power, even though that can cause tragic results for the government. Think of Wilson, Nixon, and Johnson, for example. A third type (passive-negative) is the Presidential pharaoh: one who sees himself high above the actual mundane, sordid, human conditions of low politics, thus ignoring heavy troubles of the people, as did Coolidge and Eisenhower. By contrast, the strong and direct and hopeful Presidential character is the active-positive: an energetic politician who really likes the work of democracy politics.

But even that is not enough to know about, from the stories now coming out. A President with a healthy personality does not necessarily have healthy skills. Sitting there in the White House, can a President do the needed homework, the negotiations, and the rhetoric? Those might seem obvious skills needed, but in fact we have had Presidents who failed because they lacked one or more of the skills or were weak in them. For that reason, we should check out their skills in their biographies.

But even healthy Presidential personalities with Presidential skills are not the only values we ought to apply. Beyond all of the above, we need to know: what do they believe? Not just what they say, but what do they really believe in, as their previous behavior has shown. We need a President whose statements of belief we can trust. That is obviously a real question about George Bush, who said, on the eve of his 1989 inauguration about his campaign the year before: "That's history." What did he think his campaign statements meant? Bush said, "That doesn't mean anything anymore."

What we need to assess is how truthfully the candidate is speaking about what politics he will try to make happen as President. In the past, has the candidate carried forward what he said he would carry forward? If not, watch out.

Now, as the election approaches, is the time to take time to find out what we need to know about the candidates. Most magazine articles skim the surface in a few paragraphs. This book on Bill Clinton has gone beyond the sound-bites to capture the spirit of the times that he grew up in and the forces that shaped his character.

We need to know.

James David Barber, a noted expert on the topic of presidential politics, is the author of "The Presidential Character". He is currently a professor of political science at Duke University.

THE PRESIDENTIAL
CHARACTER
by James David
Barber

How Bill Clinton Withstood the Media Storm

by Michael B. Cornfield

During the late 1970s and 1980s, several trends converged to produce waves of scandalous news about public figures. The old rules about what constituted "proper behavior" were challenged by two social movements, fundamentalism and feminism. The deadlock between the Democratic Congress and Republican White House led politicians from both parties to look for any kind of edge in their battles over the budget, the composition of the courts, and foreign relations. And media corporations blurred the once sacred line between news and entertainment.

This meant that anyone in America with a personal bone to pick with a prominent politician could: A) ally him- or herself with one of the social movements, B) find sympathetic ears in the members of the politician's opposing party, and C) stimulate the creation of a media extravaganza.

Early in 1992, a scandal wave hit Bill Clinton. Adulterer! Then another: Draft-dodger! And another: pot-smoker!

Clinton buckled, but survived, a surprising development for a presidential candidate.

How did he do it?

First, Clinton never stopped his face-to-face (as in no media) campaigning. Americans admire fighters who persist after setbacks. And Clinton was fortunate that the first wave crested while he was campaigning in New Hampshire, a small and politically sophisticated state, where direct contact with voters can have a big impact.

Second, Clinton seized the lead in distributing information about himself.

He appeared with his wife on national television after the Super Bowl, and the couple's words and body language both communicated the message that their marriage was solid. On the night of the New Hampshire primary, Clinton was the first candidate on the air. He described his second-place showing as an underdog's triumph, and the "come-back kid" label stuck because it fit.

It soon became apparent that the sensational accusations about Clinton's character were, at the least, oversimplifications. More importantly, Clinton was responding openly and credibly to them, thereby demonstrating what he was truly made of.

In his responses to some draft-dodging and marijuana-smoking questions, Clinton made several glaring mistakes. But people realized that mistakes happen when someone makes an honest effort to set the record straight. The Governor's primary opponents, to their credit, didn't seek to exploit the situation beyond the bounds of fair competition. And Clinton's ability to laugh at his mis-statements didn't hurt.

Third, because Clinton didn't issue denials and evade questions, the scandal news petered out. The media can be harsh, but they don't dwell. As soon as negative information stops flowing, they move on to the next subject.

Some in the media, to be sure, needed a little push. But fourth, and perhaps most importantly, the public stepped in to declare the story dead. The studio audience for a *Donahue* program in April turned on the talk-show host for spending too much time rehashing the scandal with guest Clinton. They recognized that paying too much attention to a celebrity's personal flaws can distract from massive, if more boring, forms of corruption, such as the S & L scandal, as well as from other pressing issues.

For these reasons, when voters judge Bill Clinton's character this fall — as they should — they are likely to do so in a comparative instead of punitive light. The outstanding question about the Democratic nominee is not whether he's been a perfect human being. It's whether he is a better man for the job of president than George Bush.

Michael Cornfield, a political scientist, teaches courses on media and politics at the University of Virginia. He has written for The Wilson Quarterly and The Washington Monthly, and his book Narrating The Presidency: White House News Stories From Truman to Bush, will be published next year by NYU Press.

Adapted by the author from his article in
The Wilson Quarterly *(Spring 1992)*

The Press and Political Campaigns

Michael Marray

During 1991 readers of American newspapers were faced with a long series of analytical articles about how the coming election campaign was going to be different from 1988. We were told that it would focus upon real issues instead of indulging in character assassination and digging through candidates' private lives. Americans struggling their way through a recession were tired of scandal, the political analysts solemnly informed us. And so were the media themselves. Times had changed.

So what happened? One answer is that despite the public soul searching within the quality press (a label commonly used in Britain, where newspapers are neatly divided into two groups— "tabloids" and "qualities") in reality media coverage of candidates is often driven by the tabloids, which decide what will or will not be published.

The tabloid press digs up some scandal, and generates enough publicity to make it "an issue" which may affect the way people vote. The serious newspapers then feel obligated to report it because it has become . . . an issue which may affect the way people vote— that is to say a legitimate news story.

Thus the same story gets reported in two different ways. The tabloids get straight to the point on the front page. Candidate A in new scandal — for sensational details turn to top of page five. The serious press are a little more coy, running a story at the bottom of page 15 entitled "How will new scandal affect voter's perception of candidate A." The sensational bits are usually there too, but buried discreetly down in paragraph seventeen.

In Bill Clinton's case this process was neatly illustrated in January. First *The New York Times* reported that there were accusations surrounding the candidate, adding that they had so far had "relatively little circulation," but it could cause damage particularly "among women voters." It might be noted that *The Times* report itself added a few more million readers to there "relatively little circulation" of the accusations.

By January 24 *The Times* was quoting — in a small story on page A14 — a story in *The Star* which was running the Gennifer Flowers accusations. By January 26, we were reading that the candidate was deflecting questions about his personal life. That same evening he went on TV after the Superbowl, putting the story well and truly into the public domain.

This is just one example of how the process works. The sensational tabloids go after a story, and once they have initiated the process the serious newspapers tend to be drawn in after them. Some of the hand ringing as they join in looks a bit overdone, but nonetheless many journalists are concerned about the privacy and muckraking — despite the current fashion to depict journalists as sharks who enjoy nothing better than a good feeding frenzy.

It can be argued that candidates running for high office must endure probing into their private life— if such matters reflect the values, prejudices and hypocrisies of the electorate. And candidates, always willing to play the "family values" card by surrounding themselves with wife and children at photo ops, do have a tendency to set themselves up on a pedestal from which it is tempting to try to knock them down.

Such arguments may be interesting for a theoretical debate, but unfortunately the debate within the media is usually conducted by a group of editors who do not actually initiate the dirt-digging process by sending reporters out to investigate candidates' private lives — but will ultimately report why a candidate's poll ratings have suddenly fallen.

Thus what does and does not become a "character issue" of public interest is being decided at editorial meetings at *The Star*, not at *The New York Times* — and debates on ethics aren't one of *The Star's* strong suits.

So with the tabloids leading the way, future candidates had better be prepared for the kind of assault which Bill Clinton faced early in 1992, and should ignore all those long articles about how this year the voters want issues and not scandal. They are being written early in the campaign season, when there isn't enough day to day action to write about. Things will soon liven up.

Michael Marray, a graduate of The London School of Economics, is a professional free-lance journalist based in New York City.

The Changing Voice of the Media in Political Campaign

by Edwin Diamond, Wendy Martens and Richard Wells

On the eve of the fall presidential race, we offer a pop-media quiz. Here are two of the biggest news stories of the 1992 campaign so far.

Story One: a team of investigative reporters fans out across town, inspecting state-court documents, pursuing published leads, knocking on doors. The reporters find several witnesses to "improprieties" involving Candidate A; they take notes, snap pictures and release their materials, which are played at the top of the network newscasts across the country. Story Two: in a small town, far from the Beltway, a hard-charging reporter unearths a plausible source who comes forward, in an exclusive arrangement with the reporter's organization; sensational revelations make page one across the country.

The question: which story was splashed first in the supermarket trash-tabloid The Star and which story was the lead on ABC News' high class "Nightline" with the respected Ted Koppel? The answer: Story One was The

Star's (the headline: "My 12 Year Affair with Governor Clinton"). Story Two was ABC News' (Koppel's opening tease on April 9:

"Allegations that while (Brown) was governor, he threw parties where cocaine and marijuana was used...We'll talk to..a former member of his police guard..making the charges").

So much for the difference between trash and class. When we went back over the full sweep of January-to-July campaign coverage in newspapers, magazines, and on the radio and television, we were struck not so much by what separated Star and Nightline but by the similarities in methods and performance. This is not the fashionable view. But by and large both High press and Low press contributed to their audience's understanding, if voters-citizens paid attention and worked their way through headlines and TV reports. Certainly, there were media howlers and hysteria, though not enough to warrant the current handwringing about journalism's feeding frenzies and the media trivialization of politics— as if there was some Golden Age that preceded our own blighted Brassy Time.

Were those good old days when, say, Andrew Jackson was accused of fathering a mulatto child or when Lincoln was called a baboon?

Once upon a time, before television, the two political parties actually ran election campaigns; party leaders picked the tickets in private, did most of the name-calling, trooped the faithful to the polls, and reaped the rewards of victory (jobs and pork.) Then came TV and the new media politics; the power to tap candidates as a deserving attention or "electable" passed from the parties to the networks and to the elite newspapers and to the news magazines. The clout of a Richard J. Daley and a David Lawrence gave way to the Mandarinic of the columnists and TV commentators. "The screening committees," David Broder of the Washington Post once called the new power brokers (Broder, of course, holds a tenured chair on the committee).

More and more in the 1992 primaries, however, big media found itself yielding some of its influence to the new populist forces, just as the party bosses had to adjust to media politics. The new power brokers starting at the upper end, and descending: CNN's 24 hour news service; local TV-news stations with their own Sam Donaldson's; tabloid TV shows such as Donahue, Oprah, Larry King, Entertainment Tonight and the McLaughlin Show mud wrestlers; The Star and the checkout-counter weeklies; and the terrorist radio talkers — Don Imus on WFAN in New York drive time, Michael Jackson on KABC in Los Angeles. These are not the kind of people either Daley or Broder would want around their clubhouses. "The idiot culture," in the words of the celebrated Watergate reporter Carl Bernstein (Washington Post, Time magazine among his High Press memberships).

The rude intruders redrew the political map in the 1992 primaries. Two appearances with CNN's Larry King and H. Ross Perot achieved national status as a presidential candidate.

During the New York primary, Bill Clinton helped turn around his prospects with a down-and-relaxed performance on Imus (Clinton explained his saxophone technique by saying that he didn't inhale). The decline of the old party machines opened up the nominating process to disenfranchised groups, including women and minorities. The new pop culture -- a term less provocative than idiot culture — is bringing the campaign to audiences not currently reached by High Press. How bad can this be, for the country or for journalism?

Consider two examples of recent big-story coverage by the mainstream; then compare them with some of the "excesses" of the pop culture.

Shadows And Smoke: The Brown Society — John McWethy of ABC News was in Long Beach, California, last March on assignment, far from his usual beat at the State Department. At an aircraft plant, checking into a story about the C-17, he started talking to one of the line workers. McWethy learned that the man used to be a state cop assigned to former Governor Jerry Brown's security force. McWethy's casual question about the governor's chances in the primaries led from one thing to another. The ex-cop talked about the house, in the Laurel Canyon section of Los Angeles, that Brown owned and used as a retreat while governor from 1974-1982. The man suggested that guests participated in pot and coke parties there. McWethy found a second, then a third, then more "sources" to back guard #1.

When ABC was satisfied it and it alone had the story, Ted Koppel devoted an entire Nightline to drugs and the candidate. Koppel intoned: "Let's begin by acknowledging the obvious. This story can be devastating for a man running for president...while no one is charging that Governor Brown himself used drugs, that charge that others used drugs...when Brown was also in the house..can be devastating." Nightline viewers saw the dim outlines of the Laurel Canyon contemporary shot through misty woods, then heard from the two ex-police sources, unidentified by name and photographed, tab-TV style, in the shadow. Later, Brown was allowed to reply, first on tape and then live with Koppel. ABC also switched to Los Angles, where

Ken Kashiwahara interviewed five Californians "who knew Brown when he was the governor." Four dismissed the drug-party story; the final sound bite came from "Don Walter, Journalist" who allowed that he "didn't find incredible" the story. Finally one on one with Koppel, Brown dismissed the ABC account as bizarre, denounced the use of anonymous informants ("what are they afraid of..I have no power"), and threatened legal action. He also worked in a plug for his 1-800 number.

That night, too, Peter Jennings began ABC's World News Tonight with the drug-parties story. The sources were presented in tab-TV silhouettes again, with voice track distorted. Jennings later told PBS talk-show interviewer Charlie Rose that WNT never had any question about running the story; nor was there much discussion about using it as the lead in the top-rated serious newscast in the country. In a matter of days, Laurel Canyon faded to obscurity (Gennifer? Laurel? Which was the blonde with roots?). We asked McWethy why the drug story broke when it did, and why it hasn't been mentioned since. Brown and the press had been attacking Clinton, McWethy explained, and Brown was "doing well" — he just won the Connecticut primary. "Any reporter who comes across information suggesting a candidate is a felon and doesn't publish it should be fired." As for why the story died: "it's hard to find cops who will talk (for the record)." Further, "Brown was no longer a viable candidate."

Bill and Hillary: Conflicts of What?— Top reporters of the two prominent newspapers in the country, The Washington Post and the New York Times, spent weeks in Arkansas early in 1992. They investigated everything from the Clinton environmental record — for example, the reported pollution of Kings Rivers in Northwest Arkansas as a result of fecal bacteria runoff from the state's chicken, turkey, and hog farms — to the lawyer Hillary Clinton and her law firm. Reporters were interested in state-private business "links," a good old journalistic word that skirts libel burdens.

The payoffs from this legwork were modest. At the top of the Post's page one for Sunday,

March 15, staff writers Michael Weisskopf and David Maraniss reported: "Hillary

Clinton's Law Firm/ Is Influential With the State." As the story unfolded it turned out that the Rose law firm has been influential in Arkansas for at least 150 years (it was founded in 1820). Twelve days later, in The New York Times of March 27, reporter Jeff Gerth reported, also on page one, that a proposed Arkansas ethics and disclosure law for public officials was "altered" to exempt from its requirements state officials (like Clinton and his wife). To learn of Arkansas' conflict of interest provisions, Gerth tracked through Little Rock law libraries and the legislative vault.

These investigative pieces generated more press. After the fecal runoff account in the Times, they became known, generically, as The Chickenshit Story. The Clinton campaign claimed that Gerth took the conflict of interest change "out of context." The context, as explained by the Clinton campaign: the provision was redrawn in order to win office holders' block support in the upcoming referendum. But the Rose law firm "link" achieved a life of its own. Jerry Brown claimed that Arkansas was "funneling" contracts to Rose.

New York Times columnist Anthony Lewis wrote on April 19 that Hillary Clinton's law firm had billed the state

236

exactly $4,226.75 over the past decade. Lewis added that the editor who "fronted the story" — put it one page one — should be working for the National Enquirer. Maraniss was particularly upset by the comments from Lewis, suggesting the columnist ought to look at the hype "in stories in his own paper." Maraniss nevertheless worried whether in fact his Post editors HAD overplayed the law firm story.

Jeff Gerth said he wanted his article to speak for itself; but in the Times' newsroom, too, there was some surprise at its prominent play. John Robert Starr, editor of the Arkansas

Democrat-Gazette, was most dismissive of all when we talked to him. The Times, the Post, the Wall Street Journal, the Los Angeles Times — "the respectables" — were doing "waving-to-their-friends journalism." The "links" of the Rose firm had been well covered by the Arkansas press, Star explained, and added, not so incidentally: "I opposed Clinton, and will do all I can to prevent him from becoming president...but this goes beyond good journalism."

Now look at the examples of sleazoid Low Press behavior: The Star's trash play of the Gennifer Flowers story, Phil Donahue's "adultery" questions to Clinton, local New York media's lubricious interest in sex, drugs, and rock-n-roll. In fact, Star reporters copied documents about Clinton's supposed girlfriends from a 1990 law suit filed by a former office holder in the Little Rock courts (not far from where Gerth tracked through the legislative vault). Donahue, after one swarmy sex-tease show, more than made up for it by inviting Clinton and Brown on camera and letting them go head to head with no moderator — the best one hour of television in the primary season. New York TV reporter Marcia Kramer wanted and got an an-

swer from Clinton about marijuana not so much because
the 1960's college boy's smoking activities were wrong but
because the 1990's political man needed to give straight
replies to her simple questions. Not that much separated
High and Low coverage. Maraniss told us, "we didn't
exaggerate. We simply wrote what we found." So did The
Star.

"Oh my, yes, maybe put it in the paper," the critics of
the Low Press begin to murmur, but then seem to get
uptight about the stock of the paper (cheap weekly news-
print) or the low-rent location of the broadcast (a.m. drive,
afternoon TV talk).

Lyndon Johnson advised political office seekers to go
hunting where the ducks were. So, too, with the political
dialogue: candidates and media need to engage their varied
publics in as many places as possible.

But Donahue does it for the ratings in as many places as
possible. The Star paid Flowers in order to sell its magazines! True, Flowers received a huge sum for her tale and
her tapes— $150,000 by some estimates. But consider the
point made in a Boston Globe editorial: if Simon and
Shuster paid Flowers a $150,000 advance and published
her memoirs in proper hardcover form, High Press would
have judged the book newsworthy and covered it above the
fold. An advance peek at the Kitty Kelly demolition of
Nancy Reagan appeared on the eve of publication - hype
for the book - in the New York Times, and on page one.

Perhaps there has been a coarsening-down of the American High press as it tries to grapple with the candidates'
character (and their spouses'); the mainstream also had to
deal with a disaffected audience and the uncouth antics of
Low Press. Or perhaps, Low Press is cleaning up its act a
bit, raising the level of its efforts, sending out reporters,

following up leads, checking court papers, finding time for the campaign during the entertainment schedules. High and Low are meeting in some inclusive middle. Politics, as Andrew Jackson and Abraham Lincoln can testify, used to be played broadly, for the grounding as well as the boxes. Let the new Brass Age begin.

Edwin Diamond is a media columnist for New York Magazine and a professor of journalism and director of the News Study Group at New York University. Wells and Martens are members of the Group.

Ethics in Politics and the Press

by Marion R. Just

With updates 1992

Humorists depict political ethics as an oxymoron, but there are serious reasons why moral behavior is problematic in politics. First, the demands of democratic compromise threaten a principled approach to policy-making. Second, almost all important policies carry with them unpredicted and unavoidable evil consequences for some present or future persons. As for individual political practitioners, history confirms that power corrupts. When people talk about the problems of ethics in American politics, however, they are always referring to individual behavior or public officials rather than the ethics of policy. The personal orientation of public discourse on ethics is largely a function of the news agenda. In ethics as in other political arenas "the press may not be successful much of the time in telling people what to think, but it is stunningly successful in telling its readers what to think about."[1]

In recent years, the American press has explored a range of ethical controversies in policy-making, official responsibility, and personal morality. The press, for example, played a critical role in laying out the ethical issues in the affirmative action debate, building the discussion around news pegs, such as the Bakke case. Coverage of issues of official responsibility in the Iran-Contra affair drew on a muckraking tradition reinvigorated by Watergate. The most constant and obtrusive feature of press coverage of political ethics, however, is its concentration on the personal ethics of public officials.

As early as 1830, Alexis de Tocqueville characterized American journalists less disposed to argue principles than "to assault the characters of individuals, to track them into private life and disclose all their weaknesses and vices."[2]. Press coverage of personal morality is distinguished by a scope and intensity unparalleled in the coverage of policy ethics. Discussions of the ethics of particular policies are often confined to a single source (such as *The New York Times* series on the hazards of nuclear weapons plants). The investigation of individual breaches of the public trust, such as the case of Robert Garcia, typically involve a larger number of media outlets, particularly in a local area. No other aspect of political ethics, however, arouses the kind of universal press response as the personal indiscretions of public figures.

Especially during election campaigns, the candidate who commits a moral offense receives inescapable and single-minded press attention, a press "feeding frenzy."[3] In the 1988 presidential campaign we witnessed a series of pack-journalist attacks focusing on Gary Hart's girlfriend, Joe Biden's plagiarism, Pat Robertson's "miracle baby," and Dan Quayle's military service. [In the 1992 presidential election, we have been subjected to tales of unproved accusations of infidelity, draft dodging, and marijuana usage.] While the confines of campaigns seem to heighten the effect, avalanche coverage is typical of the press response to the personal moral failings of public figures at other times as well. Over the years the public has been titillated by stories about John Tower, Wilbur Mills and Ted Kennedy.

Press enthusiasm for covering stories about individual indiscretions can be partly explained by the old saw that familiarity breeds contempt. The requirements of press oversight bring reporters and officials into daily proximity. Journalists inevitably become aware of any discrepancy between a virtuous public image and politicians' private behavior. That is probably why hypocrisy is particularly apt to trigger full-court press coverage.

The people share responsibility with the press for focusing ethical debate on private morality. The public's insatiable appetite for gossip about public figures sells newspapers. This overpowering curiosity creates an economic incentive for the press to "tell all" about public officials. The prestige press may have scruples about being the first to report a rumor of official indiscretion, but once the lurid details are circulated even by a small outlet, competition generally overcomes initial misgivings. Journalists rationalize professional behavior, no matter how unattractive, as "the people's right to know."

The press would probably devote even more coverage to the personal indiscretions of officials if the public was not reputed to be easily bored. In order for an issue to support continuing coverage, there has to be "news," i.e. something new to report. When a politician waffles on the issue or doesn't tell the whole story (the "partial hangout") the press has an opportunity to present the continuing revelations as news. That is why political consultants advise candidates to make a clean breast of it, as Representative Barney Frank did so excruciatingly in the Gobi affair. But the case of Jim Wright shows that once a public figure is in a serious decline, one piece of bad news leads to another. Speaker Wright's problems began with selling too many copies of the book, but when the public was unmoved by the book payoff, the press took up Wright's staff appointments, and his wife's relationship with a major campaign contributor.

Wright's problems were similar to those of an electoral candidate who has to meet the press. Consider, for example, the treatment of Jim Wright compared to that of Barney Frank. As Speaker, Wright was expected to be in daily contact with the press. He could not lie low; and whenever he came before the press, he was forced to discuss the ethics charges against him. Just as candidates who are forced from the field because their campaign message is choked off, Wright could not carry on as Speaker if he had to talk about himself rather than the Congress. Barney Frank, on the other hand, after an extensive explanation, somewhat belatedly distanced himself from the press, and the issue receded.

The public also plays a role in limiting press attention to individual moral failings. The press can only maintain an attack on personal misconduct if the revelations of official misconduct, "resonate" with the public. Whether charges of ethical misconduct "stick" to particular individuals depends on the prestige of the office, the harm to others, and the extent to which the misconduct reveals character flaws. So, for example, Senator Edward Kennedy's actions at Chappaquiddick might be acceptable in a senator but not in a president. Representative Frank's indiscretion was not as serious as Gary Hart's because Frank was not married; and Gary Hart's dalliance with Donna Rice finally became unacceptable because it putatively revealed a lack of judgement which could be disastrous in a president. In addition, the public seems to apply a "once is enough" standard to reports of ethical impropriety. The scandals over Chief Justice Rehnquist's restrictive covenant and Mayor David Dinkins's income tax filings did not "stick" the second time around.

Is it reasonable to ask the press to limit its coverage of the private lives of public officials? Ethicists generally agree that the press should confine itself to censoring only those private behaviors which threaten an individual's ability to carry out public duties. The trap here is that honesty and caution are public as well as private virtues. Therefore any indiscretion uncovered by the press means that, first, the individual was dishonest for not telling the public about it and second, somewhat a fool for allowing the action to be discovered.

If press coverage of a personal indiscretion cannot be proscribed, the point may be gained by prescribing greater press attention to ethical issues that are more publicly relevant. The press already does a very good job of covering charges of corruption or official misconduct. There are other, legal, instruments for controlling the behavior of politicians who hire family members in no-show jobs, or bureaucrats who line their pockets by selling privileged information. But the press has a unique role in promoting public discussion of the ethics of public policy.

One of the barriers to exploring the full range of policy options is that press coverage of the substance of policy often leads to charges of bias. The norm of neutrality is so deeply rooted among journalists and the public that the press naturally recoils from discussion of issues which are

244

or may become partisan. The press is especially wary of tackling the ethics of public policy during conservative administrations when criticism is marked down as "liberal bias."[4] Exploring the ethics of nuclear war or affirmative action is essential, however, for our political well-being, [while investigating exactly what Bill Clinton did with Gennifer Flowers is not]. It is simply unavoidable, however, to discuss the ethics of tax policy, racism, or military intervention without making arguments that can be used in the course of partisan debate.

Journalists will have to steel themselves against charges of bias if they shift the focus of ethical debate to public policy rather than personal indiscretion. But they cannot do it alone. The press needs the public to respond to policy stories with some of the interest and applause that is reserved for tales of sexual misadventure. Audiences have to respond with outrage when the press reveals how the mentally ill were cut from the social security roles or how the government turned a blind eye to dangerous nuclear weapons plants. The press needs the public to help it brave the cries of foul when it investigates bad policy rather than adultery. The press and the public need the courage to tackle the full range of ethical issues in politics.

Adapted by the author from his article in
Barnard Magazine *(Spring 1990)*

Endnotes

1. Bernard C. Cohen, *The Press and Foreign Policy* (Princeton, N.J.: Princeton University Press, 1963), p. 13.

2. Alexis de Tocqueville, *Democracy in America,* vol. I (New York: Vintage Books, 1945), p. 194.

3. Larry J. Sabato, *"Modelling the modern Feeding Frenzy"* (photocopy, c. 1989) and personal communication, December 18, 1989.

4. See Mark Hertzgard, *On Bended Knee: The Press and the Reagan Presidency.*

Marion Just is currently a professor of Political Science at Wellesley College.

Part Four

The Message

For what do people look in leaders, however selected? For what should they look? All of the great leaders have had one characteristic in common: it was the willingness to confront unequivocally the major anxiety of their people in their time. This, and not much else, is the essence of leadership.

John Kenneth Galbraith,
The Age of Uncertainty:
A History of Economic Ideas and their Consequences

Millions of Americans who have voted for Clinton in Arkansas and in the Democratic primaries believe that he understands their disenchantment with government and the economic problems of America. They believe that the ideas he has articulated in *Putting People First: A National Economic Strategy for America* can change its fundamental character and direction and demonstrate a clear economic policy vision for the 1990s.

Clinton, who is a practical man, is also a man of ideas. And some of his ideas are very exciting. He has already dramatically changed the Democratic Party's governing philosophy — in a way that people frustrated with big, bloated government bureaucracy will find refreshing and quite appealing. As Chairman of the National Governors Association, he has led the way on both national welfare reform and improving performance in education.

Since 1970, there have been four major proposals for welfare reform including Nixon's Family Assistance Program, Carter's Program for Better Jobs and Income, Reagan's Workfare and Senator Daniel Patrick Moynihan's JOBS package. Great ideas, but the results are mixed. In 1980, Ronald Reagan promised to reduce the size of government and cut the deficit and failed to do both. President Bush broke his "no new taxes" pledge. America is disillusioned with traditional conservative and liberal rhetoric and is ready for a completely new approach to government. Clinton's ideas incorporate new incentives into the system that can revolutionize the way government gets the job done — and make government work much better than ever before.

Bill Clinton has studied a field of new ideas and approaches and has also generated his own fresh, original thinking about the nation's problems. He believe the Americans should be encouraged to take their responsibilities as seriously as their rights. The current generation must also take responsibility for the stewardship of the environment, crumbling infrastructure, nuclear waste disposal sites, Medicare and Social Security systems as well as the massive federal debt.

This book contains a whole range of ideas which we may hear more about in a Clinton Administration. In the field of entitlements, the most important idea requires a person, in return for the right to receive welfare benefits, to assume responsibility to do work or at least take steps necessary to become self-supporting. To chronic welfare recipients, he says, "If you can work, you've got to go to work, because you can no longer stay on welfare forever."

At the heart of Clinton's *New Covenant* agenda is a new idea with ancient roots. As Amitai Etzioni writes in *The Communitarian Platform* (1989) ". . . Strong rights entail strong responsibilities. We have a sound base of rights (although they need to be constantly and vigilantly guarded). However, we have not matched our concern with the preservation of rights with a commitment to personal and social responsibilities." John F. Kennedy's oft-overused phrase, "Ask not what your country can do for you, but what you can do for your country," underpins the values of opportunity, responsibility, and community which are the core of Clinton's campaign platform. In short, Clinton's New Covenant calls for a new social contract between the American people and its government.

The idea of a social contract is not new. Although it has its roots in Arisotle's *Politics*, it found its greatest development during the British and French Enlightenment. The writings of Thomas Hobbes, John Locke, Baron de Montesquieu, and Jean-Jacques Rousseau — who wrote an essay specifically entitled *The Social Contract* — influenced the enlightened American leaders, including Thomas Jefferson, Benjamin Franklin, John Adams before and after the first American revolution.

Now, over two hundred years later, there is a serious crisis of confidence in our system of government. A new grass-roots revolution is sweeping across America. People are angry that the checks and balances of government are neither checking the waste nor balancing the budget. People are enraged with politicians who raise taxes while bureaucrats fail to solve the major problems facing America. In our democracy, we can have a peaceful and constructive Second American Revolution simply by electing new presidential leadership and reinventing the way government serves the people.

Clinton's *New Covenant* is a sacred promise to help America achieve her best potential. It echoes the bold innovation of Franklin Roosevelt's New Deal programs to help lift this nation out of the Depression. It reflects the character and principles of Harry Truman's Fair Deal for the American people. The *New Covenant* reminds us of the soaring idealism of Dr. Martin Luther King's unfinished agenda to lift people out of poverty by investing in education and economic development. Yet the *New Covenant* recognizes that government doesn't have the means to do everything, and that people must accept responsibility to help themselves.

Bill Clinton and his running mate, Senator Al Gore, have the opportunity to dramatically change the political culture of the United States, one that has been dominated by the traditional dove-hawk, liberal-conservative ideology of the Cold War era. The Clinton Era can create the foundations for a fresh start for America as a new century begins.

"I am convinced that if we are to get on the right side of the world revolution, we as a nation must undergo a radical revolution of values. We must rapidly begin the shift from a "thing-oriented" society to a "person-oriented" society. When machines and computers, profit motives and property rights are considered more important than people, the giant triplets of racism, materialism, and militarism are incapable of being conquered."

Martin Luther King, Jr.
April 4, 1967

Putting People First

A National Economic Strategy for America

by Bill Clinton

<u>Summary</u>

During the 1980's, our government betrayed the values that make America great: providing opportunity, taking responsibility, rewarding work. While the rich got richer, the forgotten middle class — the people who work hard and play by the rules — took it on the chin. They paid high taxes to a government that gave them little in return. Washington failed to put people first.

No wonder our nation has compiled its worst economic record in fifty years.

Our political system isn't working either. Washington is dominated by powerful interests and an entrenched bureaucracy. Americans are tired of blame. They are ready for a leader willing to take responsibility.

My national economic strategy puts people first by investing more than $50 billion each year for the next four years while cutting the deficit in half. These investments will create millions of high-wage jobs and help America compete in the global economy.

My strategy includes:

- **Putting America to work** by rebuilding our country, converting from a defense to a peacetime economy, revitalizing our cities, encouraging private investment, and opening up world markets.
- **Rewarding work** by providing **tax fairness** to working families, ending welfare as we know it, providing family leave and cracking down on deadbeat parents.
- **Supporting lifetime learning** by bringing parents and children together, improving schools, training high school graduates, offering every American the chance to borrow money to go to college and serve our nation, and retraining workers.
- **Providing quality, affordable health care** by radically controlling costs, reducing paper work, phasing in universal access to basic medical coverage, and cracking down on drug manufacturers and insurance companies.
- **Revolutionizing government** by cutting 100,000 federal jobs, eliminating wasteful spending, limiting the power

of special interests, stopping the revolving door from public service to private enrichment, and reforming campaign finance and practices.

It's time to **put people first!**

That is the core of my national economic strategy for America. And that will be the fundamental idea that guides my Presidency.

America is the greatest nation on earth. But for more than a decade our government has been rigged in favor of the rich and special interests. While the very wealthiest Americans get richer, middle class Americans pay more taxes to their government and get less in return. Our government has betrayed the values that make us great — providing opportunity, taking responsibility and rewarding hard work.

For twelve years, the driving idea behind American economic policy has been cutting taxes on the richest individuals and corporations and hoping that their new wealth would "trickle down" to the rest of us.

This policy has failed.

The Republicans in Washington have compiled the worst economic record in fifty years: the slowest economic growth, slowest job growth, and slowest income growth since the Great Depression. During the 1980s the wealthiest one percent of Americans got 70 percent of income gains. By the end of the decade, American CEOs were paying themselves 100 times more than their workers. Washington stood by while quick-buck artists brought down the savings and loan industry, leaving the rest of us with a $500 billion bill.

While the rich cashed in, the forgotten middle class —

the people who work hard and play by the rules — took it on the chin. They worked harder for less money and paid more taxes to a government that failed to produce what we need: good jobs in a growing economy, world-class education, affordable health care, and safe streets and neighborhoods. The working poor had the door of opportunity slammed in their face.

A decade ago, Americans earned higher wages than anyone else in the world. Now we're tenth, and falling. In Europe and Japan our competitors' economies grew three and four times faster than ours — because their leaders decided to invest in their people and Washington did not.

In the emerging global economy, everything is mobile: capital, factories, even entire industries. The only resource that's really rooted in a nation — and the ultimate source of all its wealth — is its people. The only way America can complete and win in the 21st Century is to have the best educated, best trained work force in the world, linked together by transportation and communication networks second to none.

I believe in free enterprise and the power of market forces. I know economic growth will be the best jobs program we'll ever have. But economic growth does not come without a national economic strategy to invest in people and meet the competition.

Today we have no economic vision, no economic leadership and no economic strategy.

Our political system has failed us, too. Washington is dominated by powerful interests and an entrenched bureaucracy. Too many public officials enter the revolving door and emerge as high-priced influence peddlers. Too often those we elect to lead seem to respond more quickly to special interests than to the real problems of real people.

No wonder all of us have had enough. Our government doesn't work. People who pay the bills get little value for their dollar and have no voice in Washington. They are tired of hearing politicians blame each other. They are eager for someone to take responsibility and ready for a leader who will challenge all of us again.

The strategy outlined in the pages that follow is not all-inclusive. There are many other crucial challenges that await the next President: healing the divisions that threaten our society, restoring law and order to our streets and communities, protecting a woman's right to choose, launching a war on AIDS, leading the world in protecting our environment, and securing our interests and human rights around the globe.

But we will reach our goals only if we focus on our country's greatest resource. That is why putting people first is the heart and soul of my national economic strategy — and the key to the American future.

My strategy puts people first by investing more than $50 billion each year over the next four years to put America back to work — the most dramatic economic growth program since World War II. My strategy recognizes that the only way to lay the foundation for renewed American prosperity is to spur both public and private investment. To reclaim our future, we must strive to close both the budget deficit and the investment gap.

These investments will create millions of high-wage jobs and provide tax relief to working families. They will also help move people from welfare to work, provide lifetime learning, and ensure affordable health care for every citizen.

To pay for these investments and reduce our national deficit, I will save nearly $300 billion by cutting spending, closing corporate tax loopholes, and requiring the very wealthy to pay their fair share of taxes. My plan will cut the deficit in half within four years, and assure that it continues to fall each year after that.

No American will agree with all the details of my plan. But you have a right to know what I'll do and where I stand.

Putting people first demands, above all, that we put America back to work!

For the last twelve years Washington has penalized hard work and sold out American families. As the recession sends working families into poverty, the Republicans throw up their hands instead of rolling up their sleeves.

The results have been devastating. Record numbers of Americans are unemployed and millions more must settle for insecure, low-wage, no-benefit jobs. Small businesses — which create most of the new jobs in this country — are starved for capital and credit. Washington continues to grant tax deductions for outrageous executive pay and reward American corporations who move their plants and jobs overseas.

The corrupt do-nothing values of the 1980s must never mislead us again. Never again should Washington reward those who speculate in paper, instead of those who put people first. Never again should we sit idly by while the plight of hard-working Americans is ignored. Never again should we pass on our debts to our children while their futures silently slip through our fingers.

My national economic strategy will reward the people who work hard creating new jobs, starting new businesses and investing in our people and our plants here at home. To restore economic growth, we need to help free enterprise flourish, put our people back to work, and learn again how to compete. My plan will shut the door on the "something for nothing" decade by making the wealthiest Americans pay their fair share in taxes; ending tax breaks for American companies that shut down their plants here and ship American jobs overseas; eliminating deductions for outrageous executive pay; and cracking down on foreign companies that prosper here and manipulate tax laws to their advantage.

Rebuild America.

The 1980s saw the concrete foundations of the United States crumble as the investment gap widened between America and our global competitors. By the decade's end, Japan and Germany were investing more than 12 times what we spend on roads, bridges, sewers and the information networks and technologies of the future. No wonder they threaten to surpass America in manufacturing by 1996. No wonder we are slipping behind.

To create millions of high-wage jobs and smooth our transition from a defense to a peacetime economy, we will rebuild America and develop the world's best communication, transportation and environmental systems.

As a prominent part of our strategy to put people first, we will create a **Rebuild America fund**, with a $20 billion Federal investment each year for the next four years, leveraged with state, local, private sector and pension fund contributions. User fees such as road tolls and solid waste disposal charges will help guarantee these investments.

Just as constructing interstate highways in the 1950s ushered in two decades of unparalleled growth, creating the pathways of the 21st century will help put Americans back to work and spur economic growth. States and localities will be responsible for project development and management. The creation of large, predictable markets will stimulate private industry to invest in our economy and create new high-wage jobs.

We will focus on four critical areas:

Transportation, including renovation of our country's roads, bridges and railroads; creation of a high-speed rail network linking our major cities and commercial hubs; investment in "smart" highway technology to expand the capacity, speed and efficiency of our major roadways; and development of high-tech short-haul aircraft.

A national information network to link every home, business, lab, classroom and library by the year 2015. To expand access to information, we will put public records, databases, libraries and educational materials on line for public use.

Environmental technology to create the world's most advanced systems to recycle, treat toxic waste and clean our air and water; and develop new, clean energy sources. We need not make a false choice between protecting our environment and spurring economic growth.

Defense conversion to ensure that the communities and millions of talented workers that won the Cold War don't get left out in the cold. Many of the skills and technologies required to rebuild America are similar to those now used in our defense industries. We will encourage companies that bid on projects to rebuild America to contract work to,

258

or purchase, existing defense facilities; order the Pentagon to conduct a national defense jobs inventory to assist displaced workers; and provide special conversion loans and grants to small business defense contractors.

Investing in communities.

While America's great cities fall into disrepair, Washington continues to ignore their fate. Private enterprise has abandoned our cities, leaving our young people with few job prospects and less hope. To restore urban economic vitality and bring back high-paying jobs to our cities, I will: target funding and Community Development Block Grants to rebuild America's urban roads, bridges, water and sewage treatment plants and low-income housing stock, stressing "ready to go" projects. Require companies that bid on these projects to set up a portion of their operations in low-income neighborhoods and employ local residents.

Create a nationwide network of community development banks to provide small loans to low-income entrepreneurs and homeowners in the inner cities. These banks will also provide advice and assistance to entrepreneurs, invest in affordable housing, and help mobilize private lenders.

Fight crime by putting 100,000 new police offers on the streets. We will create a National Police Corps and offer unemployed veterans and active military personnel a chance to become law enforcement officers here at home. We will also expand community policing, fund more drug treatment, and establish community boot camps to discipline first-time non-violent offenders.

Create urban enterprise zones in stagnant inner cities, but only for companies willing to take responsibility. Business taxes and federal regulations will be minimized to provide incentives to set up shop. In return, companies will have to make jobs for local residents a top priority.

Ease the credit crunch in our inner cities by passing a more progressive Community Reinvestment Act to prevent "redlining"; and requiring financial institutions to invest in their communities.

Encouraging private investment in America.

Ten years ago, the United States spent about $400 more per person than Japan in capital investment. Today the Japanese invest more than twice as much in their nation as we do. We must either change our course or continue to slide.

To help American business create new jobs and compete in the global economy, we must dramatically increase private investment. My plan would:

Provide a targeted investment tax credit to encourage investment in the new plants and productive equipment here at home that we need to compete in the global economy.

Help small business and entrepreneurs by offering a 50 percent tax exclusion to those who take risks by making long-term investments in new business.

Make permanent the research and development tax credit to reward companies that invest in ground-breaking technologies.

Create a civilian research and development agency to bring together businesses and universities to develop cutting-edge products and technologies. This agency will increase our commercial research and development spending, and focus its efforts in crucial new industries such as biotechnology, robotics, high-speed computing, and environmental technology opening up world markets. Because every $1 billion of increased American exports will create 20,000 to 30,000 new jobs, we will move aggressively to open foreign markets to quality American goods and services. We will urge our trading partners in Europe and the Pacific Rim to abandon unfair trade subsidies in key sectors like shipbuilding and aerospace — and act swiftly if they fail to respond. To ensure a more level playing field, we will:

— Pass a stronger, sharper "Super 301" trade bill: if other nations refuse to play by our trade rules, we'll play by theirs.

— Seek more open markets for American products by negotiating a fair trade agreement with Mexico that protect basic worker rights and environmental standards.

— Create an Economic Security Council, similar to the National Security Council, with responsibility for coordinating America's international economic policy.

— Reform the office of the U.S. Trade Representative by issuing an executive order banning trade negotiators from cashing in on their positions by becoming lobbyists for foreign governments or corporations. We must transform this office into a corps of trade experts whose primary aim is to serve their country, not sell out for lucrative paychecks from foreign competitors.

Rewarding work and families.

Putting our people first means honoring and rewarding those who work hard and play by the rules. It means recognizing that government doesn't raise children — people do. It means that we must reward work, demand responsibility and end welfare as we know it.

Washington has abandoned working families. Millions of Americans are running harder and harder just to stay in place. While taxes fall and incomes rise for those at the top of the totem pole, middle class families pay more and earn less. Wages are flat, good jobs have become scarce, and poverty has exploded. Health care costs have skyrocketed, and millions have seen their health benefits disappear.

Today almost one of every five people who works full-time doesn't earn enough to support his or her family above the poverty line. Deadbeat parents owe $25 billion in unpaid child support, and have left millions of single-parent families in poverty.

In the 1980s the Republicans used welfare as a wedge to divide Americans against each other. They silently hacked away at the programs that keep disadvantaged children healthy and prepare them for school. They talked about "family values" but increased the burden on American families.

My national economic strategy will strengthen families and empower all Americans to work. It will break the cycle of dependency and end welfare as we know it. It includes:

Expanding the Earned Income Tax Credit. To en-sure that no one with a family who works full-time has to raise their children in poverty, we will increase the Earned Income Tax Credit to make up the difference between a family's earnings and the poverty level. The credit will also be expanded for part time workers, giving them a greater incentive to work.

Middle class tax fairness. We will lower the tax burden on middle class Americans by asking the very wealthy to pay their fair share. Middle class taxpayers will have a choice between a children's tax credit or a signifi-cant reduction in their income tax rate. Virtually every industrialized nation recognizes the importance of strong families in its tax code; we should, too.

Welfare-to-work. We will scrap the current welfare system and make welfare a second chance, not a way of life. We will empower people on welfare with the educa-tion, training and child care they need for up to two years so they can break the cycle of dependency. After that, those who can work will have to go to work, either by taking a job in the private sector or through community service.

Family and medical leave. Parents should not have to choose between the job they need and the family they love. I will immediately sign into law the Family and Medical Leave Act. This bill will give American workers the right to take 12 weeks of unpaid leave in order to care for a newborn child or sick family member — a right enjoyed by workers in every other advanced industrial nation.

Child support enforcement. We will crack down on deadbeat parents by reporting them to credit agencies, so they can't borrow money for themselves when they're not taking care of their children. We'll use the Internal Revenue Service to collect child support, start a national deadbeat databank, and make it a felony to cross state lines to avoid paying support.

Lifetime learning.

Putting people first demands a revolution in lifetime learning, a concerted effort to invest in the collective talents of our people. Education today is more than the key to climbing the ladder of opportunity. In today's global economy, it is an imperative for our nation. Our economic life is on the line.

Government fails when our schools fail. For four years we have heard much talk about "the Education President" but seen no government action to close the gap between what our people can achieve and what we ask of them. Washington shows little concern as people pay more and get less for what matters most to them: educating their children.

Millions of our children go to school unprepared to learn. The Republicans in Washington have promised — but never delivered — full funding of Head Start, a proven success that gives disadvantaged children a chance to get ahead. And while the states move forward with innovative ways to bring parents and children together, Washington fails to insist on responsibility from parents, teachers, students — and itself.

The 1980s witnessed the emergence of immense education gaps between America and the world and among our own people. Test scores went down while violence in the schools went up. Too many children did bullet drills instead of fire drills, and too many teachers were assaulted. High school graduates who chose not to go to college saw their incomes drop by 20 percent. While college tuition and living costs skyrocketed, the Republicans tried to slash assistance for middle class families. By the decade's end, nearly one of every two college students was dropping out, most because they simply could no longer afford it.

In an era when what you earn depends on what you learn, education too often stops at the schoolhouse door. While our global competitors invest in their people, American companies spend seven of every ten dollars for employee training on those at the top of the corporate ladder. High-level executives float on golden parachutes to a cushy life while hard-working Americans are grounded without the skills they need.

My national economic strategy for America will put people first at every stage of their lives. We will dramatically improve the way parents prepare their children for school, give students the chance to train for jobs or pay for college, and provide workers with the training and retraining they need to compete in tomorrow's economy.

The main elements include:

Parents and children together. We will inspire parents to take responsibility, and empower them with the knowledge they need to help their children enter school ready to learn. As we do in my state, we will help disadvantaged parents work with their children to build an ethic of learning at home that benefits both parent and child. We will fully fund programs that save us several dollars for every one we spend — Head Start, the Women, Infants and Children (WIC) program, and other critical initiatives recommended by the National Commission on Children.

Dramatically improve K-12 education. We will over-haul America's public schools to insure that every child has a chance for a world-class education. We will establish tough standards and a national examination system in core subjects like math and science, level the playing field for disadvantaged students, and reduce class sizes. Every parent should have the right to choose the public school his or her child attends, as parents do in Arkansas. In return, we will demand that parents work with their children to keep them in school, off drugs and headed toward gradua-tion.

Safe Schools Initiative. We will provide funds for violence-ridden schools to hire security personnel and pur-chase metal detectors; and help cities and states use com-munity policing to put more police officers on the streets in high-crime areas where schools are located.

Youth Opportunity Corps. To give teenagers who drop out of school a second chance, we will help communi-ties open youth centers. Teenagers will be matched with adults who care about them, and given a chance to develop self-discipline and skills.

National Service Trust Fund. To give every American the right to borrow money for college, we will scrap the existing student loan program and establish a National

Service Trust Fund. Those who borrow from the fund will be able to choose how to repay the balance: either as a small percentage of their earnings over time, or by serving their communities for one or two years doing work their country needs as teachers, law enforcement officers, health care workers, or peer counselors helping kids stay off drugs and in school.

Worker retraining. We will require every employer to spend 1.5 percent of payroll for continuing education and training, and make them provide the training to all workers, not just executives. Workers will be able to choose advanced skills training, the chance to earn a high school diploma, or the opportunity to learn to read. And we will streamline the confusing array of publicly-funded training programs.

Quality, affordable health care.

The American health care system costs too much and does not work. Instead of putting people first, Washington favors the insurance companies, drug manufacturers, and health care bureaucracies. We cannot build tomorrow's economy until we guarantee every American the right to quality, affordable health care.

Washington has ignored the needs of middle class families and let health care costs soar out of control. American drug companies have raised their prices three times faster than the rate of inflation, forcing American consumers to pay up to six times more than Canadians or Europeans for the same drugs. Insurance companies routinely deny coverage to consumers with "pre-existing conditions" and waste billions on bureaucracy and administration. Twelve years ago Americans spent $249 billion on health care. This year we'll spend more than $800 billion.

Health care costs are now the number one cause of bankruptcy and labor disputes. They threaten our ability to compete, adding $700 to the cost of every car made in America. Our complex system chokes consumers and providers with paper, requiring the average doctor to spend 80 hours a month on paperwork. It invites fraud and abuse. We spend more on health care than any nation on earth and don't get our money's worth.

Our people still live in fear. Today almost 60 million Americans have inadequate health insurance — or none at all. Every year working men and women are forced to pay more while their employers cover less. Small businesses are caught between going broke and doing right by their employees. Infants die at rates that exceed those of countries blessed with far fewer resources. Across our nation older Americans live in fear that they will fall ill — and lose everything or bankrupt their children's dreams trying to pay for the care they deserve.

America has the potential to provide the world's best, most advanced and cost-effective health care. What we need are leaders who are willing to take on the insurance companies, the drug companies, and the health care bureaucracies and bring health care costs down.

My health care plan is simple in concept but revolutionary in scope. First, we will move to radically control costs by changing incentives, reducing paperwork and cracking down on drug and insurance company practices. As costs drop, we will phase in guaranteed universal access to basic medical coverage through employer or public programs.

Companies will be required to insure their employees, with federal assistance in the early years, to help them meet their obligations. Health care providers will finally have incentives to reduce costs and improve quality care for consumers. Savings from cost containment will help those who pay too much for health insurance today. American health care will make sense.

My plan will put people first by guaranteeing quality, affordable health care. No American will go without health care, but in return everyone who can must share the cost of their care. The main elements include:

National spending caps. The cost of health care must not be allowed to rise faster than the average American's income. I will scrap the Health Care Financing Administration and replace it with a health standards board — made up of consumers, providers, business, labor and government — that will establish annual health budget targets and outline a core benefits package.

Universal coverage. Affordable, quality health care will be a right, not a privilege. Under my plan, employers and employees will either purchase private insurance or opt to buy into a high-quality public program. Every American not covered by an employer will receive the core benefits package set by the health standards board.

Managed care networks. Consumers will have access to a variety of local health networks, made up of insurers, hospitals, clinics and doctors. The networks will receive a fixed amount of money for each consumer, giving them the necessary incentive to control costs.

Eliminate drug price gouging. To protect American consumers and bring down prescription drug prices, I will eliminate tax breaks for drug companies that raise their prices faster than Americans' incomes rise.

Take on the insurance industry. To stand up to the powerful insurance lobby and stop consumers from paying billions in administrative waste, we need to streamline the industry. My health plan will institute a single claim form and ban underwriting practices that waste billions to discover which patients are bad risks. Any insurance company that wants to do business will have to take all comers and charge every business in a community the same rate. No company will be able to deny coverage to individuals with pre-existing conditions.

Fight bureaucracy and billing fraud. To control costs and trim the "paper hospital," my plan will replace expensive and complex financial forms and accounting procedures with a simplified, streamlined billing system. Everyone will carry "smart cards" coded with their personal medical information. We will also crack down on billing fraud and remove incentives that invite abuse.

Core benefits package. Every American will be guaranteed a basic health benefits package that includes ambulatory physician care, inpatient hospital care, prescription drugs, and basic mental health. The package will allow consumers to choose where to receive care and include expanded preventive treatments such as pre-natal care, mammograms and routine health screenings. We'll provide more services to the elderly and the disabled by expanding Medicare to include more long-term care.

Equitable costs. We will protect small businesses

through "community rating," which requires insurers to spread risk evenly among all companies.

A revolution in government.

We cannot put people first and create jobs an economic growth without a revolution in government. We must take away power from the entrenched bureaucracies and special interests that dominate Washington.

We can no longer afford to pay more — and get less from our government. The answer for every problem cannot always be another program or more money. It is time to radically change the way government operates — to shift from top-down bureaucracy to entrepreneurial government that empowers citizens and communities to change our country from the bottom up. We must reward the people and ideas that work and get rid of those that don't.

It's long past time to clean up Washington. The last twelve years were nothing less than an extended hunting season for high- priced lobbyists and Washington influence peddlers. On streets where statesmen once strolled, a never-ending stream of money now changes hands — tying the hands of those elected to lead.

Millions of hard-working Americans struggle to make ends meet while their government no longer fights for their values or their interests. Washington deregulated the Savings and Loan industry and then tried to hide when it collapsed, leaving taxpayers to foot the bill. Political action committees and other special interests funnel more than $2.5 million every week to Congress, giving incumbents a 12-1 financial advantage over challengers.

During the 1980s the White House staff routinely took

taxpayers for a ride to play golf or to bid on rare stamps. High-level executive branch employees traded in their government jobs for the chance to make millions lobbying their former bosses. Experts estimate that nearly one of every two senior American trade officials has signed on to work for nations they once faced across the negotiating table.

This betrayal of democracy must stop.

To break the stalemate in Washington, we have to attack the problem at its source: entrenched power and money. We must cut the bureaucracy, limit special interests, stop the revolving door, and cut off the unrestricted flow of campaign funds. The privilege of public service ought to be enough of a perk for people in government.

I will take the following steps:

Staff reductions. I will reduce the White House staff by 25 percent and challenge Congress to do the same.

Eliminate 100,000 unnecessary positions in the bureaucracy. I will cut 100,000 federal government positions through attrition.

Cuts in administrative waste. I will require federal managers and workers to achieve 3 percent across-the-board administrative savings in every federal agency.

Cut wasteful government spending programs. I will eliminate taxpayer subsidies for narrow special interests, reform defense procurement and foreign aid, and get rid of spending programs that no longer serve their purpose.

Line item veto. To eliminate pork-barrel projects and cut government waste, I will ask Congress to give me the line item veto.

Special interest tax. To help put government back in the hands of the people, I will ask Congress to eliminate the tax deductions for special-interest lobbying expenses. I will also urge Congress to close the "lawyers' loophole," which allows lawyer-lobbyists to disguise lobbying activities on behalf of foreign governments and powerful corporations.

Stop the revolving door. I will require all my top appointees to sign a pledge that, if they work in my Administration, they will refrain from lobbying government agencies within their responsibilities for five years after leaving office. I will require senior officials to pledge never to become registered agents on behalf of any foreign government.

I will then challenge members of Congress to do the same.

Lobbyists. I will push for and sign legislation to toughen and streamline lobbying disclosure. The new law will require all special interest groups to register with the Office of Government Ethics within 30 days after contacting a federal official, lawmaker or lawmaker's aide. Lobbyists will be required to report twice a year on their contacts and expenses. I will instruct the Justice Department to strictly enforce disclosure laws and collect fines.

Campaign finance reform. I will push for and sign

strong campaign finance legislation to cap spending on House and Senate campaigns: cut political action committee (PAC) contributions in any race to the individual legal limit of $1,000; lower the cost of air time so that television becomes an instrument of education, not a weapon of political assassination; and require lobbyists who appear before Congressional committees to disclose the campaign contributions they've made to committee members.

INVESTMENTS AND SAVINGS
(in billions of dollars)

New Investments

	1993	1994	1995	1996
Putting America to work	28.30	34.60	35.40	28.30
Rewarding work and families	3.50	5.50	6.50	3.50
Lifetime learning	10.10	14.25	17.27	10.10
Total	41.90	54.35	59.17	64.10

New Savings

	1993	1994	1995	1996
Spending Cuts	26.09	32.42	36.81	44.98
Entitlement Reform	0.60	1.00	1.00	1.80
Tax Fairness	19.80	22.70	23.90	25.30
Closing Corporate Loopholes	11.30	14.40	15.30	17.30
Total	57.79	70.52	77.01	89.38

BREAKDOWN OF SAVINGS
(in billions of dollars)

	1993	1994	1995	1996
Spending Cuts				
Defense cuts (beyond Bush)	2.0	8.5	10.5	16.5
Intelligence cuts	1.0	1.5	1.5	1.5
Administrative savings	2.0	5.0	6.5	8.5
100,000 federal workers	2.0	4.3	4.5	4.5
Cut White House staff by 25 per cent	0.01	0.01	0.01	0.01
Reform debt financing	0.0	2.0	2.0	2.0
Cut Congressional staff by 25 percent	0.1	0.1	0.1	0.1
Line-item veto to cut pork barrel projects	3.8	2.0	2.0	2.0
Reform defense Department procurement mgmt..	5.7	0.0	0.0	0.0
Reform Defense Department inventory system	2.3	2.5	2.5	2.5
Create comprehensive federal agency energy conservation programs	0.0	0.85	0.85	0.85
Reducing overhead on federally-sponsored university research	0.73	0.76	0.79	0.82
Streamline USDA field offices	0.035	0.075	0.13	0.14
Special purpose HUD grants	0.12	0.12	0.13	0.13
Index nuclear waste disposal fees for inflation	0.02	0.04	0.06	0.08

continued on next page

	1993	1994	1995	1996
Spending Cuts Cont'd.				
RTC Management Reform	2.0	8.5	10.5	16.5
End taxpayer subsidies for honey producers	1.0	1.5	1.5	1.5
Consolidate overseas broadcasting system	2.0	5.0	6.5	8.5
Freeze spending on federal consultants	2.0	4.3	4.5	4.5
Consolidate Social Service programs	0.01	0.01	0.01	0.01
Reform foreign aid pipeline	0.0	2.0	2.0	2.0
Total	26.09	32.42	36.81	44.98

Entitlement Reform

	1993	1994	1995	1996
Increase Medicare-B costs for those with incomes of more than $125,000	0.6	1.0	1.0	1.8

Tax Fairness

	1993	1994	1995	1996
Increase rates on top 2% raise AMT, surtax on millionaires	17.8	20.5	21.6	23.0
Prevent tax fraud on unearned income for the wealthy	2.0	2.2	2.3	2.3
Total	19.8	22.7	23.9	25.3

Closing Corporate Loopholes

Limit corporate deductions at $1 million for CEOs	0.1	0.4	0.4	0.4
End incentives for opening plants overseas	0.3	0.4	0.4	0.4
Prevent tax avoidance by foreign corporations	9.0	11.0	11.5	13.5
Increased fines and taxes for corporate polluters	1.8	2.5	2.9	2.9
Eliminate tax deduction for lobbying expenses	0.1	0.1	0.1	0.1
Total	11.3	14.4	15.3	17.3

TOTAL NEW SAVINGS

57.79 70.52 77.01 89.38

DEFICIT PROJECTIONS

(in billions of dollars)

	1993	1994	1995	1996
Current Deficit*	323.0	268.0	212.0	193.0
Clinton Plan moderate growth	295.7	243.0	174.0	141.0
Clinton Plan strong growth	282.6	207.0	125.5	75.8

*Based on Congressional Budget Office growth assumptions

In Their Own Words

Announcement of Candidacy for President
By Bill Clinton
Old State House, Little Rock, Arkansas,
October 3, 1991.

Thank you all for being here today, for your friendship
and support, for giving me the opportunity to serve as your
Governor for 11 years, for filling my life full of blessings
beyond anything I ever deserved.

I want to thank especially Hillary and Chelsea for
taking this big step in our life's journey together. Hillary,
for being my wife, my friend, and my partner in our efforts
to build a better future for the children and families of
Arkansas and America. Chelsea, in ways she is only now
coming to understand, has been our constant joy and re-
minder of what our public efforts are really all about: a
better life for all who will work for it, a better future for

the next generation.

All of you, in different ways, have brought me here today, to step beyond a life and a job I love, to make a commitment to a larger cause: preserving the America Dream...restoring the hopes of the forgotten middle class...reclaiming the future of our children.

I refuse to be a part of a generation that celebrates the death of communism abroad with the loss of the American Dream at home.

I refuse to be a part of a generation that fails to compete in the global economy and so condemns hard-working Americans to a life of struggle without reward or security.

That is why I stand here today, because I refuse to stand by and let our children become part of the first generation to do worse than their parents. I don't want my child or your child to be a part of a country that's coming apart instead of coming together

Over 25 years ago, I had a professor at Georgetown who taught me that America was the greatest country in history because our people believed in and acted on two simple ideas: first, that the future can be better than the present; and second, that each of us has a personal, moral responsibility to make it so.

That fundamental truth has guided my public career, and brings me here today. It is what we've devoted ourselves to here in Arkansas. I'm proud of what we've done here in Arkansas together. Proud of the work we've done to become a laboratory of democracy and innovation. And proud that we've done it without giving up the things we cherish and honor most about our way of life — solid, middle-class values of work, faith, family, individual responsibility and community.

As I've traveled across our state, I've found that everything we believe in, everything we've fought for, is threatened by an administration that refuses to take care of our own, has turned its back on the middle class, and is afraid to change while the world is changing.

The historic events in the Soviet Union in recent months teach us an important lesson: National security begins at home. For the Soviet Empire never lost to us on the field of battle. Their system rotted from the inside out, from economic, political and spiritual failure.

To be sure, the collapse of communism requires a new national security policy. I applaud the President's recent initiative in reducing nuclear weapons. It is an important beginning. But make no mistake — the end of the Cold War is not the end of threats to America. The world is still a dangerous and uncertain place. The first and most solemn obligation of the President is to keep America strong and safe from foreign dangers and promote democracy around the world.

But we cannot build a safe and secure world unless we can first make America strong at home. It is our ability to take care of our own at home that gives us the strength to stand up for what we believe around the world.

As Governor for 11 years, working to preserve and create jobs in a global economy, I know our competition for the future is Germany and the rest of Europe, Japan and the rest of Asia. And I know that we are losing America's leadership in the world because we're losing the American dream right here at home.

Middle class people are spending more hours on the job, spending less time with their children, bringing home a smaller paycheck to pay for more health care and housing and education. Our streets are meaner, our families are broken, our health care is the costliest in the world and we get less for it.

The country is headed in the wrong direction fast, slipping behind, losing our way...and all we have out of Washington is status quo paralysis. No vision, no action. Just neglect, selfishness and division.

For 12 years, Republicans have tried to divide us — race against race — so we get mad at each other and not at them. They want us to look at each other across a racial divide so we don't turn and look to the White House and ask, Why are all of our incomes going down? Why are all of us losing jobs? Why are we losing our future?

Where I come from we know about race-baiting. They've used it to divide us for years. I know this tactic well and I'm not going to let them get away with it.

For 12 years, Republicans have talked about choice without really believing in it. George Bush says he wants school choice even if it bankrupts the public schools, and yet he's more than willing to make it a crime for the women of America to exercise their individual right to choose.

For 12 years, the Republicans have been telling us that America's problems aren't their problems. They washed their hands of responsibility for the economy and education and health care and social policy and turned it over to fifty states and a thousand points of light. Well, here in Arkansas we've done our best to create jobs and educate our people. And each of us has tried to be one of those thousand points of light. But I can tell you, where in Arkansas we've done our best to create jobs and educate our people. And each of us has tried to be one of those thousand points of light. But I can tell you, where there is no national vision, no national partnership, no national leadership, a thousand points of light leaves a lot of darkness.

We must provide the answers, the solutions. And we

will. We're going to turn this country around and get it moving again, and we're going to fight for the hard-working middle-class families of America for a change.

Make no mistake. This election is about change: in our party, in our national leadership, and in our country.

And we're not going to get positive change just by Bush- bashing. We have to do a better job of the old-fashioned work of confronting the real problems of real people and pointing the way to a better future. That is our challenge in 1992.

Today, as we stand on the threshold of a new era, a new millennium, I believe we need a new kind of leadership, leadership committed to change. Leadership not mired in the politics of the past, not limited by old ideologies. Proven leadership that knows how to reinvent government to help solve the real problems of real people.

That is why today I am declaring my candidacy for President of the United States. Together I believe we can provide leadership that will restore the American Dream, that will fight for the forgotten middle class, that will provide more opportunity, insist on the more responsibility, and create a greater sense of community for this great country.

The change we must make isn't liberal or conservative. It's both, and it's different. The small towns and main streets of America aren't like the corridors and back rooms of Washington. People out here don't care about the idle rhetoric of "left" and "right" and "liberal" and "conservative" and all the other words that have made our politics a substitute for action. These families are crying out desperately for someone who believes the promise of America is to help them with their struggle to get ahead, to offer them a green light instead of a pink slip.

This must be a campaign of ideas, not slogans. We don't need another President who doesn't know what he wants to do for America. I'm going to tell you in plain language what I intend to do as President. How we can meet the challenges we face — that's the test for all the Democratic candidates in this campaign. Americans know what we're up against. Let's show them what we're for.

We need a New Covenant to rebuild America. It's just common sense. Government's responsibility is to create more opportunity. The people's responsibility is to make the most of it.

In a Clinton Administration, we are going to create opportunity for all. We've got to grow this economy, not shrink it. We need to give people incentives to make a long-term investment in America and reward people who produce goods and services, not those who speculate with other people's money. We've got to invest more money in emerging technologies to help keep high-paying jobs here at home. We've got to convert from a defense to a domestic economy.

We've got to expand world trade, tear down barriers, but demand fair trade policies if we're going to provide good jobs for our people. The American people don't want to run from the world. We must meet the competition and win.

Opportunity for all means world-class schools and world-class education. We need more than "photo ops" and empty rhetoric — we need standards and accountability and excellence in education. On this issue, I'm proud to say that Arkansas has led this way.

In a Clinton Administration, students are parents and teachers will get a *real* education President.

Opportunity for all means pre-school for every child

who needs it, and an apprenticeship program for kids who don't want to go to college but do want good jobs. It means teaching everybody with a job to read, and passing a domestic GI Bill that would give every young American the change to borrow the money necessary to go to college and ask them to pay it back either as a small percentage of their income over time or through national service as teachers or policemen or nurses or child care workers. In a Clinton Administration, everyone will be able to get a college loan as long as they're willing to give something back to their country in return.

Opportunity for all means reforming the health care system to control costs, improve quality, expand preventative and long- term care, maintain consumer choice, and cover everybody. And we don't have to bankrupt the taxpayers to do it. We have to take on the big insurance companies and health care bureaucracies and get some real cost control into the system. I pledge to the American people that in the first year of a Clinton Administration we will present a plan to Congress and the American people to provide affordable, quality health care for all Americans.

Opportunity for all means making our cities and our streets safe from crime and drugs. Across America, citizens are banding together to take their streets and neighborhoods back. In a Clinton Administration, we'll be on their side — with new initiatives like community policing, drug treatment for those who need it and boot camps for first-time offenders.

Opportunity for all means making taxes fair. I'm not out to soak the rich. I wouldn't mind being rich. But I do believe the rich should pay their fair share. For 12 years, the Republicans have raised taxes on the middle class. It's time to give the middle class tax relief.

Finally, opportunity for all means we must protect our environment and develop an energy policy that relies more on conservation and clean natural gas so all our children will inherit a world that is cleaner, safer, and more beautiful.

But hear me now. I honestly believe that if we try to do these things, we will still not solve the problems of today or move into the next century with confidence unless we do what President Kennedy did and ask every American citizen to assume personal responsibility for the future of our country.

The government owes our people more opportunity, but we all have to make the most of it through responsible citizenship.

We should insist that people move off welfare rolls and onto work rolls. We should give people on welfare the skills they need to succeed, but we should demand that everybody who can work go to work and become a productive member of society.

We should insist on the toughest possible child support enforcement. Governments don't raise children, parents do. And when they don't their children pay forever, and so do we.

And we have got to say, as we've tried to do in Arkansas, that students have a responsibility to stay in school. If you drop out for no good reason, you should lose your driver's license. But it's important to remember that the most irresponsible people of all in the 1980s were those at the top — not those who were doing worse, not the hard-working middle class, but those who sold out our savings and loans with bad deals and spent billions on wasteful takeovers and mergers, money that could have been spent to create better products and new jobs.

Do you know that in the 1980s, while middle-class income went down, charitable giving by working people went up? And while the rich people's incomes went up, charitable giving went down. Why? Because our leaders had an ethic of get it while you can and to heck with everybody else.

How can you ask people who work or who are poor to behave responsibly when they know that the heads of our biggest companies raised their own pay in the last decade by four times the percentage their workers' pay went up. When they ran their companies into the ground and their employees were on the street, what did they do? They bailed out with golden parachutes to a cushy life. That's just wrong.

Teddy Roosevelt and Harry Truman and John Kennedy didn't hesitate to use the bully pulpit of the Presidency. They changed America by standing up for what's right. When Salomon Brothers abused the treasury markets, the President was silent. When the rip-off artists looted our S&L's, the President was silent. In a Clinton Administration, when people sell their companies and their workers and their country down the river, they'll get called on the carpet. We're going to insist that they invest in this country and create jobs for our people.

In the 1980s, Washington failed us, too. We spent more money on the present and the past and less on the future. We spent $500 billion to recycle assets in the in the S&L mess, but we couldn't afford $5 billion for unemployed workers or to give every kid in this country the chance to be in Head Start. We can do better than that, and we will.

A Clinton Administration won't spend our money on programs that don't solve problems and a government that doesn't work. I want to reinvent government to make it more efficient and more effective. I want to give citizens more choices in the services they get, and empower them to make choices. That's what we've tried to do in Arkansas. We've balanced the budget every year and improved services. We've treated taxpayers like our customers and our bosses, because they are.

I want the American people to know that a Clinton Administration will defend our national interests abroad, put their values into our social policy at home, and spend their tax money with discipline. We'll put government back on the side of the hard-working middle-class families of America who think most of the help goes to those at the top of the ladder, some goes to the bottom, and no one speaks for them.

But we need more than new laws, new promises, or new programs. We need a new spirit of community, a sense that we are all in this together. If we have no sense of community, the American Dream will continue to wither. Our destiny is bound up with the destiny of every other American. We're all in this together, and we will rise or fall together.

A few years ago, Hillary and I visited a classroom in Los Angeles, in an area plagued by drugs and gangs. We talked to a dozen sixth-graders, whose number one concern was being shot going to and from school. Their second worry was turning 12 or 13 and being forced to join a gang or be beaten. And finally, they were worried about their own parents' drug abuse.

Nearly half a century ago, I was born not far from here, in Hope, Arkansas. My mother had been widowed three months before I was born. I was raised for four years by my grandparents, while she went back to nursing school. They didn't have much money. I spent a lot of time with my great-grandparents. By any standard, they were poor. But we didn't blame other people. We took responsibility for ourselves and for each other because we knew we could do better. I was raised to believe in the American Dream, in family values, in individual responsibility, and in the obligation of government to help people who were doing the best they could.

It's a long way in America from that loving family which is embodied today in a picture on my wall in the Governor's office of me at the age of six holding my great-grandmother's hand to an America where children on the streets of our cites don't know who their grandparents are and have to worry about their own parents' drug abuse.

I tell you, by making common cause with those children we give life to the American dream. And that is our generation's responsibility — to form a New Covenant ... more on opportunity for all, more responsibility from everyone, and a greater sense of common purpose.

I believe with all my heart that together we can make this happen. We can usher in a new era of progress, prosperity and renewal. We can. We must. This is not just a campaign for the presidency — it is a campaign for the future, for the forgotten hard-working middle class families of America who deserve a government that fights for them. A campaign to keep America strong at home and around the world. Join with us. I ask for your prayers, your help, your hands, and your hearts. Together we can make America great again, and build a community of hope that will inspire the world.

The New Covenant: Responsibility and
Rebuilding the American Community
Georgetown University, Washington, DC,
October 23, 1991.

Thank you all for being here today. You are living in
revolutionary times. When I was here, America sought to
contain Communism, not roll it back. Indeed, most respected academics held that once a country "went Communist," the loss of freedom was irreversible. Yet in the last
three years, we've seen the Berlin Wall come down, Germany reunified, all of Eastern Europe abandon Communism, the Soviet Coup fail and the Soviet Union itself
disintegrate, liberating the Baltics and other republics. The
Soviet Foreign Minister is trying to help our Secretary of
State make peace in the Middle East. And in the space of
one year, Lech Walesa and Vaclav Havel both came to this
city to thank America for supporting their work for freedom. Nelson Mandela walked out of a jail in South Africa
he entered before I entered Georgetown in 1964. He now
wants a Bill of Rights like our for his country.

We should be celebrating. All around the world, the
American Dream — political freedom, market economics,
national independence — is ascendant. Everything your
parents and grandparents stood for from World War II on
has been rewarded.

Yet we're not celebrating. Why? Because our people
fear that while the American Dream reigns supreme abroad,
it is dying at here at home. We're losing jobs and wasting
opportunities. The very fiber of our nation is breaking
down: Families are coming apart, kids are dropping our of

school, drugs and crime dominate our streets. And our leaders here in Washington are doing nothing to turn America around. Our political system rotates between being the butt of jokes and the object of scorn. Frustration produces calls for term limits from voters who think they can't vote incumbents out, resentment produces votes for David Duke — not just from racists, but from voters so desperate for change, they'll support the most anti-establishment message, even from ex-Klansman who was inspired by Adolf Hitler. We've got to rebuild our political life together before demagogues and racists and those who pander to the worst in us bring this country down.

People once looked to our President and Congress to bring us together, solve problems, and make progress. Now, in the face of massive challenges, our government stands discredited, our people disillusioned. There's a hole in our politics where a sense of common purpose used to be.

The Reagan-Bush years have exalted private gain over public obligations, special interests over common good, wealth and fame over work and family. The 1980s ushered in a gilded age of greed, selfishness, irresponsibility, excess, and neglect.

S&L crooks stole billions of dollars in other people's money. Pentagon contractors and HUD consultants stole from the taxpayers. Many big corporate executives raised their own salaries when their companies were losing money or their workers were losing their jobs. Deadbeat fathers were more likely to make their car payment than their child support. Some people stayed on welfare even though they could work.

And government, which should have been setting an example, was even worse. Congress raised its pay and guarded its perks while most Americans were working harder for less money. Two Republican Presidents elected on a promise of fiscal responsibility advanced budget policies that more than tripled the national debt. Congress went along with that, too. Taxes were lowered on the wealthiest people whose incomes rose, and raised on middle class people whose incomes fell.

And through it all, millions of decent, ordinary people who worked hard, played by the rules, and took responsibility for their own actions were falling behind, living a life of struggle without regard or security. For 12 years, the forgotten middle class watched their economic interests ignored and their values run into the ground. Responsibility went unrewarded and so did hard work. It's no wonder so many kids growing up on the street think it makes more sense to join a gang and deal drugs than to stay in school and go to work. The fast buck was glorified from Wall Street to Main Street to Mean Street.

To turn America around, we need a new approach founded on our most sacred principles as a nation, with a vision for the future. We need a New Covenant, a solemn agreement between the people and their government, to provide opportunity for everybody, inspire responsibility throughout our society, and restore a sense of community to this great nation. A New Covenant to take back to ordinary people.

More than two hundred years ago, the founding founders outlined our first social contract between government and the people, not just between lords and kings. More than a century ago, Abraham Lincoln gave his life to maintain the Union the contract created. Sixty years ago, Franklin Roosevelt renewed that promise with a New Deal that offered opportunity in return for hard work.

Today we need to forge a New Covenant that will repair the damaged bond between the people and their government and restore our basic values — the notion that our country has a responsibility to help people get ahead, that citizens have not only the right but a responsibility to rise as far and as high as their talents and determination can take them, and that we're all in this together. We must make good on the words of Thomas Jefferson, who said, "A debt of service is due from every man to his country proportional to the bounties which nature and fortune have measured him."

Make no mistake — this New Covenant means change — change in our party, change in our national leadership, and change in our country. Far away from Washington, in your hometown and mine, people have lost faith in the ability of government to change their lives for the better. Out there, you can hear he quiet, troubled voice of the forgotten middle class, lamenting that government no longer looks out for their interests or honors their values — like individual responsibility, hard work, family, community. They think their government takes more from them than it gives back, and looks the other way when special interests only take from this country and give nothing back. And they're right.

This New Covenant can't be between the politicians and the established interests. It can't be another back-room deal between the people in power and the people who keep them there. That's why the New Covenant for change must be ratified by the people in the 1992 election. And that's why I'm running for President.

Some may think it's old-fashioned, even naive, to talk about restoring the American Dream, through a covenant between the people and their government. But I believe with all my heart that a New Covenant is the only way we can hold this country together, and move boldly forward into the future.

Over 25 years ago, Professor Carroll Quigley taught in his Western Civilization class here at Georgetown that the defining idea of our culture in general and our country in particular is "future preference," the idea that the future can be better than the present, and that each of us has a personal, moral responsibility to make it so.

I hope they still teach that lesson here, and I hope you believe it, because I don't think we can save America without it.

In the weeks to come, I will outline my plans to rebuild our economy, regain our competitive leadership in the world, restore the forgotten middle class, and reclaim the future for the next generation. I will put forth my views on how to promote our national security and foreign policy interests after the Cold War. And I will tell you what the President and the Congress owe the people in this New Covenant for change.

But there will never be a government program for every problem. Much of what holds us together and moves us ahead is the daily assumption of personal responsibility by millions of Americans from all walks of life. I can promise to do a hundred different things for you as President. But none of them will make any difference unless we all do more as citizens. And, today, I want to talk about the responsibilities we owe to ourselves, to one another, and to our nation.

It's been 30 years since a Democrat ran for President and asked something of all the American people. I intend to challenge you to do more and to do better.

We must go beyond the competing ideas of the old

political establishment: beyond every man for himself on the one hand and the right to something for nothing on the other.

We need a New Covenant that will challenge all our citizens to be responsible. The New Covenant will say to our corporate leaders at the top of the ladder: We'll promote economic growth and the free market, but we're not going to let you erect special privileges. We'll support your efforts to increase profits and jobs through quality products and services, but we're going to hold you responsible to be good corporate citizens, too.

The New Covenant will say to people on welfare: We're going to provide the training and education and health care you need, but if you can work, you've got to go to work, because you can no longer stay on welfare forever.

The New Covenant will say to the hard-working middle class and those who aspire to it: We're going to guarantee you access to a college education, but if you get that help, you've got to give something back to your country.

And the New Covenant will challenge all of us in public service: We have a solemn responsibility to honor the values and promote the interests of the people who elected us, and if we don't, then we don't belong in government anymore.

The New Covenant must begin here in Washington. I want to revolutionize government and fundamentally change its relationship to people. People don't want some top-down bureaucracy telling them that to do anymore. That's one reason they tore down the Berlin Wall and threw out the Communist regimes in Eastern Europe and Russia.

Now, the New Covenant will challenge our government to change its way of doing business, too. The American people need a government that works at a price they can afford. The Republicans have been in charge of the government for 12 years. They've brought the country to the brink of bankruptcy. Democrats who want the government to do more — and I'm one of them — have a heavy responsibility to show that we're going to spend the taxpayer's money wisely and with discipline.

I want to make government more efficient and more effective by eliminating unnecessary layers of bureaucracy and cutting administrative costs, and by giving people more choices in the services they get, and empowering them to make those choices. That's what we've tried to do in Arkansas — balancing our budget every year, improving services and treating taxpayers like our customers and our bosses, giving them more choices in public schools, child care centers, and services for the elderly.

The New Covenant must challenge Congress to act responsibly. And here again, Democrats must lead to way. Because they want to use government to help people, Democrats have to put Congress in order. Congress should live by the laws it applies to other work places. No more midnight pay raises. Congressional pay shouldn't go up while the pay of working Americans is going down. Let's clamp down on campaign spending and open the airwaves to encourage real political debate instead of paid political assassination. No more bounced checks. No more bad restaurant debts. No more fixed tickets. Service in Congress is privilege enough.

We can't go on like this. We have to honor, reward and reflect the work ethic, not the power grab. Responsibility is for everybody, and it begins here in the nation's capital.

The New Covenant will also challenge the private sector. The most irresponsible people in the 1980s were those in business who abused their position at the top of the totem pole. This is my message to the business community: As President I'm going to do everything I can to make it easier for your company to compete in the world, with a better trained work force, cooperation between labor and management, fair and strong trade policies, and incentives to invest in American economic growth. But I want the jet-setters and the "feather-bedders" of corporate America to know that if you sell your companies and your workers and your country down the river, you'll get called on the carpet. That's what the President's bully pulpit is for. It's simply not enough to obey the letter of the law and make as much money as you can. It's wrong for executives to raise their pay by four times the percentage their workers' pay goes up and three times the percentage their profits go up — and that's exactly what they did. It's wrong to drive a company into the ground and bail out with a golden parachute to a cushy life.

The average CEO at a major American corporation is paid about 100 times as much as the average worker — compare that to a ratio of 23 to 1 in Germany and only 17 to 1 in Japan. And our government today rewards that excess with a tax break for executive pay, no matter how high it is. That's wrong. If a company want to overpay its executives and under invest in the future, it shouldn't get any special treatment from Uncle Sam. There should be no more deductibility for irresponsibility.

The New Covenant will also challenge the hard-working middle-class families of America. Their challenge centers around work and education. I know Americans worry about the quality of education in this country and want the best for their children. The Clinton administration will set high school national standards based on international competition for what everybody ought to know, and a national examination system to measure whether they're learning it. It's not enough to put money into schools. We need to challenge the work-place between management and workers, and a continuing effort to move toward high-performance work organizations.

There's a special challenge in the New Covenant for the young men and women who live in America's most troubled urban neighborhoods, the children like those I met in Chicago and Los Angeles who live in fear of being forced to join a gang or getting shot going to and from school.

Many of these young people believe this country has ignored them for too long, and they're right. Many of them think America unfairly blames them for every wrong in our society — for drugs, crime, poverty, the breakup of the family and the breakdown of the schools — and they're right. They worry that because their face is of a different color, their only choice in life is jail or welfare or a dead-end job, that being a minority in an inner city is a guarantee of failure. But they're wrong — and when I'm President, I'm going to do my best to prove they're wrong.

I know these young people can overcome anything they set their mind to. I believe America needs their strength, their intelligence, and their humanity. And because I believe in them and what they can contribute to our society, they must not be let off the hook. All society can offer them is a chance to develop their God-given abilities. They have to do the rest. Anybody who tells them otherwise is lying — and they know it.

As President, I'll see that they get the same deal as everyone else: they've got to play by the rules, stay off drugs, stay in school and keep out of the street.

There's a special challenge in the New Covenant for the

young men and women who live in America's most troubled urban neighborhoods, the children like those I met in Chicago and Los Angeles who live in fear of being forced to join a gang or getting shot going to and from school.

Many of these young people believe this country has ignored them for too long, and they're right. Many of them think America unfairly blames them for every wrong in our society — for drugs, crime, poverty, the breakup of the family and the breakdown of the schools — and they're right. They worry that because their face is of a different color, their only choice in life is jail or welfare or a dead-end job, that being a minority in an inner city is a guarantee of failure. But they're wrong — and when I'm President, I'm going to do my best to prove they're wrong.

I know these young people can overcome anything they set their mind to. I believe America needs their strength, their intelligence, and their humanity. And because I believe in them and what they can contribute to our society, they must not be let off the hook. All society can offer them is a chance to develop their God-given abilities. They have to do the rest. Anybody who tells them otherwise is lying — and they know it.

As President, I'll see that they get the same deal as everyone else: they've got to play by the rules, stay off drugs, stay in school and keep out of the streets. They've got to stop having children if they're not prepared to support them. Governments don't raise children. People do.

And for those young people who do get into trouble, we'll give them one chance to avoid prison, by setting up community boot camps for first-time non-violent offenders — where they can learn discipline, get drug treatment if necessary, continue their education, and do useful work for their community. A second chance to be a first-rate citizen.

The New Covenant must be pro-work. That means people who work shouldn't be poor. In a Clinton Administration, we'll do everything we can to break the cycle of dependency and help the poor climb out of poverty. First, we need to make work pay by expanding the Earned Income Tax Credit for the working poor, creating savings accounts that make it easier for poor people even on welfare to save, and supporting micro-enterprise grants for those who want to start a small business. At the same time, we need to assure all Americans that they'll have access to health care when they go to work.

The New Covenant can break the cycle of welfare. Welfare should be a second chance, not a way of life. In a Clinton Administration, We're going to put an end to welfare as we know it. I want to erase the stigma of welfare for good by restoring a simple, dignified principle: no one who can work can stay on welfare forever.

We'll still help people who can't help themselves, and those who need education and training and child care. But if people can work, they'll have to do so. We'll give them all the help they need for up to two years. But after that, if they're able to work, they'll have to take a job in the private sector, or start earning their way through community service. That way, we'll restore the covenant that welfare was first meant to be: to give temporary help to people who've fallen on hard times.

If the New Covenant is pro-work, it must also be pro-family. That means we must demand the toughest possible child support enforcement authority, and find new ways of catching deadbeats. In Arkansas, we passed a law this year that says if you owe more than a thousand dollars in child support, we're going to report you to every credit agency in the state. People shouldn't be able to borrow money before they take care of their children.

Finally, the President has the greatest responsibility of all — to bring us together, not to drive us apart. For 12 years, this President and his predecessor have divided us against each other — pitting rich against poor, black against white, women against men — creating a country where we no longer recognize that we're all in this together. They have profited by fostering an atmosphere of blame and denial instead of building an ethic of responsibility. They had a chance to bring out the best in us and instead they appealed to the worst in us.

I pledge to you that I'm not going to let the Republicans get away with this cynical scam anymore. A New Covenant means it's my responsibility and the responsibility of every American in this country to fight back against the politics of division and bring this country together.

After all, that is what's special about America. We want to be a part of a nation that's coming together, not coming apart. We want to be part of a nation that brings out the best in us not the worst. And we believe that the only limit to what we can do is what our leaders are willing to ask of us and what we are willing to expect of ourselves.

Nearly sixty years ago, in a famous speech to the Commonwealth Club in the final month of his 1932 campaign, Franklin Roosevelt outlined a new compact that gave hope to a nation mired in the Great Depression. The role of government, he said, was to promise every American the right to make a living. The people's role was to do their best to make the most of it. He said: "Faith in America demands that we recognize the new terms of the old social contract. In the strength of great hope we must all shoulder our common load."

That's what our hope is today: A New Covenant to
shoulder our common load. When people assume responsibility and shoulder that common load, they acquire a
dignity they never knew before. When people go to work,
they rediscover a pride that was lost. When fathers pay
their child support, they restore a connection they and their
children need. When students work harder, they find out
they all can learn and do as well as anyone else on Earth.
When corporate managers put their workers and their long-
term profits ahead of their own paychecks, their companies
do well, and so do they. When the privilege of serving is
enough of a perk for the people in Congress, and the
President finally assumes responsibility for America's problems, we'll not only stop doing wrong, we'll begin to do
what is right to move America forward.

And that is what this election is really all about —
forging a New Covenant of change that will honor middle-
class values, restore the public trust, create a new sense of
community, and make America work again. Thank you.

A New Covenant for the Environment
Drexel University, Philadelphia, Pennsylvania,
Earth Day, April 22, 1992.

Twenty-two years ago today, thousands of Americans
marched and met and spoke out across the country to raise
a new concern onto our nation's agenda: the protection of
America's environment. The first Earth Day in 1970 awak-
ened our nation to the ticking of a different kind of biologi-
cal clock — a clock that measured the careless degradation
of America's air, water, land and natural resources.

Many of you were not even born yet. And it's only

worth recalling the whirlwind of change and progress that followed that day. Within two years, our nation created the Environmental Protection Agency, passed the Clean Air, Clean Water, and Endangered Species Acts, and banned DDT. For my generation, it was a heady, hopeful experience.

Two decades later, all those efforts seem dwarfed by the enormity of old and new threats to our communities, our resources, and our planet.

We restricted open dumping into our rivers, but now we see used hypodermic needles washing up on our beaches.

We banished lead from our gas tanks, but still find it concentrated where children of our cities live and play.

We pinpointed the nation's toxic waste dumps, but have only cleaned up a handful.

We confronted the acid raid killing our trees, but not the rush of development that is wiping our woodlands at home and rain forests abroad.

We stopped building nuclear power plants, but now see our addiction to fossil fuels wrapping the earth in a deadly shroud of greenhouse gasses.

We opened our eyes to the treats posed by oil-soaked beaches, smoggy skies, and burning rivers; yet we still struggle to comprehend less apparent dangers, such as an invisible hole in a distant ozone layer that allows unseen rays to plant the microscopic seeds of cancer.

The question that falls to your generation is this: will the march that began 22 years ago move forward, or will we stand in place?

Over the past generation, much has changed our thinking. Children now teach their parents to sort their garbage. Colleges like Drexel train young people in environmental engineering. A Big Mac at McDonald's comes in a recyclable cardboard container in a recycled paper bag.

Yet while the thinking of most Americans has changed, the thinking of our recent leaders has not. For more than a decade, we've had no national energy strategy, no environmental strategy, no economic strategy to capture the markets of the future with new technologies that are energy-efficient and environmentally sound.

Within the past decade, climate change, ozone depletion, and other global environmental problems have emerged as threats to our very survival. Dependence on foreign oil has been the cornerstone of our energy policy, and oil imports now make up half of our trade imbalance. The collapse of Communism and the end of the Cold War have created new markets and a new urgency for environmental cleanup. We have an unprecedented opportunity to protect the earth and make our economy grow.

Too often, on the environment as on so many issues, the Bush Administration has been reactive, rudderless, and expedient. Under George Bush and Ronald Reagan, presidential leadership on the environment has become an endangered species.

George Bush promised to be the Environmental President, but a photo op at the Grand Canyon is about all we have to show for it.

He made Boston Harbor a prop in his negative campaign in 1988, but for years later has done precious little to help clean it up.

He promised "no net loss" of America's precious woodlands, then tried to hand half of them over to developers.

He invoked Teddy Roosevelt's devotion to preserving our natural heritage, then called for opening the Arctic wilderness to oil drilling.

He talked about the need for an energy policy, then

went to Detroit on the eve of the Michigan primary to promise American auto makers that he wouldn't raise fuel efficiency standards for American cars.

He called for an international summit on the environment but now is single-handedly blocking an historic meeting in Rio de Janeiro of a hundred nations to control global warming.

And just yesterday, I read in the paper that he wants to make another attack ad, this time about problems along the White River in Arkansas. We're fighting the battle to clean up the White River, and I welcome the President's attention.

So, Mr. President, when you return from Rio, I hope you'll visit Northwest Arkansas and the White River. I'll show you what the problems are and what progress we've made. I'll show you the rivers you can fish in, and streams kids can swim in.

And if you really want to clean up the problem, I'll make an agreement with you. We'll outline federal and state responsibilities — and we'll get results. Our people are tired of the politics of blame. But this is no Boston Harbor. If you want to place blame, you'll have to shoulder some.

Let me be clear. I don't believe President Bush is bent on destroying the environment. But his views were shaped in another era, when the world faced other threats, and economic growth and environmental protection were seen as mutually exclusive.

I've spent the last decade as Governor of a poor state, fighting to keep jobs and make up for lost time. I know how much our people are hurting after the longest recession and slowest economic growth in the last 50 years.

In the '80s, I also faced the old short-term trade-offs between jobs and the environment, made tougher by cutbacks in federal aid and the lack of clear policies in some areas which allowed states to be played off against one another. In this context, I've had the choice for jobs in a poor state without enough jobs for federal help for environmental protection and cleanup.

But over the years, I've learned something that George Bush and his advisors still don't understand, to reject the false choice between economic growth and environmental protection. Today, you can't have a healthy economy without a healthy environment, and you don't have to sacrifice environmental protection to get economic growth.

Our competitors know you can't have one without the other. One of the reasons German workers make 25% more than the average American worker is that their economy uses half the energy to produce the same amount of goods. Japanese companies enjoy a 5% competitive advantage in the global marketplace because of higher energy efficiency. Our competitors are rushing to develop new environmental technologies that will enable them to capture the markets of the future. Only the United States is heading toward the 21st Century without a long-term strategy to achieve sustainable economic growth.

The Bush Administration doesn't understand that perpetuating the false choice between environmental protection and economic growth is bad for the environment and bad for the economy. Our lakes will be dirtier and our air will be more dangerous because George Bush put Dan Quayle in charge of the Competitiveness Council, a group which lets major polluters in through the back door at the White House to kill environmental regulations they don't like. And the most disturbing thing is, they call it competitiveness.

Over the long run, the Bush Administrations isn't doing

American business any favors by pretending that energy efficiency and improved environmental protection are at odds with economic growth. If we're going to compete and win in the world economy, if we want to improve our quality of life as well as our standard of living, we need to learn to use environmental protection as a tool for economic growth.

That is what I've tried to do in Arkansas. As Governor, I've worked hard to pursue both environmental quality and economic growth, In my first term, I took on one of my state's strongest special interests when I tried to focus our utilities more on conservation than construction of new power plants. Today that approach is called "least cost planning," and nearly half the state use it to conserve resources and save rate payers money. Back then, the name didn't exist and the utilities fought it tooth and nail. By the end of the'80s they had come around, and Arkansas consumers and businesses will save lots of money in the future.

We did other things too. We set up one of the nation's first state-level paper recycling programs, helped establish nearly 40 new wildlife preserves and parks to protect our rivers, forests, woodlands, and prairies, and created a new statewide reforestation program that has planted 25 million trees in the last two years. We've provided Arkansas business a 30% tax credit for installing waste reduction and recycling facilities — a measure that is protecting Arkansas's environment and creating Arkansas jobs.

There was a time in this country when environmental protection was viewed as best a necessary burden for industry to bear. Today that idea just isn't true. Technology has changed; the stakes have changed; and it's time for our thinking to change, too. In today's economy, there doesn't have to be a trade-off between growth and environmental protection. We now have the tools and the need to choose both.

What we need today is a New Covenant for Environmental Progress. That covenant is built on a renewed commitment to leave our children a better nation — a nation whose air, water, and land are unspoiled; whose natural beauty is undimmed; and whose leadership for sustainable global growth is unsurpassed. This New Covenant will challenge Americans and demand responsibility at every level — from individuals, families, communities, corporations, and government agencies — to do more to preserve the quality of our environment and our world.

A New Covenant for environmental progress will have three priorities: exerting new American leadership to protect the global environment; preserving the quality of our environment here at home; and finding ways to promote innovation and growth consistent with firm environmental goals.

The first part of a New Covenant for environmental progress must be for the U.S. to exert international leadership for the health of the planet. The Cold War is over, and we have entered a new era in which treats to our security are less evident, but no less dangerous, than before. As Senator Gore has dramatized in his recent book, *Earth in the Balance*, if we do not find the vision and leadership to defeat the unprecedented new threats of global climate change, ozone depletion, and unsustainable population growth, then those threats may defeat us instead.

This June, the nation of the world will meet in Rio to negotiate reduction in their output of carbon dioxide and other greenhouse gasses; to end the destruction of the ozone layer; and to find rules for sustainable development to ensure that our species does not outlive its welcome on this planet. Nearly a hundred heads state have firmly committed to attend. But, yesterday the President said he can't decide whether or not to go.

We've seen eight of the hottest years in history in the last decade. The world's rain forests are disappearing at the rate of one football field a minute. An ozone hole is growing over Kennebunkport. And the leaders of nearly every nation on earth are waiting while the President of the United States makes up his mind whether to act.

I say this is one foreign trip George Bush can't afford to miss.

If the President does decide to go, simply showing up in Rio is not enough. Unless he makes the U.S. a leader against global warming and removes the obstacles he has thrown in the way of a climate change treaty, nothing will come of the Rio meeting. President Bush should commit the U.S. to limit U.S. carbon dioxide emissions to 1990 level by the year 2000; and to join new efforts to protect the planet's biodiversity and preserve its forest. As Senator Gore says, this is now the most important global environmental challenge.

In a Clinton Administration, the U.S. will take the lead in promoting sustainable development. We'll call on major banks and multilateral institutions like he IMF and the World Bank to negotiate debt-for-nature swaps that allow developing nations to reduce their crippling international debt burden by setting aside precious lands. We should explore establishing the international equivalent of the Nature Conservancy, a fund contributed to by developed nations and pharmaceutical companies to purchase easements in the rain forests for medical research. These easements and the profits for new drugs could make not developing the forests more profitable than tearing them down.

We can also lead the quest for sustainable development by supporting efforts to stem global population growth. As

Al Gore has noted, it took mankind 10,000 generations to reach a population of 2 billion. Yet we will likely see that number triple in my lifetime. The earth's resources and delicate eco-systems are straining and breaking under this unsustainable burden. President Bush was once a strong supporter of efforts to limit global population growth, and it is shameful that he blocked our contributions to those efforts to appease the anti- choice wing of his party. A Clinton Administration will restore U.S. foreign aid to support Planned Parenthood.

But we cannot lead the fight for environmental progress abroad unless we do more here at home. The U.S. constitutes just five percent of the world's population, yet we consume over a quarter of its oil. We need to reduce our oil consumption and increase our energy efficiency dramatically if we are to lead the fight against global warming, sharpen our competitive edge in trade, and reduce our vulnerability to cutoffs in the availability of foreign oil.

For the past 11 years, we have had no national energy policy. In a Clinton Administration, we'll have an energy policy the day I take office:

— We'll accelerate our progress toward more fuel-efficient cars, and seek to raise the average goal for auto makers to 45 miles per gallon.

— We'll increase our reliance on natural gas, which is inexpensive, clean-burning and abundant, and can reduce our carbon dioxide emissions. I'll start with an executive order to purchase natural gas powered vehicles for the federal fleet, following the lead of Gov. Ann Richard in Texas.

— We'll push for revenue-neutral incentives that reward conservation and make polluters and energy-wasters pay. California, for example, has proposed giving purchasers of fuel- efficient cars rebates paid for by a special fee on those who buy gas-guzzlers.

— We'll invest more in the development of renewable energy sources. Federal funding for renewables has dropped from $850 million to $144 million in the last decade. There's no reason why 60 percent of the Department of Energy's money should still be going to nuclear weapons, with nuclear power and fossil fuels getting most of the rest. We'll encourage the use of new energy sources like wind and solar, and new ways to get better results out of the sources we already have. In a Clinton Administration, we will designate as wilderness the Arctic National Wildlife Refuge and stop the crusade for new drilling off our costs.

— As part of an effort to convert come of our Cold War military spending to civilian purposes, we'll use research and development funds to develop light rail, which can speed travel, save fuel, and provide transportation for people less able to afford it.

—Finally, we'll make energy conservation and efficiency central goals in every field of policy — in designing our offices, planning our communities, designing our transportation systems and regulating our utilities. My goal is to improve America's overall energy efficiency by 20 percent by the year 2000.

We also need a policy to prevent pollution. Since 1970,

we've made great strides in controlling pollution "at the pipe" -- regulating how much could be dumped and where. Now we need to expand our efforts earlier in the process and move from control to prevention.

One of the most urgent challenges is to reduce the amount of solid waste we generate. A Clinton Administration will find new ways to prevent pollution in the first place:

— We'll create a system of tradeable credits that will reward companies that recover a greater portion of their waste and penalize those that don't.

— We'll create incentives for firms and government to recycle and use federal purchasing power to create markets in recycled materials.

— We'll pass a national bottle bill to encourage recycling by creating small deposits on all glass and plastic bottles.

To improve the quality of our water, we need to turn greater attention to the polluting effect of water running off our agricultural fields, icy streets, and suburban developments. We need a new Clean Water Act with standards for non-point-source pollution and incentives that will unleash the creative and technological potential of our firms, farmers, and families to reduce and prevent polluted run-off at the source.

We also need to strengthen our efforts on toxic wastes. The Super Fund program has been disastrously mismanaged. We've spent $13 billion to clean up only 80 of the 1200 deadliest dump sights — with much of the money squandered on legal fees and cost overruns to contractors who bought Rolex watches and art for their walls.

The Super Fund program was a historic breakthrough in 1980. In my first term, Arkansas was the first state in the country to have an EPA-approved hazardous waste management program. Super Fund enabled us to contain the most immediate risks, and provided a powerful deterrent against toxic dumping. Now those of us who care are about the environment must take the lead to explore every possible improvement that might get more sites cleaned up sooner for less, without letting responsible parties off the hook.

We also need to improve America's resources by preserving our natural heritage for future generations. As President, I will protect our old growth forests and other vital habitats, and make the "no net loss" promise on woodlands a reality. I'll rededicate the agencies that manage our national parks and wilderness lands to a true conservation ethic. And I'll expand our efforts to acquire new parklands and recreational sites with the funds already available under the federal Land and Water Conservation Fund. Every year, millions of American families vacation in national parks, from Yosemite to Yellowstone. They deserve an administration that cares about America' parks as much as they do.

All of our efforts to improve the nation's resources ultimately depend on enforcement and public awareness. In a Clinton Administration, we'll stop shortchanging EPA's enforcement efforts, and ensure that we hold companies and polluters responsible for their behavior. When corporate executives deliberately violate environmental laws, they must pay the price.

The third priority I want to speak about today is he need to bring powerful market forces to bear on America's pollution problems. Many of our environmental efforts in the past were based on a "command and control" approach to regulation that told firms how much pollution to produce and what kinds of technology to use. While that approach produced important successes, it sometimes stifled innovation by locking firms into a specific kind of equipment, and increased regulatory cost and burdens by taking such a detailed and inflexible approach.

I believe it is time for a new era in environmental protection which uses the market to help us get our environment back on track — to recognize that Adam Smith's invisible hand can have a green thumb. While we need to maintain tough guidelines and goals for reducing pollution, charging companies for their pollution would give them daily incentives to find progressively cleaner technologies and manufacturing processes. In certain settings, this results-oriented approach can cut compliance costs, shrink regulatory bureaucracies, enlist corporate support, take environmental policy away from the specialists and lobbyists, and open it up more to the general public.

But freeing up our companies to find cost-effective pollution control methods is not the only step we need to take. It is time we recognized that environmental sectors of the 21st Century. The market for environmental technology and services is already around $200 billion a year, and developing nations will need to install a trillion dollars' worth of energy technology over the next 15 years.

Unfortunately, we're losing that battle. In 1980, the U.S. had three quarters of the world sales of solar technology. By 1990, German and Japanese competition had cut our share to 30 percent. We need to recognize that the nation that pioneered the environmental movement will be the world's foremost producer and exporter of environmental technology and services.

As I have travelled across his country campaigning for President, I have been struck by the yearning I see among Americans of all backgrounds, incomes, and colors to be united again in common purpose. If there is one thing that has united Americans across dozens of generations, it is the feeling we have for this rich and expansive land. Our forebears were passionate about it. They were farmers and pioneers, who made these two billion acres we call America the canvas of their dreams.

That stubborn, protective love of the land, which flows like a mighty underground current through our national character, is what burst to the surface of American life on April 22, 1970. And it was the will-spring for one of the most important marches for progress we have known in our time.

For over a decade, that progress has been arrested. And for too many of those years, we have walked backwards. Too many times we told that trees cause pollution and that sunglasses are the best answer to the ozone problem. And far too many times we were divided against ourselves, falsely told to choose between our quality of life and our standard of living. I believe now it is time to move past the false choices, unite our nation again, and resume our progress for the land we cherish, the values we share, and the only earth we have.

A generation ago, conservationist Aldo Leopold wrote that, "History consists of successive excursions from a single starting point, to which man returns again and again to organize yet another search for a durable set of values." One of the starting points for America will always be our devotion to our natural heritage. And today I ask you to join me in beginning an excursion from that starting point anew. Thank you.

On to the White House: Election Night Victory Speech
Los Angeles, California, June 2, 1992.

Thank you very much. Thank you. Thank you so much. On behalf of Hillary and on my own behalf, I want to begin by thanking the millions and millions of people who voted for this campaign and its promise of change all across this country.

I want to thank the people who volunteered literally millions of hours of their time to make this campaign work. I want to thank the friends of my lifetime who stood by me, the people who worked on our campaign across the nation and back home. And I want to say a special word of thanks to those who worked in my administration who kept our government going and working hard and made it possible for me to make this campaign.

All of you tonight, this is your victory. It is not mine, and I hope you're proud of it.

When I got into this race, the President was at an historically high point in popularity and most people did not think there would be much of a race this year. But I was convinced then and I am convinced now that this country needs profound change.

For too long Washington has rigged our system for the benefit of the few, the quick buck, the gimmick, and the short run. For the first time since the twenties, one percent of the American people control more wealth than the bottom ninety percent.

For this we were promised jobs, but instead we got pink slips and insecurity, worries about health care and education and safe streets. We have tried it that way and now we have to change. I am tired of seeing the people who work hard and play by the rules get the shaft.

And tonight, with this delegate count, we want to put the forces of the status quo and short term greed on notice: the party is over, we are in for a change, we want our country back.

It's time to invest in this country again, reward those who play by the rules, punish those who don't and get on in to the future that the people in this country deserve. It is time to make sure that everybody knows, as great as I am for what has happened, that this campaign is not about delegate count, it is about making people count.

Tonight, I can't help thinking back over these last several months and all of the brave Americans I have met along the way. The people with whom I started in New Hampshire, Ron Macos Jr., who couldn't get a job with health insurance because he had a two year-old child who had open heart surgery. He played by the rules and was going to be punished because he lives in the only advanced nation where the government stubbornly refuses to control health care costs and provide affordable health care to all Americans. We are going to change that.

Tonight, I think of that wonderful immigrant father, I met in New York, who grabbed me as I was walking toward a speech and said, "Governor, my ten year-old studies politic in school, and he said, you should be President, so I am going to vote for you," but he said, "I came here because America is the land of the free. But my boy is not free, he can't even walk to school unless I go with him. If you become President, make my boy free."

I'll tell you one thing, if this government helps cities put more police of the street in community policing, provided boot camps for first-time offenders, and passed the

Brady Bill, that boy would be freer — and I intend to do that.

I think about the women that I met — the working mother in Livingston, New Jersey, in Sacramento, California, — who worry about how they can balance the demands of motherhood and work, how they can do right by their children.

Well, I'll tell you one thing, if we had a President who would sign instead of veto the Family and Medical Leave Act, they'd be better off. And I am going to give that to them.

I think about that wonderful couple, Marie Annie and Edward Davis, I met and broke down and cried as I hugged them, telling me that every week they were choosing between food and medicine because they live in the only advanced nation that doesn't have health care including a decent long-term health system. And I'm going to give it to them if you will help me be President of the United States of America.

For twelve years, Americans have tried to do the right things and they deserve a government that will do right by them. Doing right by our people means rebuilding our economy by investing in their jobs, their education, in their health care. It means honoring work and demanding responsibility.

At the end of World War II, this great nation of ours did a wonderful job rebuilding Europe and Japan. It's time at the end of the Cold War for us to rebuild America. That's where our work is today.

To do that, rebuilding America begins with a commitment to educate and train all of our people. It's the best investment we will ever make, and to do it, we need a real education President — someone who has paid the price and done the work.

I have heard all of the talk about what a wonderful program Head Start is. It's time we had a President who would fund it so the children in this country had their parents would know how wonderful it is.

And there needs to be something for these young people on the other end of school too. For those who don't choose to go to college but don't want to be in dead-end jobs, we should join the ranks of advanced nations and provide a two-year apprenticeship program to every non-college bound student so they can get those good jobs and we can restore the dignity to the blue collar work in this country.

Finally, I want to make it possible for every young American and every not so young American who wants to go to college to borrow the money to do it. We must end the attempt to make it impossible for people to go to college and provide the funds necessary for any American to go.

At the end of World War II, we rebuild our country in large measure because we provided, through the GI Bill, the opportunity for any soldier who wanted to go to college.

When John Kennedy was President, we helped rebuild a lot of the rest of the world through the Peace Corp. I propose to take the best of both ideas. Let anybody borrow the money to go to college and let them pay it back by giving a couple of years of service to our nation here at home to rebuild America as teachers, or police officers, or nurses.

Investing in our people means also having the courage to take on the insurance companies and the health care bureaucracies and the government and providing affordable health care to all Americans.

Tonight, even as we celebrate, there are thousands of

318

people all across American lying awake wondering whether they are going to lose their jobs or their health insurance or whether the next illness will bankrupt them. That's because we have stubbornly refused to do what the competition does. Vote for me and together we'll provide affordable health care to the people of this country.

Investing in America also means creating jobs for the people who are educated and healthy to do. Every last dollar by which we reduce defense must be reinvested in America to build an economy for the 21st century — every dollar — for high-speed rail, for short haul aircraft, for fiber optics communication, for modern environmental systems, to clean up our water and to recycle our solid waste.

We can have growth and environmental protection if, but only if, we are committed to reinvesting in this country. That's the way we are going to create jobs and we are going to do it by investing in America for a change.

Finally, if we want these changes, we are going to have to insist that all of our citizens accept the challenge to do their part and to be more responsible. There are millions of good people in business in this country today making the free enterprise system go. But our tax system does not reward them.

It does not reward investment in a new plant and equipment. Instead, it rewards unlimited executive compensation — even for companies that are losing money. It rewards moving plants overseas instead of moving plants here at home with new plant and investment .

And I tell you, we need a new responsibility ethic in our tax system — more incentives to invest in America, no incentives for executive compensation that is excessive or moving our plants overseas.

We also need a new family policy in this country — more incentives for child care and maternal and health care for the kids. We need family leave. But, we need the toughest possible child support enforcement. I am tired of people running off and leaving their children for the government to raise, and we can stop it.

We need a new policy toward the poor. We need to lift those who work 40 hours a week and have children at home above the poverty line. We need to say to those on welfare as we know it, we will invest more in your education and training and support for your children. But then you must work. We have got to end the system as we know it.

My fellow Americans, change is never easy, but I have worked hard for more than a decade to make change and I have learned a few things about it. You have to be willing to take on organized groups and fight for change even if they are against you. You have to be willing to pay the price of time and you have to know, that in the end, words have to give way to deeds.

Commencement Address (Hillary Clinton) Wellesley College, Wellesley, Massachusetts, June, 1992

President Keohane, trustees, faculty, students, parents, friends, and, most of all, honored graduates of the Class of 1992.

This is my second chance to speak from this podium. The first was twenty-three years ago when I was a graduating senior. My classmates selected me to address them as the first Wellesley student ever to speak at a Commencement.

I can't claim that 1969 speech as my own; it reflected the hopes, values and aspirations of my classmates. It was full of the uncompromising language you only write when you are twenty-one. But it's uncanny to me the degree to which those same hopes, values and aspiration have shaped my adulthood.

We passionately rejected the notion of limitations on our abilities to make the world a better place. We saw a gap between our expectations and realities, and we were inspired, in large part by our Wellesley education, to bridge that gap. On behalf of the Class of 1969, I said then, "The challenge now is to practice politics as the art of making what appears to be impossible, possible." That is still the challenge of politics, especially in today's far more cynical climate.

The aspiration I referred to then was "the struggle for an integrated life . . . in an atmosphere of . . . trust and respect." What I meant by that was a life that combines personal fulfillment in love and work with fulfilling responsibility to the larger community.

When the ceremonies and hoopla of my graduation were over, I commenced my adult life by heading straight for Lake Waban. In those days and probably still now; swimming in the lake, other than at the beach, was prohibited. But it was one of my favorite rules to break. I stripped down to my swimsuit, put my clothes in a pile on the ground, took off my coke-bottle glasses that you have now seen in a hundred pictures and publications from one end of this country to the next and waded off in Tupelo Point.

While I was happily paddling around, feeling relieved I had survived the day, a security guard came by on his rounds, picked up my clothes and my glasses and carried them off. Imagine my surprise when I emerged to find neither clothes nor glasses and, blind as a bat, I had to feel my way back to Stone-Davis.

I'm just glad that picture hasn't also come back to haunt me. You can imagine the captions: "Girl offers vision to classmates and then loses her own." Or, better still, the tabloids might have run something like: "Girl swimming blinded by aliens after seeing Elvis."

While medical technology has allowed me to replace those glasses with contact lenses, I hope my vision today is clearer for another reason: the clarifying perspective of experience. The opportunity to share that experience with you, the honored graduates of the Class of 1992, is a privilege and a kind of homecoming to me, and I want to be somewhat personal.

Wellesley nurtured, challenged, and guided me; it instilled in me, not just knowledge, but a reserve of sustaining values. I also made friends who are still among my closest friends today.

When I arrived as a freshman in 1965 from my "Ozzie and Harriet" suburb of Chicago, both the College and the country were going through a period of rapid, sometimes tumultuous changes. My classmates and I felt challenged and, in turn, did challenge the College from the moment we arrived. Nothing was taken for granted. We couldn't even agree on an appropriate, politically correct cheer. To this day when we attend Reunions, you can hear us cry: "1-9-6-9 Wellesley Rah, one more year, still no cheer."

There often seemed little to cheer about. We grew up in a decade dominated by dreams and disillusionments. Dreams of the civil rights movement, of the Peace Corps, of the space program. Disillusionments starting with President Kennedy's assassination, accelerated by the divisive war in Vietnam, and the deadly mixture of poverty, racism, and despair that burst into flames in the hearts of some of our cities then and which is still burning today. A decade when speeches like "I Have a Dream" were followed by songs like "The Day the Music Died."

I was here on campus when Martin Luther King was murdered. My friends and I put on black arm bands and went into Boston to march in anger and pain — feeling as many of you did after the acquittals in the Rodney King case.

Much has changed in those intervening years — and much of it for the better — but much has also stayed the same, or at least not changed as much as we had hoped or as irrevocably.

Each new generation takes us into new territory. But while change is certain, progress is not. Change is a law of nature; progress is the challenge for both a life and a society. And what better place to speak of those challenges, particularly to women, and the challenge of leading an integrated life than here at Wellesley, a college that not only vindicates the proposition that there is still an essential place for an all-women's college, but which defines its mission as seeking "to educate women who will make a difference in the world."

And what better time to speak about women and their concerns than in the spring of 1992.

I've traveled all over America in the last months, talking and listening to women who are: struggling to raise their children and somehow make ends meet; women who are battling against the persistent discrimination that still limits their opportunities for pay and promotion; women who are bumping up against the glass ceiling; who are watching the insurance premiums on themselves and their families increase; who are coping with inadequate or non-existent child support payments after divorces which lead to precipitous drops in their standard of living; women who are existing on shrinking welfare payments with no available jobs in sight; and women who are anguishing over the prospect that abortions will be criminalized again. These women and their voices are there to be heard and seen and listened to by any of us.

I have also talked to women about our common desires to educate our children, to be sure they do receive the health care they need, to protect them from the escalating violence in our streets, to wonder how we ever got to a position in our country where we have children in schools that do bullet drills instead of fire drills. Worrying about our children is something women do and something mothers are particularly good at doing.

Women who pack lunch for their kids, or take the early bus to work, or stay out late at the PTA or spend every spare minute tending to their aging parents don't need lectures from Washington about values. They don't need to hear about an idealized world that never was as righteous or as carefree as some would like to think. They and we need understanding and a helping hand to solve our own problems. Most of us are doing the best we can to find the right balance in our own lives.

For me, the elements of that balance are family, work, and service.

First, your personal relationships. When all is said and done, it is the people in your life, the friendships you form and the communities you maintain that give shelter to that life. Your friends and your neighbors, the people, at work or church, wherever you come into contact with them, all who touch your daily lives. And if you choose, a marriage filled with love and respect. When I stood here before, I could never have predicted — let alone believed — that I would fall in love with someone named Bill Clinton and that I would follow my heart to a place called Arkansas. I have to tell you, based on the years that stand between you and me, I'm very glad I had the courage to make that choice.

Second, your work. For some of you, that may overlap with your contribution to your community. For some of you, the future might not include work outside the home (and I don't mean involuntary unemployment); but most of you will at some point in your life work for pay, maybe in jobs that used to be off-limits for women or for those that are still the backbone of the kind of nurturing and, caring professions that are so important. You may choose to be a corporate executive or a rocket scientist, you may choose to run for public office, you may choose to stay home and raise your children — but now you can make any or all of those choices and they can be the work of your life.

And the third element for me, and I hope for you, of that integrated life I alluded to those years ago is service. As students, we debated passionately what responsibility each individual has for the larger society and we went back and forth as to just what our College's Latin motto meant — "Not to be ministered unto, but to minister." The most eloquent explanation I have found of what I believe now and what I argued then is from Vaclav Havel, the play-wright and first freely-elected president of Czechoslovakia. In a letter from prison to his wife, Olga, he wrote: "Every-thing meaningful in life is distinguished by a certain tran-scendence of individual human existence — beyond the limits of mere 'self-care' — toward other people, toward society, toward the world. . . .Only by looking outward, by caring for things that, in terms of pure survival, you needn't bother with at all . . . and by throwing yourself over and over again into the tumult of the world, with the intention of making your voice count — only thus will you really become a person."

I first recognized what service I cared most about while I was in law school where I worked with children at the Yale New Haven Hospital and Child Study Center and represented children through legal services. And where during my first summer I worked for the Children's Defense Fund. My experiences gave voice for me to deep feelings about what children deserved from their families and their government. I discovered that I wanted my voice to count for children.

Some of you may have already had such a life-shaping experience; the arts, the environment, other human rights issues — whatever it might be — for many, it lies ahead. Recognize it and nurture it when it occurs.

Because my concern is making children count, I hope you will indulge me as I tell you why. The American Dream is an inter-generational compact. Or, as someone once said, one generation is supposed to leave the key under the mat for the next. We repay our parents for their love in the love we give our children — and we repay our society for the opportunities we are given by expanding the opportunities given to others. That's the way it's supposed to work. You know too well that it is not. Too many of our children are being impoverished financially, socially, and spiritually. The shrinking of their futures diminishes us all. Whether you end up having children of your own or not, I hope each of you will recognize the need for a sensible national family policy that reverses the absolutely unforgivable neglect of our children in this country in this year.

If you have children, you will owe the highest duty to them and will confront your biggest challenges in parting them. If, like me at your age, you now know little (and maybe care less) about the mysteries of good parenting, I can promise you there is nothing like on-the-job training.

I remember one very long night when my daughter, Chelsea, was about four weeks old and crying inconsolably. Nothing from my courses in my political science major seemed to help at all. Finally, I looked at her in my arms and I said, "Chelsea, you've never been a baby before and I've never been a mother before, we're just going to have to help each other get through this together." So far, we have. For Bill and me, she has been the great joy of our life. Watching her grow and flourish has given greater urgency to the task of helping all children.

There are many ways of helping children. You can do it through your own personal lives by being dedicated, loving parents. You can do it in medicine or music, social work or education, business, or government service. You can do it by making policy or making cookies.

It is, though, a false choice to tell women — or men for that matter — that we must choose between caring for ourselves and our own families or caring for the larger family of humanity.

In their recent Pastoral Letter, "Putting Children and Families First," the National Conference of Catholic Bishops captured this essential interplay of private and public roles: "No government can love a child and no policy can substitute for a family's care," the bishops wrote, but "government can either support or undermine families. . . . There has been an unfortunate, unnecessary, and unreal polarization in discussions of how best to help families. . . . The undeniable fact is that our children's future is shaped both by the values of their parents and the policies of our nation."

As my husband says, "Family values alone won't feed a hungry child. And material security cannot provide a moral compass. We need both."

Forty-five years ago, the biggest threat to our country came from the other side of the Iron Curtain, from the nuclear weapons that could wipe out life on the entire planet. While you were here at Wellesley, that threat ended.

Today, our greatest threat comes not from some external Evil Empire, but from our own internal Indifferent Empire that tolerates splintered families, unparented children, embattled schools, and pervasive poverty, racism, and violence.

Not for one more year can our country think of children as some asterisk on our national agenda. How we treat our children should be front and center of that agenda, or it won't matter what else is on it.

My plea is that you not only nurture the values that will determine the choices you make in your personal lives, but also insist on policies that include those values to nurture our nation's children.

"But, really Hillary," some of you may be saying to yourselves, "I've got to pay off my student loans. I can't even find a good job, let alone someone to love. How am I going to worry about the world? Our generation has fewer dreams, fewer illusions than yours."

And I hear you and millions of women like you all over the country. As women today, you do face tough choices. You know the rules are basically as follows:

If you don't get married, you're abnormal.

If you get married but don't have children, you're a selfish yuppie.

If you get married and have children, but then go work

outside the home, you're a bad mother.

If you get married and have children, but stay home, you've wasted your education.

And if you don't get married, but have children and work outside the home as a fictional newscaster, then you're in trouble with the vice president.

So you see, if you listen to all the people who make all those rules, you might conclude that the safest course of action is just to take your diploma and crawl under your bed. But let me end by proposing an alternative.

Hold onto your dreams. Take up the challenge of forging an identity that transcends yourself. Transcend yourself and you will find yourself. Care about something you needn't bother with at all. Throw yourself into the world and make your voice count.

Whether you make your voice count for children or for another cause, enjoy your life's journey. There is no dress rehearsal for life, and you will have to ad-lib your way through every scene. The only way to prepare is to do what you have done: get the best possible education; continue to learn from literature, scripture and history, to understand the human experience as best you can so that you do have guideposts charting the terrain toward whatever decisions are right for you.

I want you to remember this day and remember how much more you have in common with each other than with the people who are trying to divide you. And I want you to stand together as you appear to me from this position: beautiful, brave, and invincible, and to have a sense of celebration that you carry with you.

Congratulations to each of you. Look forward to and welcome the challenges ahead. And I hope that over the next years you look back on this day as a truly great opportunity that leads you to transcend and to forge an identity that is uniquely your own.

Godspeed.

Acceptance of the Democratic Party Nomination for the Presidency
Democratic National Convention, New York, New York, July 16, 1992.

Governor Richards, Chairman Brown, Mayor Dinkins, our great host, my fellow delegates and my fellow Americans:

I am so proud of Al Gore. He said he came here tonight because he always wanted to do the warm-up for Elvis. Well, I ran for president this year for one reason and one reason only: I wanted to come back to this convention and finish that speech I started four years ago.

Last year, Mario Cuomo taught us how a real nominating speech should be given. He also made it clear why we have to steer our ship of state on a new course.

Tonight I want to talk with you about my hope for the future, my faith in the American people, and my vision of the kind of country we can build, together.

I salute the good men who were my companions on the campaign trail: Tom Harkin, Bob Kerrey, Doug Wilder, Jerry Brown and Paul Tsongas. One sentence in the platform we built says it all: "The most important family policy, urban policy, labor policy, minority policy and foreign policy America can have is an expanding, entrepreneurial economy of high-wage, high-skill jobs."

And so, in the name of all those who do the work, pay the taxes, raise the kids and play by the rules — in the name of the hard working Americans who make up our forgotten middle class, I proudly accept your nomination for the Presidency of the United States.

I am a product of that middle class. And when I am President you will be forgotten no more.

We meet at a special moment in history, you and I. The cold war is over; Soviet Communism has collapsed, and our values — freedom, democracy, individual rights, free enterprise — they have triumphed all around the world. And yet just as we have won the cold war abroad, we are losing the battles for economic opportunity and social justice here at home. Now that we have changed the world, it's time to change America.

I have news for the forces of greed and the defenders of the status quo: your time has come—and gone. It's time for a change in America.

Tonight, ten million of our fellow Americans are out of work. Tens of millions more work harder for lower pay. The incumbent President says unemployment always goes up a little before a recovery begins. But unemployment only has to go up by one more person before a real recovery can begin — and Mr. President, you are that man.

This election is about putting power back I your hands and putting government back on your side. It's about putting people first.

You know, I've said that all across America. And whenever I do, someone comes back at me, as a young man did just this week at a town meeting at the Henry Street Settlement on the Lower East Side of Manhattan. He said, "That sounds good, Bill. But you're a politician. Why should I trust you?"

Tonight, as plainly as I can, I want to tell you who I am, what I believe and where I want to lead America.

I never met my father.

He was killed in a car wreck on a rainy road three months before I was born, driving home from Chicago to Arkansas to see my mother.

After that, my mother had to support us. So we lived with my grandparents while she went away to Louisiana to study nursing.

I can still see her clearly tonight through the eyes of a three-year-old: kneeling at the railroad station and weeping as she put me back on the train to Arkansas with my grandmother. She endured that pain because she knew that sacrifice was the only way she could support me and give me a better life.

My mother taught me. She taught me about family and hard work and sacrifice. She held steady through tragedy after tragedy. And she held our family, my brother and I, together through tough times. As a child, I watched her go off to work each day at a time when it wasn't always easy to be a working mother.

As an adult, I've watched her fight off breast cancer. And again she has taught me a lesson in courage. And always, always she taught me to fight.

That's while I'll fight for high-paying jobs so that parents can afford their children today. That's why I'm to make sure every American gets the health care that saved my mother's life. And that women's health care gets the same attention as men's. That's why I'll fight to make sure women in this country receive respect and dignity — whether they work in the home, out of the home or both. You want to know where I get my fighting spirit? It all started with my mother. Thank you, Mother. I love you.

When I think about opportunity for all Americans, I think about my grandfather.

He ran a country store in our little town of Hope. There were no food stamps back then, so when his customers — whether they were white or black — who worked hard and did the best they could came in with no money, well, he gave them food anyway, Just made a note of it. So did I. Before I was big enough to see over the counter, I learned from him to look up to people other folks looked down upon.

My grandfather just had a high-school education — a grade-school education. But in that country store he taught me more about equality in the eyes of the Lord than all my professors at Georgetown; more about intrinsic worth of every individual than all the philosophers at Oxford, more about the need for equal justice under the law that all the jurists at Yale Law School.

If you want to know where I come by the passionate commitment that I have to bringing people together without regard to race, it all started with my grandfather.

I learned a lot from another person, too. A person who for more than 20 years has worked hard to help our children. Paying the price of time to make sure our schools don't fail them. Someone who traveled our state for a year. Studying, learning, listening. Going to PTA meetings, school board meetings, town hall meetings. Putting together a package of school reforms recognized around the nation. Doing it all while building a distinguished legal career and being a wonderful loving mother.

That person is my wife.

Hillary taught me. She taught me that all children can learn, and that each of us has a duty to help them do it. So if you want to know why I care so much about our children and our future, it all started with Hillary.

Frankly, I'm fed up with the politicians in Washington lecturing the rest of us about "family values." Our families have values. But our government doesn't.

I want an America where "family values" live in our actions, not just our speeches. An America that includes every family, every traditional family and every extended family, every two-parent family, every single-parent, and every foster family, every family.

I want to say something to the fathers in this country who have chosen to abandon their children by neglecting their child support: Take responsibility for your children or we will force you to do so. Because governments don't raise children; parents do. And you should.

And I want to say something to every child in America tonight who's out there trying to grow up without a father or a mother: I know how you feel. You're special, too. You matter to America. And don't you ever let anybody tell you you can't become whatever you want to be. And if other politicians make you feel like you're not a part of their family, come on and be part of ours.

The thing that makes me angriest about what's gone wrong in the last 12 years is that our government has lost touch with our values, while our politicians continue to shout about them. I'm tired of it.

I was raised to believe the American Dream was built on rewarding hard work. But we have seen the folks in Washington turn the American ethic on its head. For too long, those who play by the rules and keep the faith have gotten the shaft. And those who cut corners and cut deals have been rewarded. People are working harder than ever, spending less time with their children, working nights and weekends at their job, instead of going to PTA and Little League or Scouts, and their incomes are still going down, their taxes are going up, and the cost of health care, housing and education are going through the roof. Meanwhile, more and more of our best people are falling into poverty — even though they work 40 hours a week.

Our people are pleading for change, but government is in the way. Its been hijacked by privileged, private interests. It's forgotten who really pays the bills around here. It's taking more of your money and giving you less in service.

We have got to go beyond the brain-dead politics of Washington and give out people the kind of government they deserve: a government they deserve: a government that works for them.

A President ought to be a powerful force for progress. But right now I know how President Lincoln felt when General McClellan wouldn't attack in the Civil War. He asked him, "If you're not going to use your army, may I borrow it?" And so I say, George Bush, if you won't use your power to help America, step aside. I will.

Our country is falling behind. The President is caught in the grip of a failed economic theory. We have gone from first to 13th in the world in wages since Reagan and Bush have been in office. Four years ago, candidate Bush said America is a special place, not just "another pleasant country some where on the U.N. roll call, between Albania and Zimbabwe." Now, under President Bush America has an unpleasant economy stuck somewhere between Germany and Sri Lanka. And for most Americans, Mr. President, life's a lot less kind and a lot less gentle than it was before your Administration took office.

Our country has fallen so far, so fast, that just a few months ago the Japanese Prime Minister actually said he felt "sympathy" for the United States. Sympathy! When I am your President, the rest of the world won't look down on us with pity but up to us with respect again.

What is George Bush doing about our America's economic problems?

Well, four years ago he promised 15 million new jobs by this time, and he's over 14 million short. Al Gore and I can do better.

He has raised taxes on the people driving pickup trucks and lowered taxes on the people riding in limousines. We can do better.

He promised to balance the budget, but he hasn't even tried. In fact, the budgets he has submitted to Congress nearly doubled the debt. Even worse, he wasted billions, and reduced our investments in education and jobs. We can do better.

So if you are sick and tired of a Government that doesn't work to create jobs, if you are sick and tired of a tax system that's stacked against you, if your sick and tired of exploding debt and reduced investments in our future, or if, like the great civil rights pioneer Fannie Lou Hamer your just plain old sick and tired of being sick and tired, then join us, work with us, win with us — and we can make our country the country it is meant to be.

Now George Bush talks a good game. But he has no game plan to rebuild America, from the cities to the suburbs to the countryside so that we can compete and win again in the global economy. I do.

He won't take on the big insurance companies and the bureaucracies to control health costs and give us affordable health care for all Americans but I will.

He won't even implement the recommendations of his own Commission on AIDS, but I will.

He won't streamline the Federal Government and change the way it works; cut 100,000 bureaucrats and put 100,000 new police officers on the streets of American cities, but I will. He's never balanced a government budget, but I have. Eleven times.

He won't break the stranglehold the special interests have on our elections and the lobbyists have on our government, but I will.

He won't give mothers and fathers the simple chance to take some time off from work when a baby is born or a parent is sick, but I will.

We're losing our farms at a rapid rate and he has no commitment to keep family farms in the family, but I do.

He's talked a lot about drugs, but he hasn't helped people on the front line to wage that war on drugs and crime, but I will.

He won't take the lead in protecting the environment and creating new jobs in environmental technology. But I will.

You know what else? He doesn't have Al Gore, and I do.

Just in case—just in case you didn't notice, that's Gore with an E on the end.

And George Bush—George Bush won't guarantee a women's right to choose. I will. Listen, here me now: I am not pro-abortion. I am pro-choice strongly. I believe this difficult and painful decision should be left to the women of America. I hope the right to privacy can be protected, and we will never again have to discuss this issue on political platforms. But I am old enough to remember what it was like before *Roe v. Wade*. And I do not want to return to the time when we made criminals of women and their doctors.

Jobs. Education. Health Care. These are not just commitments from my lips. They are the work of my life.

But, my fellow Democrats, it's time for us to realize that we've got some changing to do too. There is not a program in government for every problem. And if we want to use government to help people, we've got to make it work again.

Because we are committed in this convention and in this platform to making these changes, we are, as Democrats, in the words that Ross Perot himself today, a revitalized Democratic Party. I am well aware that all those millions of people who rallied to Ross Perot's cause wanted to be in an army of patriots for change. Tonight, I say to them: join us and together we will revitalize America.

But I can't do it alone. No president can. We must do it together. It won't be easy and it won't be quick. We didn't get into this mess and we won't get out of it overnight. But we can do it—with our commitment, our creativity, our diversity, and our strength. I want every person in this hall and every citizen in this land to reach out and join us in a great new adventure to chart a bold new future.

As a teenager, I heard John Kennedy's summons to citizenship. And then, as a student at Georgetown, I heard the call clarified by the professor I had named Carroll Quiqley, who said America was the greatest country in the history of the world because our people always believed in two great ideas: first, that tomorrow can be better than today and second, that each of us has a personal, moral responsibility to make it so.

Let that be our cause, and our commitment and our New Covenant.

I end tonight where it all began for me: I still believe in a place called Hope.

Acknowledgements

I owe a great debt of thanks to the many people who helped turn my idea into reality. Four people in particular worked hard to help make this book happen: Shawn Landres, a gifted thinker and researcher, helped organize this book and spent weeks editing the manuscript. He developed many of the contacts with the Friends Of Bill (FOBs) and coordinated the flow of information. Kathy Shandling, gave us some insight into the implications of media power in the political world today, through her work on Part Four. She extended my contacts with FOBs through her research and helped encourage many to contribute. Jason Wertheim wrote fact-filled research memos about key topics. He reviewed every article and speech and edited the manuscripts with intelligence and insight. Mason Kirby spent hours typing and editing manuscripts, essays, and speeches, and contributed valuable editorial suggestions.

The following people offered valuable editorial assistance: Arthur Wertheim, Harold and Gail Snider, Fred Williams, Natalie Riggs-Figueroa, Ralph Figueroa, Michael Gauldin, and Robert and Anna Ware. Special thanks to Harold and Gail Snider, both of whom happen to be blind, who offered to edit the entire manuscript. Harold has experience with political biographies such as this, having written one as his D.Phil thesis. We sent them a disk which he converted with a computer program into Braille for editing. They both speed-read Braille at over 400 words a minute, and have written and edited professionally. They did an excellent job, typing editorial notes about the text on a Braille word processor. Robert Ware also made valuable contributions in many hours of editing.

I am indebted to the staff of Shaposky Publishers, Inc. — especially the publisher, Ian Shapolsky; Annie Cohen, his assistant; Sherrel Farnsworth; George Partruzio, the art director, and Stacy Wike, the publicity director. Production of this book was made easier thanks to the creative and technical expertise of Julian Serer, Heather Rockwell, Ron Logsdon, and Jim McGuiness.

Special thanks to Saul Benjamin, one of the FOBs who originally proposed in Little Rock that I contact 10 or more FOBs for anecdotes about Bill Clinton's life. It made this instant book a much richer volume with credible primary sources. Jan Emberton, of the Little Rock Public Library, assisted us greatly with her original research, as well as Arkansas newspaper clippings going back to 1974.

Much appreciation to all the FOBs and others who contributed time and thoughts about Bill. Thanks to the media professionals and academics who contributed their work and their support to this project. A number of others helped this project in a variety of ways: David E. Shaw, Terence Duffy, Catherine Greenwood, Betsey Wright, Kathy Ford, Max Parker, Bruce Lindsey, Dana Hyde, Richard Strauss, Harry Thomason, and George Stephanopoulos for their encouragement and support.

I am grateful to Sierra Capital's staff for their assistance: Kevin McCrary, Karen Perez, Anatoly Veltman, and Alexander Belozertzev. Thanks to my friends, Drs. Jacqueline and Eytan R. Barnea as well as Herb Moskowitz,

M.D., Irwin M. Rosenthal, Esq. and Andrew F. Capoccia, Esq. for their kind understanding and for encouraging me to be involved with their projects---despite the book, which was a major distraction, I remain strongly committed to assisting and believe in their important medical research.

Our goal was to create a balanced, comprehensive and error-free biography. This book was written with a great time pressure because we wanted it to come out before the election to offer another source of information for voters. It was intended to be a general introduction to Bill Clinton's background and is by no means a definitive biography. We hope that the reader will understand that any errors in fact were completely unintentional and hopefully innocuous.

About the Contributors

ROBERT E. LEVIN, Author. Robert is the president of Sierra Capital Management, Inc., a Wall Street-based investment management firm with affiliated offices worldwide including London, Frankfurt and Moscow. A lifelong Democrat, he is the founder of the Wall Street Democrats, an economic policy forum, a foreign policy educational foundation and an international trade forum. Robert Levin has been active in several Jewish and pro-Israel organizations. He is a graduate of the University of California, Berkeley, where he co-founded the California Public Interest Research Group (CALPIRG) which conducted research and lobbied on environmental and consumer issues. He studied political science at the University of Bordeaux. He earned a MBA in Finance at the New York University's

Stern School of Business. He is the author and editor of *Democratic Blueprints: National Leaders Chart America's Future*, published in 1988.

J. SHAWN LANDRES, Editor. Shawn is studying American History at Columbia University, and intends to pursue a career in academia and public service. He is an expert in student financial aid issues, having testified in Congress on various aspects of the Higher Education Act. Shawn has appeared on NBC's *Today Show* as an advocate for broader access to postsecondary education. He has won writing awards, and has been honored for his academic and public service accomplishments.

JASON ALBERT WERTHEIM, Associate Editor. Jason is currently enrolled at the Massachusetts Institute of Technology. He has served as editor-in-chief of a number of prize-winning publications. He has studied journalism at Oxford University, at Yale University, and at Northwestern University's Medill School of Journalism, and is the recipient of numerous awards for his accomplishments. Jason's interview credits include such political figures as South Africa's Archbishop Desmond Tutu and exiled Haitian President Jean Bertrand Aristide.

KATHY M. SHANDLING, Associate Editor. Kathy Shandling is a publishing executive with the Meredith Corporation in New York City. A graduate of Wellesley College and The London School of Economics, she has worked on political campaigns both in England and in the United States. While an undergraduate, she was actively involved with the MIT News Study Group. Kathy is a member of numerous professional organizations, including the Foreign Policy Association. She has authored several magazine articles on the media and media personalities.

MASON R. KIRBY, Assistant Editor. Mason is a student at Columbia University studying urban studies and architecture. He attended the Governor's School for Citizen Leadership in Washington state in 1989 where he discussed ethical and moral issues which the world will face in the years ahead.

If you have any opinions about this book, the author and the editors would like to hear from you. Please send a postcard or letter to:

Clinton Bio c/o SPI Books,
136 West 22nd Street,
New York, N.Y. 10011.

You may also send a fax to (212) 633-2123, attn: Clinton Bio. All inquiries will be responded to personally if you include your return address or fax number.

INDIVIDUAL SALES
If you would like to order this book for your family, friends, Perot supporters, Reagan Democrats or enlightened Republicans, please write or send a fax with instructions to the number above.

QUANTITY SALES
Corporations, organizations or groups can order in bulk with or without special imprints, messages, and excerpts to meet your needs.
Please allow 2 weeks for delivery unless a rush order is requested.